We would like to dedicate this book
to our in-class tutors, all the members of the
editorial board who helped us put this book
together, our families, and our school.

Most of all we would like to thank
Mr. Rose and Ms. Leathers, who pushed
us a lot, but we got there.

Published May 2010 by 826 Valencia
Copyright © 2010 by 826 Valencia
All rights reserved by 826 Valencia and the authors

ISBN: 978-1-934750-17-9

Printed in Canada by Printcrafters
Distributed by PGW

We The Dreamers

Young Authors Explore
the American Dream

We the Dreamers

Young Authors Explore
the American Dream

Written by

students of John O'Connell High School

with a foreword by Daniel Alarcón

TABLE
of
CONTENTS

It unites us even when we're far away

Wave at me out the window when you see me speeding by

I had never seen a big red bridge and couldn't imagine one

Foreword
THINGS GET INTERESTING

by DANIEL ALARCÓN

ALMOST TEN YEARS AGO, I taught a photography and writing class in a neighborhood on the outskirts of Lima, Peru, called 10 de Octubre. My students were mostly first-generation city-dwellers, the sons and daughters of those who had fled political violence in the provinces, young people growing up and finding their way on the edges of the chaotic and often-bewildering Peruvian capital. 10 de Octubre, when I was living there, was a friendly but difficult place. Everything was (and, years later, remains) under construction. Understand how new this area was: the name referred to the date it had been founded, October 10, 1984 (or '85, I can't recall for certain), and in 2001, stark memories of those first years were still quite fresh. Any adult could tell you, with a little prodding, the history of the place: what it felt to leave everything they'd ever known to start over; the imagination and faith required to see this bare, stony mountainside—isolated and dry and far from everything—and call it home. For years after it had been settled, 10 de Octubre, like dozens of similar neighborhoods scattered throughout Lima, appeared on no map. Schools had to be built, roads paved, electricity lines strung, water trucked in—but for this arduous process to begin, the authorities had first to be convinced of two important facts: that there were people living there, and most importantly, that they were there to stay.

While the city may have been ambivalent about places like 10 de Octubre, the young people, at least, were less conflicted regarding the city. Most, I discovered, thought of themselves as Limeños, no matter how the city they lived in differed from the official image Lima might hope to project. If these young people were familiar with two cultures—the rural Andean traditions of their parents and the severe, surreal modernity of life in a fully globalized place like Lima—they had, for the most part, opted for the latter. They had few memories of the provinces they'd fled, and the stories their parents told—of war and dislocation, of killings and fear—seemed remote, even irrelevant. The older generation might speak Quechua and Spanish, but their children made a point of only speaking Spanish, the language of the city. They liked house music or salsa or reggaeton, but had little use for the lugubrious, funereal Andean melodies their parents were so moved by. They had become Limeños, a category of Peruano not easily defined; and, like true Limeños, they felt no need to define it. Nor did they feel any compunctions about rewriting the staid, outdated definition of the city itself—their music, their dance, their slang, and their concerns became paramount. Their dreams, by sheer force of numbers, became the city's dreams too.

Part of my project when I was living in 10 de Octubre was to gather the photos my students took, and go to the provinces to show them to young people in rural communities—young people who hoped to move to the city one day. I'm reminded of this now because it strikes me that the American Dream isn't all that different from the dream of Lima, or of any city, actually. Opportunity is the keyword; however that diffuse concept might be interpreted, it is real. Many people in the rural areas of Peru think of the capital as a place to make it; while many people in Lima think the same of the United States. When the photos of 10 de Octubre were shown to young people in rural areas, they couldn't believe what they were seeing. We had long, troubling discussions about my students' images of life in 10 de Octubre. These half-built shanties, these dusty neighborhoods, this poverty and need—could this really be Lima? Could this really be the place they'd been dreaming of?

In this book, the students of John O'Connell High School have collectively accomplished something very important: they have begun to document and dissect one of the central myths of our society, that of the American Dream. In the process of composing these moving essays, they claim that dream as their own. Just as my students in 10 de Octubre had inherited their parents' decision to migrate, many of the writers featured in this collection are first-generation immigrants, and have begun the complicated task of deciding where exactly they fit in. They do not receive definitions uncritically, nor should they—if the American Dream is to have any relevance at this late date, it must be elastic, renewable. It must be, as these young writers prove again and again, an intensely personal construct; a negotiation with reality, with tradition, with one's own past and family history; and, in no small part, a wager on the future. And in the United States, as in Peru, as in any country real or imagined—when dreams meet reality, that's precisely the moment when things get interesting.

Every year in Peru, one of the universities conducts a survey, asking ordinary citizens a hypothetical: if you had the chance to emigrate, to leave the country and start a new life, would you? The percentages vary, depending on the fluctuations in the economy, the relative stability of the political scene, but generally speaking, more than half of those surveyed respond *yes*. I've seen the percentage as high as 70 percent, and among young people, those who have less to lose and more to gain, the numbers are often higher. These numbers, even to someone like me—a child of immigrant parents who examined their options, their possible futures, and chose to leave—even to me, the numbers are always surprising. Imagine—what if everyone magically got their wish? Consider: a country where two-thirds of the population vanished one day! Can you picture it?

Like much of the developing world, Peru has been reshaped by decades of rural-to-urban migration. These yearly surveys prove that the process remains unfinished. For further proof, as if it were necessary, we need only take a look at the changing complexion of American cities and towns. Take a walk around San Francisco's Mission District. Around Oakland, or Fremont, or any city in the Bay Area. The question in the survey is hypothetical, of course; but here they are—these Peruvians, Afghans, Filipinos, Chinese, Mexicans, no longer hypothetical, but very real—remaking the country in the image of the place they'd dreamed of.

As I see them, the essays in this collection are actually a response to the question posed in the Peruvian survey—the continuation of the thought process, an examination of the consequence of that hypothetical decision. Because nowhere in the Peruvian survey is that *yes* broken down, or analyzed, or taken to its logical conclusion. The survey doesn't differentiate between a flip, reflexive impulse to emigrate and a careful, nuanced, embattled, even reluctant one. *Yes, I'd like to leave*—but then what? What impact will that have on my life, on the lives of my children? A hypothetical is safe, I suppose, because it doesn't carry the weight and trauma of a real emigration. These essays, thankfully, do. They carry the full weight—the beauty and terror of it all, the challenges, the joys and triumphs. We hear a family's heartbreak, or its successes, as narrated through the eyes of its youngest members. The dreams contained within these essays, be they as simple as driving a car of one's own, or as transcendent as being reunited with an incarcerated loved one, are important because they are *real*, because they offer a unique take on this complex American moment.

As I read through this collection, I kept coming back to one thought: what if these essays could be translated into Spanish, mailed back to Peru—one of the many countries where a version of the American Dream has been exported—and handed out to everyone who answered *yes* to that survey? What would happen then? Would everyone still answer the same? Would the harsh, often poetic truths contained within cause anyone to reconsider their choice?

These essays, however, are not just for those living abroad; they are also for us, for those of us who've lived here in the United States for most of our lives, for those of us who have never left, and have no plans to. They are for young people at schools all over the United States, who have pondered, with a mixture of trepidation and hope, what the future might hold for them here. These essays are, most significantly, a way of stating facts, those same facts the residents of 10 de Octubre once had to prove to the mapmakers of Lima: Yes, we're here. No, we're not leaving. And, by the way, our dreams matter too.

Daniel Alarcón is the author of two works of fiction, War by Candlelight *and* Lost City Radio. *He is the Associate Editor of* Etiqueta Negra, *a magazine published in his native Lima, Peru, as well as Visiting Scholar at the Center for Latin American Studies at UC Berkeley. He currently lives in Oakland.*

INTRODUCTION

by STUDENT EDITORIAL BOARD

ANGELICA VERDUGO, BRIAN HIBBELER,
CRISTIAN SOTO, JAIZEL ROBLES, KAREN MARTINEZ

THIS BOOK IS A COLLECTION of perspectives about the American Dream by juniors and seniors from John O'Connell High School of Technology in San Francisco. Some of our essays describe struggles, like trying to find a permanent home in San Francisco's Mission District or staying safe on the neighborhood bus. Others describe goals we have, like being the first in the family to go to college or becoming a veterinarian. Some describe the ways we take inspiration from anyone who has a dream and follows it—from people close to us, like older brothers and YMCA counselors, to people we don't even know, like musicians and fictional characters.

The students at O'Connell High School are mostly minorities from immigrant backgrounds. Our school gets more diverse every year. Despite differences among the students, we have one important thing in common: many of our parents came to this country because they dreamed of a better life for us and because they wanted us to achieve higher levels of education than they did. We the dreamers have heard what our parents told us and want to show them that we can make it through every obstacle we encounter. We can reach our highest goals. We can set an example.

We go to a school that was recently listed as one of the lowest-performing schools in the city. We want to show the government and anyone who looks down on us or our school that we can reach just as high—and go even higher—than they expect.

This book started as an assignment. We responded to three prompts that asked us to think about our American Dream and relate it to a memory, a person, or an object. Writing three essays required so much thinking that sometimes we didn't know what to say. (Some of us thought it was torture!) But then the tutors from 826 came and brought new life to the project. They asked question after question, and we talked and talked, and it changed how we looked at things. The first week we worked with the tutors, each student settled on one essay to finalize for this book. The tutors helped us make decisions about what would go in our essays, but they always left the final choices to us. Their help made it easier for us to expand our essays and figure out how to focus them.

As time passed, the project became more personal, more than just writing. Many of us hadn't thought before about what our dream was. Now we had the chance to take something out of ourselves, words that we may have never said to anyone, and put them on paper. We got the chance to reflect on our own experiences, to see how hard some of them have been, and to see how strong we have been. The essays became our life stories.

Sometimes it was challenging to work with the tutors. Each of us worked with more than one, and our different tutors sometimes had different ideas about what was best for our essays. Through the process, we realized we could each pick one approach, *we* could decide what would get printed in this book.

At the end of six weeks of in-class tutoring, it came time to edit our essays and put together our book of dreams. Two nights a week for a month, at least five of us headed over to 826 Valencia, where we worked with about thirty adult volunteers. We started by editing all the essays, which meant doing a lot more than fixing commas. Overall, we had fun working with the adults and learning to edit. We also got to look back at our own essays, and sometimes we felt surprised (thought, *Wow, I wrote that?*) by the power of what we had written.

Once editing was done, we decided how to group the essays within the book. The 826 staff, the adult volunteers, and our fellow students had tons of ideas. It was very entertaining to watch the wild debate! In the end, we decided to group the essays by the writing prompt they responded to (memory, object, or person), since that is how the authors conceptualized them.

Coming up with a title for this book was the most challenging task we undertook. We threw about one hundred ideas onto the board! We all felt that the final title fit the full variety of stories in the book. The title *We the Dreamers* also fits us as authors, because we are living the dreams in this book.

When you get published, a book *is* your voice—but it's a voice that will be around forever. A book is more permanent than a song or a film because it's a physical thing. It's an expression of you as a person, and it will live on well past the time you will. We've been given the opportunity to have our voice be heard widely, to express other American experiences—not the glamorized one of rags to riches, but more common struggles. Through the process of creating this book, each of us clarified what our own American Dream is—and learned the American Dreams of fifty of our peers too. We realized, as well, that we are shaping the American Dream for our country. We are grounding it in the reality of the era in which we are growing up. We are building on the dreams of past generations, and we think that future generations can do the same thing—so that the American Dream can continually evolve over time.

Like the process of crafting this book, finding the voice inside us to put into these essays was the product of many weeks and forms of collaboration. Nobody reaches a dream without help. Sharing each of our voices with so many people has helped us better see the dream. It has helped the dream create us just as much as we created it.

It unites us even when we're far away

FREEDOM
Taken for
GRANTED

by CATHERINE ESMERALDA OLVERA

I AM SITTING IN THE KITCHEN with my two older brothers, Gabriel and Anthony. Gabriel and I are sitting on brown wood chairs, and there is a big round table along with it. I'm smelling sausages in the black frying pan. I see the biscuits rising. I can also see the yellow and white eggs with little black dots of pepper. Anthony is working hard making breakfast for me and my second-oldest brother Gabriel because I'm recovering from a cold. The reason I'm excited is because no one's ever done anything like this for me before. I go to the living room and watch Rugrats *while waiting for breakfast. After my show's over, Anthony calls me to the kitchen. We serve ourselves. Then we go to the living room to eat and watch our favorite show in the whole wide world:* South Park! *The food is so delicious that every time I take a bite, my mouth starts to water. All three of us are having the greatest time in our pajamas.*

My name is Catherine Esmeralda Olvera, and this is my story about freedom, support, and achieving a dream that will not be possible for a long time.

It all started when my brother got kicked out of his father's house. He had nowhere to go, so he called my mom, asking her where he could spend the night. She told him to call his girlfriend to see if he could stay at her house. We would've let him stay at our house, but we lived in Richmond and it was about two o'clock in the morning. So he ended up at his girlfriend's house. Later on that morning we got a call from my brother, who was now at "eight-fifty jail." He told my mom that he had gotten a little drunk and injured a neighbor across the street from his girlfriend's house. I overheard my mom talking to him, and she sounded really worried. Later that day my brother's girlfriend told me the whole story. That's when I knew my life was going to change forever. My brother had been to jail a couple of times, but the reasons were never serious and the stays never lasted long. But this time, I found out that the neighbor my brother had injured was pressing charges. And my brother's girlfriend was pregnant! I just wished she would've talked my brother out of his bad choices. He could get angry sometimes, but he's very reasonable. It didn't really matter anymore, though. A week later my mom hired a lawyer. In the beginning the lawyer did an okay job, but later he got really lazy. My mom got furious, so we fired him. Then my brother got another lawyer, and the new lawyer was free because everyone has a right to a public defender. The new lawyer tried to lower my brother's sentence. The new lawyer was pretty good, because he told the judge why my brother should be bailed out. So the new lawyer actually defended my brother.

It took almost a whole year just to know how long my brother Anthony would be in jail. My mom and my brother's girlfriend were in the courtroom when the judge said "seven to ten years." My mom was devastated. She watched my brother leave the courtroom with those sad, slightly curved, big brown eyes.

When I heard the news later that day, I was so angry I punched the wall and bruised my knuckles. But what else could I do? I didn't have any money to bail him out, and I couldn't hug him or say that everything was going to be okay. It felt like the more I went into the water, the more I started to drown.

Two months later, we were able to see my brother at "eight-fifty jail." The way the visits there went was first you walked inside and took off everything that was metal. You put your stuff in a bin, and it went through a machine to check if there was anything suspicious. Then you walked through a metal detector to see if you had any weapons on you. Just going through all of that made me feel like *I* was in jail.

Next you went up in an elevator, which looked pretty old. On the inside was a hard black fuzzy floor with dirt all over. It was pretty disgusting. The elevator took you to whatever floor your inmate was placed on. Then you ended up in a long hallway full of people. My family and I had to wait in line to make an appointment to see my brother. When we finally got to the front of the line there was a guard at a big wood podium. My mom told the guard my brother's name. He asked for my mom's and my brother's girlfriend's IDs. The guard wrote down their names, along with "two minors." He checked us off for whatever appointment was available and we left to waste time. We always woke up early to make an appointment, because anyone could make an appointment to see my brother. And if we got there too late all the spots could be full, which would suck because then we would be there for nothing.

Soon two other guards would open big red doors, and then we would walk inside a room with a hard, cold floor. There was also a black, shiny payphone to talk on. Finally, we would see my brother and talk to him last. I told him that I'd missed him and that I would always be there for him.

Every time we came back for a visit, we went through the whole process again. And since then I have become really close to my brother. He's like my best friend. We only ever had a short amount of time to see him, because the visits were thirty minutes. It sucked seeing him that way, but it was better than nothing. I got to see him almost every Saturday until he was transferred to San Bruno Jail. See, every time an inmate is transferred, lots of paperwork has to be turned in and approved so you can visit your inmate. So we had to schedule our visits to San Bruno Jail over the phone. It took hours to get through to the person who put in our appointment, but it was worth it. I would tell them the number of adults who were going and how many minors, but only five visitors total were allowed per visit. The visits only lasted thirty minutes. Sometimes they would give us an extra ten minutes, but only if the nice guards were on duty. Unfortunately, most of the guards in San Bruno Jail were mean and grumpy. I couldn't stand them! Before each visit, you had to wait outside in the cold to be taken up to the jail. A worker would call the name of an inmate, and whoever was there to see that person would get in a big, shiny, white van to take them up to the jail. And then came the routine: take all metals off, go through the metal detectors, all that stuff. Except San Bruno was more strict. You couldn't wear red or blue, and no cell phones or iPods were allowed; if you broke any of these rules, your visit was cancelled.

As time passed, I didn't get to see my brother as much because my niece was born! I remember when I found out she was finally here. My mom called my dad at six o'clock in the morning; I was still asleep until my mom woke me up. That same day, August 7, 2009, we went to St. Luke's Hospital, so me, my sister, and my little brother could meet our niece. My dad took us to the tenth floor and we went into a medium-sized room with a big window overlooking the Mission. But the only thing that caught my eye was my beautiful, tiny niece. She was wrapped in a pink blanket with colored teddy bears all over it, and she wore a matching tiny hat. When I finally held her, I felt so complete and happy. It felt like we were floating on a fluffy white cloud. Even though my brother wasn't there, it felt like a piece of him was with me because of her.

Now that my niece is here, I have to step up my responsibilities. I want to be her hero, her role model, the person she goes to when something's good or bad. So far I've been doing a good job. Every Saturday I take care of her along with my family, too. When my brother left, it felt like a big huge hole had been punched through my chest. But now that my niece is here it feels like the hole never even existed. When I'm with her, our bond just blossoms into a beautiful red rose. When she laughs it sounds like my favorite piano solo, by Debussy, called "Clair de Lune." The song sounds so calming, precious, and happy. Just like she is.

I'm excited to be an aunty because I've never had a responsibility like this before. I have two younger siblings and I take care of them all the time, but it's not the same. When you finally hold your niece or nephew, you feel so invincible, like you're the protector of this little baby. I never felt a love so strong for anyone in my life before my niece was born. After my niece was six weeks old, she went to go see her daddy for the first time. I also went. I saw my niece looking through the window at my brother. It was so sad because she couldn't touch him, but at least they got to see each other for the very first time.

About four months later, my brother and his girlfriend decided to get married. They'd been together for about five years so they wanted to make it official. They signed a whole bunch of papers and turned them in. Then the jail set the date and hired a person to read their vows to them. The only person that could go was my niece. The way the wedding went was two guards set two chairs next to each other. My brother and his soon-to-be wife sat in the chairs and held hands. My niece was on my soon-to-be sister-in-law's lap. My brother and his girlfriend both said their vows and kissed for about five or ten seconds. After that I had a new member of the family, Mrs. Cecilia Urbina. I loved having a new member of the family; the bigger the better.

Three months later my brother was transferred to San Quentin Prison. Only my mom, my sister-in-law, my niece, and my dad got see my brother in San Quentin, because he was only there for about two months. Then he was transferred to Soledad Prison, where he is now. That place is so far away, it's almost at the border of L.A.

I remember the first time I visited my brother at Soledad Prison. I was excited, as were my mom, little sister, niece, and sister-in-law, because not only would the visit be three hours long, but we actually got to see my brother in person. I ran to him and gave him the biggest hug ever. I was so happy that I almost cried. My niece ran into his arms and gave him a big wet kiss on his tan cheek. My brother was stunned to see her, because she had turned one and was already walking. My mom hugged him and started to cry. His wife did the same. My brother looked really slim. He used to weigh 250 lbs, but now he weighs 180 lbs. In prison you don't get a lot of activities to do. So he chose working out.

My American Dream is to give my brother freedom. Every day I wish he could be by my side through everything. The only thing I could use to bail him out is, of course, money. But what's so ridiculous is how much the bail costs. It would take me years to get my hands on that kind of money. If I had it I would bail him out in a heartbeat, but I know that it's not possible. So I'm just glad that he's healthy and doing well. I miss him so much! There isn't a day that goes by that he's not on my mind.

For now, my niece is my ray of hope because she reminds me of my brother, especially the way she smiles. Every minute I spend with her is like eating breakfast with my two older brothers while watching *South Park*. When my niece grows up, I want her to have a good life. I don't want her to feel the pain that I feel about the whole disaster. I miss you bro, and I hope to see you soon.

GOING THROUGH
Open Doors

by JENNIFER NERON SINGH

IN A SMALL VILLAGE in Cambodia, my grandparents' home sheltered my two aunts, three uncles, my mother, and my grandparents. In order to support the family and for the love of his country, my grandfather worked in the army; he wanted to do what he could to protect his country. The rest of the family farmed, harvested crops, and raised animals. Nature provided them with plenty of edible fruits as well as ingredients for cooking, so they were very gratified. They were poor—their house was made from bamboo, and there was no electricity or running water. They had to travel miles to get to school, and they had to do it barefooted. School was a time to relax and study; however, after school they had to walk back home for another journey. They had to bring the cattle far from home to feed them water. By the time they finished all their work, it would be late at night, after they'd eaten, and they still had to do their homework. They'd sleep for a few hours, then wake up early in the morning to cook and do other work before leaving for school. It may have been a new morning, but the same lifestyle continued every day. Life was difficult, but they were all glad to have each other.

My mom was eight years old and my uncle Phon was ten years old when the Communists took over Cambodia. The Khmer Rouge were forcing other Cambodians to join them. My uncle's mother would try to cook soup for her sick three-year-old son, but food was scarce. So my uncle Phon had to sneak into the fields to steal pumpkins so that my grandmother could cook for his little brother. As he snuck through the pumpkin field, he passed through cold rice paddies. His only source of light was the moon and the stars. One day the Khmer Rouge caught him. They beat him and tied him to a horse with a thick, coarse rope. The galloping horse dragged him for miles. My uncle was covered with painful cuts everywhere. By midnight they tied him to a huge palm tree, where he passed out for hours. At dawn he regained consciousness. He was no longer tied up and the soldiers were gone. He didn't know why, but without questioning it, and in spite of his throbbing wounds, he desperately sprinted home. He reached home safely, only to hear that his brother had died. The family was very mournful and became even more distraught when their parents passed away a couple days later due to starvation. The massacre in Cambodia continued to spread throughout their cities. My uncles, aunts, and mom decided to risk their lives and escape.

They finally reached Thailand, where they lived along the border for about a year. They slept wherever they could and ate what they could find. Soon the family got out, thanks to the American Red Cross. They were sent to live in a more secure location in Thailand, in an old, poor refugee camp. Eventually one day, they became one of the chosen families to start a new life in the United States.

It was the first time the family had seen an airplane. My uncle looked outside the window for most of the trip. His eyes widened as he stared at the beautiful land, big blue ocean, and the large, plump clouds. After a couple of nights, they arrived in San Francisco, where each family had one motel room to stay for the night. The next day each family was sent off to different destinations. My uncle's family stayed in San Francisco and began their new life together. They still didn't have enough money for basic necessities.

My uncle is the third of five children. He's a handsome, loving, and successful man. He helps us anytime we need money, and he asks about our health every time he talks to us. After all his struggles in Cambodia, Thailand, and America, he is now a wealthy man. He owns a huge two-story house that is warm and welcoming with beautiful furniture. Uncle Phon didn't just magically get a better life. He had to struggle and work for it with his own sweat and blood. He did his best in high school and learned many lessons in life. Living here in America was a really drastic change for all of his family. He's married now, and continues to work hard. He still takes very good care of his brothers and sisters. He moved to Massachusetts before I was born, and I met him when I was five. In 1998, when he and his family came to visit us, I loved him almost immediately. He took us out every day around San Francisco, and we had such a sensational time. When they left I was morose and cried, but I often wrote letters to stay close with him. During holidays or birthdays, he never forgot us and sent us cards and money. We went to visit him a few times and he was very excited.

A few years ago, he called my mom one day and informed her that he was getting his bachelor's degree. I was surprised, because he already seemed like the smartest man I knew. He studied management, and we were all very proud of him. He was our first uncle to graduate from college.

Even though he went through a lot back home, my uncle doesn't let the past ruin his life. Many people who go through tragedies, like my mom's family did, let it ruin their lives or they take it out on others. I admire my uncle that much more, because he took his past as an experience and a lesson. He started a new life, yet he still cared for his family and the people around him. He started off poor, but eventually succeeded.

He's a very hard-working man who doesn't ever want much more than to see his family happy. I have never heard him ask anyone for anything. I only see him give. His new life has brought him happiness by seeing his family members' smiles and how they enjoy their lives. His dream would have been hard to achieve without patience, strength, determination, and most importantly, self-confidence.

I remember the last time I visited him, he advised, "Make sure you do good in school, honey. I don't ever want to see any of you guys failing. Always focus and remember that you have parents to take care of and make proud. Take advantage of the opportunities around you—they don't come easy. I never had anything, but now look at me, I feel like I have everything I need for myself and my family. Don't ever stop. Things tend to turn out better sooner or later. Don't ever forget that I can help you; I will do my best. If you ever need anything, please don't hesitate to ask." His dream is accomplished.

In speaking with my uncle that day, I realized it's possible to achieve something if you really want it. His speech really made a click in my head...*things don't just happen on their own; you have to make them happen.* I constantly remind myself, if my uncle went through all that he did and got what he always wanted for his family and himself, then why can't I? It's my responsibility to take advantage of the things I have, because there are others who don't have those opportunities.

I was born in San Francisco. Life is easy for me compared to what my mom's family has been through. I live in a nice, cozy home with modern devices. Lights are a switch away, water a twist away. We always have enough food to feed the family. I don't know how it feels to work really hard day and night. Like my uncle, I'm planning on a big future ahead and I'm not leaving my family behind. I want to pursue a career in art or writing. I hope I can become at least a quarter of what my uncle has become. My dream is to become successful, not only for myself, but also for my family. I'm very thankful for what I have. I'm never going to quit trying.

No matter who you are, you have a dream and it's a dream shared with many people; Americans are not the only dreamers. I believe we all must help each other in order to reach our dreams and help others reach theirs. I know for sure that it's possible to achieve a dream no matter who you are. Even people that come from a different country can achieve their dreams. Uncle Phon is someone that not only dreamed, but also succeeded. I learned from my uncle about going through open doors rather than staying behind closed ones. Motivation is what I need to reach my goals.

Life Is a STRUGGLE

by LEONARDO AGUILAR

MY MOTHER, MARIA, was born in Honduras in the early 1970s. Later she had to leave Central America for a better life. She had to leave her family behind—brothers, sisters, her mother, and her father. She left me, my younger brother Jorge, and my little sister Selena. I remember that day. It was really sad for me and my family, because I knew she was going to San Francisco, California. I thought she was lying when she told us that she would come back soon and take care of us and move us out of poverty.

One of the reasons my mother had to leave the country was that she had too much responsibility in her life. Being a young, single mother of three kids was hard for her living in Honduras, because there is a lot of poverty in that country. There is not much help, and people are not hired for jobs because they lack education. My mother had no choice but to come to the United States at the age of twenty-three. My little sister was sick, she had brain damage at one month old because of her head hitting the ground. Every time my mother had to go to the hospital, she paid for all medical charges. In Honduras, there is no medical insurance.

Our family started immigrating to San Francisco, California in the early '80s for the same reasons that my mother later had to leave the country: poverty, hopes, and dreams. My uncle Jorge was one of the first in the family who came to San Francisco, in 1983. My aunt Lucy came next, in 1985. Years later, she became an American citizen. After that, all the family immigrated to San Francisco because that was where the majority of the family lived in the early '80s. When my mother reached, the United States in 1996, it was hard for her. When she got to San Francisco, she didn't waste time. My mother started working in a supermarket as a cashier. She started sending money to Honduras to help the family she'd left behind.

In 1998, my mother could no more stand leaving everything that she loved back home in Honduras. One day, my mother was packing when my uncle Rosel walked into her apartment. She told him, "I am moving back to Honduras." When my uncle heard that, he said, "You are making a mistake if you go. I wouldn't help you if you try to come back to San Francisco." Then he said, "If I go back to Honduras, I will bring your kids to you." My mother was surprised and happy, and she could not believe what my uncle was proposing. My uncle told my mother just to give him $1,000, and the next month he would fly back to Honduras.

When it was time to go, I remember there was wind and it was a cold morning. All I remember seeing is my grandmother outside the house waving good-bye. That was the last time I saw the house where so many memories were. I left home at the age of five years old; my brother was four. Part of me was really excited and happy, but when we were leaving Honduras, we left behind my little sister Selena. I don't remember saying good-bye to her. Now that I am a young adult, it makes me feel bad. I was a kid and I didn't know what was going on.

When we got to the United States, our first city was Los Angeles, California. My mother waited for us in San Francisco. My mother's friend named Jose, who owns "El Cachanilla" restaurant on 20th Street and Folsom, went all the way to Los Angeles to get us. I will always appreciate that and be thankful. Waking up the next morning in San Francisco was really big for me. I saw my mother and I jumped into her hands. It was the happiest moment we had, my brother and me. The first place we went to was my mother's apartment downtown, where we lived for about six years. Our first school that we went to was Mission Education Center. My mother put us in an after-school program to catch up on what we had missed in school. It was hard to adapt to a new place, a new culture, and a new language that we needed to speak. Our English was not that good; I understood but didn't know how start a conversation. We ended up in Bessie Carmichael Elementary School. It was hard for us; we had about two years in San Francisco, plus a new school, new classmates, new teachers. I remember I used to get called a clown in class because my English was not that good. I thought all problems could be fixed by using violence and verbal words, but I was wrong. I got help at school and was sent to an anger management program that helped in some ways.

November 7, 2002, was one of the tragic days of my mother's life. At the time, she was working for a company, Merry Maids. She was leaving work when she received a call to meet my uncle Oscar at his apartment in the Mission District where he lived with my cousins Johanna and Katherine and my aunt. When my mother arrived to my uncle's apartment, she saw my uncle waiting outside for her with news that was not good. My uncle spoke to my mother as everybody was quiet and a sad look was on everybody's faces. My uncle gave her a hug and told her, "Your daughter was pronounced dead earlier today." My mother just covered her face and cried. My mother always thought that she would see her daughter alive again.

Before my mother was going to go to the United States, she had a talk with her father. The last words my mother told her father were "I am coming back soon." My grandfather responded, "This will be the last time I will see you." My mother responded in a strong positive way: "Don't say that. I will be back soon, in one year." But inside her heart, she cried and gave a sad look when she saw her father for the last time. Her father knew that was the last time he was seeing his daughter. Even though my grandfather was brave and strong, tears dropped while saying it this last time. On November 21, 2006, ten years after that, my mother was in San Francisco when she got the bad news that my grandfather gave his last breath. He was no longer on earth, at the age of eighty-four. My mother cried like I have never see her cry before, far from being the strong woman with all the struggles she's been through. But we still keep our heads up.

My mother was going through a lot of things. A big issue was that the economy was bad and she was trying to own a house but the mortgage was going up. She had paid the bank a really high percentage of money. But my mother was not alone in this one; she had support from her brother Oscar to help her in the house, because he and my mother were the only two owners who were trying to buy the house. The same year that my grandfather passed away, 2006, was the year my mother was buying the house and couldn't. Her daughter and her father were dead and gone … what's next?

The American Dream has taken a lot from my mother since 1996, when she came here. She never looks at the bright side of the American Dream, at the person she was before and at who she is now: independent and a hard worker. Bringing my brother and me to the United States and the suffering she has had will one day come back at her and be a blessing. She hopes one day to move back to her country, to live a peaceful life and rest from all her struggles from being a hard worker to give us things she never had when she was growing up. She feels betrayed and at the same time successful for being here. My mother has done positive things in her life. She has had the chance to own houses, a business, and cars in the United States. That's a lot of things she accomplished in the United States, because in Honduras she never would have had the things she has now. Whatever help she needs, I am going be there for her.

I appreciate my mother for all the hard work she has done to make it in her life. I will always remember positive things in life, what she has done to keep us on track and stay in school, and for being a single mother, because I know it is not easy raising kids on her own. I never had support from a father, but my mother was there in all the times that I needed support and anything else.

THREE PARTS
Make a Whole

by SAMANTHA MATTOS

THE UNITED STATES has always been a place where people come to start over, to get a better life for themselves. This country was built on immigrants coming for better jobs, better education, and better lives. America is a place of hope. My father was born in this country, and my mother was adopted as an infant from Mexico by an American couple, so my parents didn't come here as immigrants, but they are great examples of people who never gave up on their dreams. Even when they were at their lowest, when most people would have given up, they still had hope.

My father, an African American born in 1962, was raised in a segregated neighborhood in Chicago. He had a pretty good life growing up. He was close to his parents and sisters, especially his sister Sherri. He grew up in a huge, two-story house with big, wide front and back yards. When I visit my grandparents, who still live in this house, my dad always says that his room hasn't changed at all. Rap posters cover the walls, books line the shelves, and his bed and dresser are exactly how he left them. My dad went to a private school where he was one of only a handful of black students. My grandmother was a beautician and my grandfather worked in construction. You could say my dad's family was upper middle class.

Since my father had a pretty good life, what could go wrong? Surrounding himself with bad influences is what. My father will tell you himself, from experience, that his friends were doing drugs, so like any normal teen, he became curious. One thing led to another. My dad began to do drugs, and he became even more curious. Soon he was becoming an alcoholic and doing stronger drugs. He became completely addicted and was not able to attend college as a result. His parents were heartbroken to see that their one and only son was heavily addicted to drugs. They knew he was capable of so much more. His sisters felt the same way, most of all Sherri, who was devastated to find that her brother was a substance user.

Seeing the pain in his parents' eyes, seeing the heartbreak of his sister, and hating the segregated, drug-infested streets of Chicago, he knew he had to leave. He had always wanted to go to California, so he set out for a better life. Unfortunately, that didn't come right away. In fact, in California, his addiction to drugs became even stronger.

In San Francisco, my dad was literally at rock bottom, with no family, no home, no money, and a drug addiction. He slept in dark and lonely doorways, or he would stay in an abandoned bathroom at a car wash. Occasionally he would stay in a shelter, like Glide, in the Tenderloin District. Then, out of nowhere, something clicked in my father's head. He wanted to change his life for the better; he was tired of drinking and doing drugs, and he hated his everyday routine. It was as if he saw a stroke of sunlight for the very first time, shining through his dark hole. My father knew, at that moment, that this wasn't the life for him anymore. He realized his dream was still out there, waiting for him to achieve it.

My dad finally found the strength to become clean and sober. He took himself to rehabilitation facilities and meetings. This whole process was one of the hardest things my dad ever had to do. When telling me about it, he compared it to the *Twilight* saga, the book and movie series, so that I could understand. I love *Twilight* so much; I know every little aspect of the series. So my dad said to me, "Try to imagine giving up *Twilight*." That's when I was like, "Say no more, daddy, I can hardly imagine that!" I understood how hard it was. But as difficult as it was for my dad, he obviously had the strength to do the impossible. Finally, after a lot of struggle, my father became clean and sober, and he began to live his life—the life he always wanted.

I am proud to know how hard my dad worked to turn his life around. After he got sober, he worked as a security guard at Safeway stores and stayed in a few motels. It may not seem like much, but it was a start compared to that dark hole he was in before, and most importantly, he was not using drugs anymore.

But even though my father had come very far, he still felt like there was something important missing. He was all alone in California. He started praying to God for a family because family was so important to him. He needed and wanted that support and dedication that a family could bring. It was just about this time that my mother and I came into the picture.

• • •

My mother had a tough life similar to my dad's. She was adopted from Mexico as an infant and brought to San Francisco, where she lived in a very nice house with her three brothers. She attended a private girls' school, and like my father, she got into drugs when she was a teen because of peer pressure and trying to "fit in" with her so-called friends. My mother was never accepted for who she was growing up. She was too short, her hair was too curly, her skin was too dark, she had too many freckles, and she wore glasses. She always had that pressure to be some-one she was not. She felt insecure, alone, and not loved.

My mother had always felt very distant from her own mom; she didn't really feel love from her. Her mom was very strict and never let her hang out with her friends. She was very hard to communicate with and she never showed any affection toward her adopted daughter. My mom is the sweet, affectionate type. For my mom, just hearing *I love you* isn't enough; she needs to be able to see and feel love in order to know that she is loved.

When my mother first started using, she was at a friend's birthday party. She had surrounded herself with a bad group of friends and did everything they told her to do, even though deep inside she knew it was very wrong. After that day, things began to go downhill. My mom felt alone and unaccepted to the point where she, like my dad, decided moving away from her home was the best option for her. She didn't know how to face her inner problems in life, so, by leaving, she felt like she was fixing them. My mother had this huge gap of emptiness inside her, and to fill that space, she turned to drugs. Even if it was only for that short moment, as long as something took her pain away, my mother would use it. She was very emotionally unstable and vulnerable at the time.

Just when it seemed like things couldn't get any tougher for my mom, she got pregnant. This may seem like a huge burden for some people. However, this was a life-changing experience for my mother. The big difference between my mother and my father was that my mom never became heavily addicted to drugs. So when she became pregnant, she stopped thinking about just herself. She wanted the best for me; she wanted to give me the life she wasn't able to have for herself; she wanted to be the mother to me that she felt she never had. Not only did she stop abusing drugs, but she became an adult as well. She had no choice but to grow up and be that role model for me. It wasn't easy. My mother was riding solo, as my birth father wasn't in the picture. My mom was on her own for everything, and even though raising a child by herself was going to be very hard, my mom didn't mind it—not one bit. She didn't care about how hard the struggle would be; she was happy that she had somebody to love who would love her back.

My mother and father met each other through a friend of theirs. My dad always had eyes for my mom, but that was not the case for my mom. They hung out a few times with friends, and then he finally had the courage to ask her to dinner. At first my mom said no, but that didn't stop my dad; he wouldn't give up until she said yes. Finally they went on a date. Ever since that first date, they have been together. They are opposites, yet they mesh well with each other, and the one thing they do have in common is that they both are understanding people. My parents could relate to each other so much. But then, there was the problem of me!

Since it had just been the two of us for my whole life, I became very protective of my mom, especially when it came to men. I never had a father figure, so I didn't open up to anyone other than my mother. Even when I went to therapy, I didn't open up to my therapist. I had no father, I was with my mom 24/7, and I was only three years old. I had had a tough childhood up to that point. I was homeless, antisocial, and in need of a father. I had a hard time opening up to people. If I let anyone make me laugh, it would be a miracle. My mother would date a guy or two here and there, but whenever it was time for me to meet them, I would never let them get too close to my mom. If I didn't react well to the guy, then most likely he wouldn't be in the picture for too much longer. No matter what, I just didn't let them into my life.

When I first saw my father, it was in a Safeway store on Church Street. I loved going to Safeway because there was an old mechanical horse with chipped paint right in the front entrance. I loved to ride that horse whenever I had the chance. So when we got to Safeway, I asked, "Please mommy, can I ride the horse? Please?" Then I saw this big open hand appear, and it was filled with quarters. The man spoke to me. "Here, Samantha. Don't be shy. Go ride the horse." I wasn't sure why this large, dark man was speaking to me, but right there he won me over. He made me laugh, and if someone can make me laugh, it is the first step to me opening up to him. I still love how my father touches my face with his finger and how he smiles like he did that first day. Later, my dad told me that when he first met me, it was "love at first sight," and he knew he had found the daughter he always wanted.

My father and mother have both accomplished many things. My father is now an engineer, a dream he had since he was a child. He is financially stable, and he has a family of his own that he loves. My mother stopped doing drugs all on her own and has given me the life she always wanted. And for me: I have a place to grow, a dad to ask for advice, a mother whom I can go to for anything, and so much more. Some say the American Dream can no longer be achieved. Many are unemployed; others have lost their homes; and the future is uncertain. Yet my mother and father have taught me something different. My parents never gave up, even when things got very tough. They fought and created a dream for themselves. With determination, hard work, and a lot of love, they both reached their dreams. Now it is my turn to achieve my dreams, even if they may seem far away.

Even Superheroes DREAM

by ANGELICA VERDUGO

IT'S CLOSE TO THE TIME of his return. Anxiously, I bug him every day, asking when they are sending him home. "Sometime this week, maybe in a few days." Okay. I can wait a few days, it's only been *six months* since he's been able to be home for more than a week or so. I can wait; it's only my brother Louie, the person I've looked up to for most of my life. I get a picture message from him on my phone, and when I open it I think, "What?" It is of him with BART in the background. But there isn't a BART station in North Carolina, where he was stationed for the Marine Corps. So I call him. "Where are you?" I ask.

"Just here," he responds suspiciously.

"Here where?" I feel anxious to know where he is. "Are you back? 'Cause I know there aren't any BART stations in North Carolina, dude," my voice cracking at the end.

"But there is a BART," he lies.

"LIAR! BART is Bay Area—"

"Okay, okay. I'm at the airport," he finally says. I feel a rush of excitement come over me. He's home! He's finally home! He's done with training, boot camp, Marine Corps Training (MCT), and Military Operations Specialty (MOS). He's back, here to save the day.

Louie has always set the bar high when it comes to goals to achieve. He has enthusiasm, drive, and determination that make him feel that he can reach any goal he sets for himself, and he continues going higher. This is part of why I look up to him so much, more than anyone, and why he has such great influence over me now. He has learned to control what didn't work for him in order to make his goals more reachable.

Louie and I once had a conversation about why he set his goals the way he did, and he gave me an amazing, deep-from-the-heart lecture. My brother told me not to settle for average. "'Cause if you settle for average, then that's all you're going to get. Set the bar to becoming the best; once you're the best, go higher. Once you're the best, look up, set the bar to the sky; once you've reached the sky, go for the galaxy, then go for the universe." The American Dream is an idea that consists of specific ideals, a utopian lifestyle. This ideal life, filled with perfection, is impossible. Nobody or anything is perfect. There also doesn't seem to be a line dividing needs and wants. We want to have it all plus a whole bunch more. There can't be a single national dream based on a nation that isn't even united. We can't have a national dream when the dream really depends on the individual. This dream is more of an idea, or a goal to reach, and I see my brother's dream forming. The obstacles that are in the way of finding his dream, in the end, help build his dream and bring it closer.

In addition to setting his goals high, my brother would often choose goals that would be a real challenge for him. Most of them were tied to his main obsession: wrestling. He started wrestling during his sophomore year of high school, and I started going to his tournaments when I was in third grade. Wrestling was a physical challenge, and it made him self-disciplined. In order to make weight, he had to follow a strict high-protein diet, which he managed to stick to, so he kept his weight in control. Every match was an obstacle: two-minute rounds of wrestling against someone else's weight, body, strength, and movement. Louie had to know how to move, to get them down and get the most points or pin them.

I remember a round in which my brother and his opponent were evenly matched, but the score turned out to be twelve–fourteen; Louie had twelve. The coach argued that he had earned more points, so the coaches and the referee talked about it for a minute. During that time, all that was going through my brother's head was keeping his body warm (in case he had to keep wrestling) by playing the song "She's a Maniac," which always kept him pumped up. The coaches and referee concluded that the score was really fourteen–fourteen, meaning Louie and the other wrestler had to go into overtime (lasting thirty seconds to a minute). During the first overtime round, which was for one minute, neither wrestler scored any points. They had already wrestled for three straight two-minute rounds and one overtime round, and now they had another overtime match to see who would score a point first and win. In double overtime, since Louie had scored points first, he got to choose his position, top or bottom. He picked bottom. He needed to score points and score fast. This guy was good, but Louie needed to be better. When the round began, Louie started to move fast. He got up and started to peel the opponent's hands off, but as he did, he was getting too close to the boundary line. He couldn't afford to step out of the boundary line, so he maneuvered to the right. Escape! He managed to escape and gain a point, so the match was over! Fifteen–fourteen, Louie had won.

Louie also ran two to three miles and worked out whenever he could. He would run before school, during breakfast time, lunch time, after school (before practice), after practice, to work, and back home. During practice, after he had already finished running the two-mile warm-up, he would run two extra laps and overtake his teammates. But it still wasn't enough to put him in the spot he wanted. He was determined to do better and be better.

When high school was over, college was Louie's next step in life. He went to Chabot College in Hayward and joined the wrestling team. By the end of his first year in college, he still didn't know what he wanted to major in. Because wrestling ties into most of Louie's life, it was a big reason why he went to college. Louie didn't stay in college long, and he regretted not going anymore. When I saw that my brother was going to college as a full-time student, I told myself that was what I was going to do. Even though he didn't stay, I still want to go to college and get a great career out of it.

A lot happened from then until the summer of 2009, but that summer really changed things for my brother and my family. During that time, Louie told us that he had signed up for the Marine Reserves. He told us at first that he wasn't going until December or January, but there was an open spot for recruits in August. He accepted the spot, and I was devastated. I was happy that we had gotten so much closer than we used to be. Even when we weren't around each other as much, I looked up to him and saw him as the person that will always protect me. I hated the fact that we had barely started to create this brother-sister bond, and now it might cease to exist. But I supported his decision, even though I didn't want to let him go.

As time passed, we received letters from Louie. He was at Marine Corps Recruitment Depot (MCRD), also known as boot camp. He would tell me stories and write to me about the things that kept him strong. He always had something that pushed him and urged him to go forward.

From January to mid-February, Louie was completing his Military Operations Specialty (MOS), which is training for a specific job in the Marine Corps. When I spoke to my brother, I saw and heard his dream forming. He sounds like a different person at times, more mature and certain of life. He's more sure of what he wants to do in life and for himself. I see a dream within him, growing and growing as the days go by. When he talks to me, and even when he lectures me, I hear what that dream may be.

Louie became an assistant coach at Clayton Valley High School for a few years and is now a regular coach there. He wants to go back to college and now knows what he wants to do there. He loves math and coaching his wrestlers, so he wants to teach math and P.E. I think he'd be great at teaching, especially math, because he has always helped me when I don't understand my homework. I hope to be going to college in the fall of 2011. Louie has inspired me. My urge to push forward and reach to the highest is growing.

When I asked Louie what his goals were in life, he told me that he wants to be a superhero, even though he doesn't have superpowers. He has always loved Spider-Man; he would often say that he *was* Spider-Man. But there is a difference between the superhero he wants to be now and Spider-Man or any of those other characters: they had powers that helped them fight crime, and he wants to prevent crime. Instead of fighting in order to stop crime, he wants to prevent the criminal from ever forming. He wants to do so by getting kids to join wrestling, to teach them self-discipline and motivation. Being on any school team requires the players to keep their grades up, so the kids would have to do well in school, too. The student-wrestlers would be more focused on school and wrestling, rather than being on the streets.

Louie is now twenty-two years old. As he is still growing up, he is beginning to set clearer goals for himself. Not an American Dream, not a false, nationwide dream, but a dream that comes from deep down inside of an individual. The dreams of millions do not narrow down into one. Many people may have similar dreams, but they are all unique in their own ways. As for my own dreams, I believe I can achieve them in due time. I am still not sure of my lifelong goals, but I do know that attending college (hopefully NYU!) is a part of that dream of mine. I will do my best and get to my dreams when it is time to. I will show the world what I'm capable of, mature even more, and become a person that has lived her dream. In time, I will find my dream, fulfill it, and live a better life.

Our Family's
EDUCATION

by JAVIER LOPEZ

MY MOM AND DAD did not finish high school. They both dropped out of the ninth grade. They didn't finish high school because my mom was pregnant with my sister and my dad had to start working to support my family. They don't have the same education as I do, because I already passed the ninth grade. Even though I passed them, they still expect me to finish high school because they know how hard it is to get a good job without a high school diploma. My sister is the only person in my family who has graduated from high school, so it's important for me to graduate. They want our family to start doing better in school. If we start doing better, we will have better jobs and more money. Money would make my family's life a lot easier.

When my parents dropped out of high school, they got an apartment together in San Francisco to raise my sister. While my mom stayed home to take care of my sister, my dad would work a lot to support them. My mom was new at taking care of a baby, so it was hard for her. She also had to take care of the house. Since my dad didn't finish high school, he didn't have a lot of job options. He got a job at a shoe factory making shoes all day. After my sister was a little older and started school, my mom also started to work at the factory with my dad. My mom had to stop working a year later, because she was pregnant with me.

I don't think that my parents ever cared about their jobs. They both knew that if they had stayed in school their lives would have been easier.

They acted like it never bothered them, because they have a lot of pride in whatever they do. Because they were working in the shoe factory, they never had a chance to learn what their talents were. They just knew that they didn't want me or my sister to work like that. That's another reason why it is very important to them that my sister and I graduate from high school and go to college. They want us to figure out what we are good at, because success is also about working with your talents.

My family believes that going to school is about acquiring knowledge. I believe this is what they want for my sister and me. They don't see school as a place to learn about who you are. My experience with school shows this to be true. At school you don't get to choose what you want to learn; you are just expected to pass the classes they give you. I hope that when I go to college, I will be able to find what makes me happy and what my talents are. I think an important part of college is to find out who you are, even though my parents never talked about this. They want us to find jobs that make us happy and fulfill us.

Before my sister, no one in my family had ever graduated from high school. Getting a high school diploma is a big expectation in my family. Most of my family dropped out of high school either because they had to work, had a baby, or just couldn't stay. When my sister made it to the twelfth grade, there was a lot of pressure for her to graduate. She felt that if she messed up, the whole family would be disappointed with her. She was even the class president. When she graduated, it was the proudest day for my family. She was the first one to do it. When she went to San Francisco State on a scholarship, my parents had even more pride in the family. My family expects me to do the same as my sister. They want me to graduate from high school and go to college too, because they feel that if my sister could do it then I can do it too.

My sister is good at school, but I am not. School for me is very hard, and I already feel like dropping out; I don't like going and I never get along with my teachers. Teachers always assume I'm doing something wrong, even when I'm not. I remember when I was in the ninth grade, a teacher told me that I would never amount to anything. I thought that the teacher was a good teacher, so ever since then I felt that every teacher was like that. Most of my teachers never give me a chance. They expect me to fail. This unfairness makes me feel misunderstood, so I don't want to even try. I hope that when I get to college, things will be different.

My mom doesn't want me to leave school, because she knows that I am going to regret leaving, like she feels now. My mom told me that if she hadn't gotten pregnant, she would have stayed in school and studied to become a nurse. After I graduate from high school, she is planning to go back to school. She wants to show me and my sister that she can also get her high school diploma.

When I was ready to give up, I found out I was going to be a father. My girlfriend told me she was pregnant, and I felt I must stay in school because I want to be able to support my child. My mom told me she wasn't going to let me drop out. She was going to help me, because she wanted me to stay in school for my baby.

When my son was born it was a very hectic day because it happened very fast. I took my girlfriend to the doctor's for her check-up, but they told her that they needed to induce the labor. I had to call our parents to rush to the hospital because they had no idea the baby was about to be born. We stayed at the hospital for a long time and everyone was excited because of a new baby. Finally, when the baby came out we were all happy, and the doctor told me to cut the umbilical cord. I felt a lot of pride when I first saw him and held him.

After his birth, the doctor told us that he had to stay in the hospital for a couple of days because he was born jaundiced. I remember that seeing him at the hospital made me think about life and the things I was doing. My mother had told me that all the males on her side of the family had jaundice, including me. This made me feel responsible for my son because I might have passed it on to him. The experience made me think about all the things I could pass on to my son. I want to pass on something good to him.

Even though I have a baby and I know that I have to stay in school, I still feel that it is hard. Having a baby has made it more difficult for me because I have more responsibilities now. Besides school, I take care of my kid and work. Yet having a kid also inspired me to stay in school. My child gave me that extra push that I needed to finish. He inspired me because now it's not just trying to be like my sister or making the family proud; it is now about my kid's future. It's about making sure I am able to take care of him and give him everything he needs. I want to make sure my son is able to take care of himself later.

I also want to be an example for him to follow. I want to be part of the change in my family, that way the next generation has a more likely chance of staying in school, studying, and going to college. They will see that by doing this, life will be easier. When I was growing up I only saw my family dropping out of school and working a lot. I have to try more, even though I still don't like school. I know that it isn't about liking school or not; it's about finishing it for my son, so that he can have a better future and a lot of options of what he wants to be. For me, my mom was a role model because she taught me how to be independent, a leader, and a person who gets things done; qualities that make you successful in life. My mom taught me how to be like that, and that's what I want to teach my kid so that he doesn't have to depend on anybody.

I also want to teach him that the process of being happy and successful is going to be very hard, and sometimes you just want to quit. Because sometimes to be happy and successful you have to do things that you don't want to do. My teacher, Mr. Rose, loves his job and teaching is his success; at times it is hard for him, but it's what he loves to do. That's why I want to be a good role model and show my son that work can be very hard too, but it pays off.

That is a big goal for my family: to live better than the last generation. We want to have more opportunities for the next generation. I want my son to have more than what I had, and to give more to his kids. For my family to live our dream we need to stay in school, go to college, and find good jobs. The next generation will have a greater chance of following our footsteps if they can see how we did it.

What My Father Had to GO THROUGH

by ALI SHARHAN

MY FATHER WENT THROUGH A LOT to bring us to the United States for better jobs, school, and a better life. The dream was just to bring the family together. For me it is different, because I am already here and I am thinking about how I can become more independent. I want to go to college because my father didn't even go to middle school. Still, family is important to me, and the last thing I am going to do is go off and leave my family.

When my father was twelve years old, he got married to my mother, who was also twelve. He was working three different jobs to support his family. One of his jobs was working construction. He built houses and sometimes came back to the house with his hands bleeding from the work he had done. His second job was farming. He worked on the weekends at a small ranch. He worked with tomatoes and other vegetables. The third job was to watch a big building as a security guard. The owner of the building was a friend of my father's. All those jobs were not enough to support the family in his country, Yemen. He loved his country, but the money in Yemen was hard to get. To get a better paying job, my dad decided to move to Saudi Arabia because it was the closest country. He left my mother and went there. The trip was a long drive with his brother across the desert. He didn't go back to his home country for seven years, but he sent money and other things for my mom and brother. He was not allowed to bring his family to Saudi Arabia. So he knew that he would need to bring them to a country that has good jobs and where he could live with them.

After seven years, he decided to go to see his family because he missed them. He went back and stayed in his home country for two months. When he and his two brothers were in a car going back to where they came from, it was exciting because they were going to see their families. Also, their wives were waiting for them to get home. When my father and mother first saw each other, they both cried. They were so happy to see each other again. He was also happy to finally see his son.

My dad went back to Saudi Arabia to apply for a green card so he could come to the United States. He got accepted and planned to move to the United States for a better life for him and his family. Once he had his green card in his wallet, his next goal was to work so he could make money for the airplane ticket. When he had the money for the ticket, he left for the United States.

In the United States, it was hard for him because he needed to speak a new language. He didn't know anyone, so he moved into an Arabic-speaking neighborhood. He lived in one room with other people who spoke Arabic. The people were cool with him. He was trying to speak a new language, and if he didn't know a word, he asked people for the meaning of it.

My father worked at car shops for about seven years. He liked the people he worked with, and the people liked him because he was a hard worker. The job was good for my father because it paid better than the jobs in his home country. Also, he was sending money to my mother for food. That much money in my country was worth a lot. While my father was going through all that, my mother was doing all the work at the house and taking care of my older brother. Without my father at home, my mom had to do a lot of things. My father sent most of his money to my mother, and she saved it for him. My mother is a strong lady. She was without her husband for a lot of years. She trusted my father because she knew that he was working for the family. My father trusted her too.

While my mother did all that, my father was trying to bring his family over to the United States. He was looking for the best for his family. When my father got his citizenship, he wanted to bring my mother to the United States, so he went back to his country to apply from there for my mother, brother, and sister to move to the United States. My father came back to Yemen in 1992. A year afterward, I was born in the capital city. I grew up in the city and went to a school that had about eight hundred students. My school in Yemen was different from the school I attend now. One teacher taught all subjects, and the classrooms were small and packed with students. My brother was older than I was, but he was still a young boy and my father was sending money to him. My brother also worked construction with his friend. He built houses and other things. My brother was trying to help my father by working and taking care of the family. My brother only went to school for half days. He went every day, though, because he liked school and wanted a higher education. My sister took care of me and helped my mom at the house. She wanted to go to school, but no one could help my mother, so she didn't go to school. She always says that family comes first, before education. But she wanted to learn to read Arabic so she would be able to read books and other things. My brother taught her how to read.

My father stayed in Yemen for about a year. After the year finished, he came back to the United States because he didn't have enough money. He spent all his money on passports for his family and a vacation. When he went back to the United States, he worked and finished his government papers so he could bring his family there. While he waited for the papers to come, he worked to make money for the airplane ticket.

It took about six years for the papers to come. When he got the paperwork, he sent money to my mother so she could bring us to the United States, where he would be able to work and go home and see his wife at the house and she would take care of him. One of his friends told him that he had a better job for him in California, so my father decided to go to California. When we came to the United States, we were so happy because we were going to a new place. At the airport, we were excited. That was my first time riding on an airplane. It took us about eighteen hours to get to the United States. When we arrived, my father was waiting in front of the airport. When we saw my dad, we were so happy that we, as a family, had finally made it. He had gone out and looked for a house that he could rent. We all thought the house he rented was a good house because it was better than the house we used to live in. Everything was ready at the house, so we could just start living there. Inside, the house was white, and the outside was also white. The house was big, too, and I liked it because my brother and I didn't have to share a room. The house was a symbol. I want to have a good life and have the family together. My dream (and my father's dream for me) is to have a better life than my father has had and to have a higher education. My mother was tired of not living with my dad. They always wanted to live together, and now they don't have to leave each other. Staying together made the family's dream come true. My father went through a lot to bring me here.

Remember
THE NAME

by EDUARDO CAAMAL

THE MORNING OF my fourteen-year-old brother's game, you could barely see the sun because it was foggy. Roldanier woke up feeling normal, like it was a regular school day. He took a shower and woke me up. We ate his favorite cereal, Cocoa Puffs, but the whole time I was with him he never said anything about his game. My family was anxious to see the game and I was looking forward to it, too, but I knew that it wasn't my game but my brother's. We took him in the van because there are a lot of people in our family and we couldn't fit in the car. I remember that my two uncles came with me, and also my mom, my dad, my sister, her boyfriend, and my brother. We got to 26th and Harrison at the soccer field, and I saw that my brother was listening to his favorite song on his iPod, "Remember the Name" by Fort Minor, with the volume up. He says that this song inspires him to work harder and push himself to the limit. He listens to a song, and he only listens to this one, when he wants to be prepared for something.

After we arrived at the soccer field, he got out the car and he walked to the field by himself. I wanted to walk with him, but I thought that he wanted to concentrate alone. He walked away with a big smile and looked so confident.

Soccer, for me and my brother, is like a language. When we want to express our feelings, we play. When we are sad, we play to forget what made us sad. When we are mad, we play to calm down. It might sound a little crazy, but this is why we play soccer. It's not just about winning.

Soccer is important to me because it's a bond we share that nothing will break, not even death. It unites us even when we're far away from each other. When I play and he's not there, I know that he's thinking about me and is wishing me luck.

My family and I sat in the bleachers. We were nervous because we thought that it was going to be a tough game. The home team looked so prepared and organized. I saw my brother from far away and I thought that he wasn't ready for this game. He was acting different than usual; he looked too calm. This was a championship game and was really important, but he acted like it wasn't.

When the game started, my brother was good; he was always behind the ball, passing it to his teammates well. The two best players on the other team were brothers. Roli was stopping them from playing their usual game. I could see that they were mad at him. I saw one of them push him so hard that he fell on the grass. I was mad and scared at the same time that something bad was going to happen to my brother. I wanted to jump the fence, to see if he was okay, but I froze up. When he moved, I came back to my senses and started breathing again. I thought that my brother was going to be mad and do something that he'd regret later. But he actually just tried to stand back up. Before he could, one of the brothers stepped on Roli's hand with his soccer shoes. My brother couldn't hold his temper anymore so he started fighting with the guy who stepped on his hand. My brother lifted his fist, which was bleeding. His face really changed; he looked out of control. I was scared because last time I saw him that mad was when we got in our first fistfight. I knew what he was capable of doing in that state. Before Roli could do anything, though, the referee told him to sit down and relax. My brother thought about it and sat down, holding his bleeding hand away from his shirt because he didn't want his shirt to get blood on it. If he had blood on his shirt, he wouldn't be able to play—that's the rule. Roli told the referee that the brothers were trying to force him out of the game. The referee didn't believe him. Since my brother couldn't argue with him, he just wrapped his hand with a shirt and tried to make it stop bleeding. It took several minutes for the bleeding to stop.

The first half ended and he was able to get back in. I didn't want him to play because I thought that he was going to try to get revenge on the brothers. I know Roli really well. If I make him mad, he always gets me back. Either he hits me or he thinks up a way to get revenge, which is like mentally torturing me. My brother's team was losing by only one goal, and at the beginning of the second half they tied it up. Minutes were passing by so fast, and the game ended in a tie. Since the game was a championship, a team needed to win, so the referee added two ten-minute periods. At the beginning of the second period, both teams were fouling each other; they were pushing, pulling shirts, or talking trash to their opponents. They seemed to want to end the game with a big fight. I was scared that Roli's blood would boil and he'd lose his temper, but he wasn't paying attention to them, he was focused on the game.

After the second ten-minute period, the game was still tied. The referee told them that they needed to go to penalty shots. All the spectators were paying so much attention that you could only hear the sound of the wind and the players praying for their teammates. Both teams were scoring. Then one player from the other team missed; he looked nervous and kicked the ball so hard that it went flying out the park. After that it was my brother's turn to kick the ball.

Roli was smiling and looking confident and sure of himself. That's one of his problems—he thinks he's the best one and that the whole team needs him. Roli is the same way off the soccer field. Just because he's the tallest in our family, he feels superior to the rest of us. But he's wrong. I don't like telling him he's wrong, because if I do, we'll start arguing. He says that he's always going to take care of me, but he forgets that I'm older and that I'll be the one taking care of the family when my dad can't. His favorite soccer player is his role model, Cristiano Ronaldo. Every soccer player knows Ronaldo is one of the best. But no one seems to notice that he sometimes hogs the ball. My brother wants to be like him, but I tell him that he can be better. I tell him to play with his teammates—that's what soccer is about. It's not about only showing off, because that will only make you get tired and run out of breath. I tell him that last time I checked, there's no I in TEAM and that one player can't win a whole ninety-minute game. I know this because I tried playing by myself but I can't; I get wiped out fast. My brother always has a comeback, though. He says that by hogging the ball you can have fame and other people will want you to play on their team. I tell him that by playing together with your teammates, you can beat whatever team, even if they are the best ones in the world. I've seen really good teams get beat by a weak team. All it takes is communicating with your teammates and working together.

My brother says that I'm not a good player, that he's better than me. I tell him that my dream is not to have fame but to help other people. I'm the same way off the soccer field as I am on it. When I need help, I ask for help. And I help when people ask for help. Fame will end soon enough. You might enjoy it, but what has a start always has an end. My dream won't end, because I want to be a doctor so that I can help people. Roli always says that if someday he gets hurt, he'll know a doctor who will always cure him, and that his fame will come back to him no matter what happens. But someday something might happen to him that I won't be able to cure. He could get old and not be able to play anymore. There's no cure that makes you able to go back to the days when you were young. He always gets mad at me when we have a conversation like this. I've learned how to avoid the mistakes that he's making before he's even achieved his goal. Once, I worried only about myself and didn't care about anyone else. I almost lost my friends because of that, but I changed before it was too late.

My brother says that he doesn't need help with his plans, but when we were at the game and it was his turn to kick the ball, I could see him panicking; he was shaking. He was thinking about what would happen if he missed. He was finally thinking about others. And I saw him from afar and I screamed, "You can do it, bro!" He looked at me and smiled. I didn't know if I should smile back or just stand still; I just laughed. His confidence came back and he kicked the ball and he scored. He started celebrating as if it was the last game in his life and his last goal.

From that day, I remembered that he needs me by his side so he can accomplish his goals. I see that when I'm around he can do whatever it takes to achieve what he wants. And I need him, too. I want him to be there for me when I need him or when I'm struggling to achieve my goals. I want him to be there for me when I go to a college or a university. I want him to tell me that I'm doing well or that I need to do better.

When I need someone, I know that my brother will always be there. I need him because he's the thing that I care about the most. He and I are always together and we have differences but that doesn't really affect us at all. We sometimes fight, but we talk it out and end up laughing. I remember when he was small and I used to take care of him.

I want to always be with my family, no matter what. But I want most to be with my brother. That's my dream, to see him succeed, because with my help he will. I know that people will tell me that I need to talk about me. But me, I am just a kid who is trying to make someone else happy. I will help my brother achieve his goals, and we will share it together.

I AM THE ROSE
that Grew from
THE CONCRETE

by THALIA ANDRADE

Journal Entry, January 21, 2010

SO WHILE I SIT HERE and tell you how I feel, I can't stop thinking about the boundaries I hit at home. All I can do is cry about how I feel, but I am going to try to spill it all out along with my tears. Sometimes all I can think of is the hard time my dad gives me and how mad he gets at me, but I never stop and think about why he is the way he is. I never thought about stepping in his shoes to realize what he's going through and why he's going through it. I know my dad does what he does to push me further so that I can have someone to prove wrong, but I just feel like the harder he pushes me, the harder it is to crawl back up and regain my confidence. My father is the only man who can say he has given me the world, and it was all said and done the day he felt confident and told himself, "I have decided to come to America to get permission to work legally, and give my future family what I have never had."

My father left Mexico at the age of fifteen. He immigrated to the United States after the death of his mother. He was the second oldest, so he had to watch over his younger siblings. My father decided to immigrate to help his grandmother with a little extra money to provide for his brothers and sisters. He had one older sister, one younger sister, and three younger brothers, but since he was the oldest guy, he was in charge of all the man work, while his older sister was in charge of taking care of everyone. My dad didn't have a father while he was growing up and neither did any of his brothers or sisters, and the majority have different fathers, so my dad was always the male figure to them.

My father came over here on a bus that had to go through a mountain. The whole way he was anxious. He didn't know how to feel. He didn't know if he was scared, happy, or sad to leave his family. He was with two of his friends from the same town as him, called Tabasco, in the state of Zacatecas, which is a small town in Mexico where everyone knows everyone. My dad was devastated to leave his family, but happy because he knew it was a new beginning.

When my dad moved out here, he was living with a lady who charged him $280 a month to sleep in a living room while working at a carpentry job for only $3.25 an hour. At the end of the month, the little $3.25 an hour had to get split between his rent and money that he sent to Mexico. The rest was for him to eat. My dad never missed a rent, but somehow the landlord did; she didn't pay the water bills or light bills, so my dad had to take cold showers and lived with no lights. It got to the point where the next-door neighbor would let my father come and take showers at her house. It was just sad because my father gave his rent money and managed to get $280 for rent and money for Mexico out of his little $3.25 an hour, but the lady still didn't give him what he paid for.

This is all I knew until the day I went to my best friend's house and her grandmother asked me, "Are you Trino's daughter?" Back then that's what they used to call him, Trino. She reclined in her chair and she told me I looked so familiar. And that's when she told me my dad moved in with her when he first came from Mexico. He came with two other guys, one was a "drunkie" and the other was an "angel" who was always saying, "Bible this, church that."

She said to me, "Your dad knew what he wanted and his mind was set that he had come here to make money and not to play." And I will never forget when she told me that both of those guys fell on their faces and my father was still standing with his head held high, and that she knew that my dad was going to accomplish his goal and keep his word of why he came here. All I was able to do was smile at her because I felt good for his accomplishments, because that's my dad. And right then and there I knew that he was not like the others who just come to America to fool around. He actually came for the right reason.

But that's when it all came tumbling down. I asked my father about what she told me and he sat back and crossed his arms and asked, "Do you think it was that easy?" and I didn't want to answer that question because I didn't want to be wrong. I stayed quiet and he explained to me that it wasn't easy at all for him to go through that. He fell into a lot of trouble, such as gang affiliation. But my dad learned a lot before it was too late. He managed it and looked at the situation from different perspectives. He always kept his goal, which is now my American Dream, in his mind. He thought to himself, "What doesn't kill me makes me stronger, and I am going to strive to get my family where they need to be and I'm coming home with a story to tell them how we made it to where we needed to be."

Journal Entry, February 18, 2010

I just can't picture a fifteen-year-old young man having to go through all of that! To me, it feels like my dad had to grow up in a short period of time, and when I say "grow," I mean emotionally and mentally. He had to hide how he feels about his mother's death, and struggle to get his family where they need to be, and most importantly go through all of this without one sign of emotion. As for myself, I am a crybaby. I can't hold a tear in, and I can just imagine how much strength my father had to use to hide all of the emotions that must have been eating him up inside. Writing this hurts me in so many ways. I am feeling sad, ungrateful, demolished, and crushed because I have realized everything my father went through and I never stopped to think about him.

I ask myself, "How did I plan to move forward without knowing all of this?" My father went through too much for me not to just show him a piece of appreciation. It would have meant a lot to him just to show him that I understand and that I am grateful for him and his past, and to be able to tell him, "Your past is something that you do not need to hide, it's something worth glorifying."

Every day my dad and I are closer to our dream. The reason why I say "our" dream is because my father worked hard to get me everything that I wanted, so now it's my turn to return the favor. My mom and dad always taught me to be able to do things on my own. For example, my father told me I did not need a job because he wanted me to focus on school, but the way my parents raised me didn't allow me to let them pay for everything. I was tired of having my mom and dad spend everything they worked for on my needs, or should I say wants.

My father never told me what his dream was, but my guess is "us," and by "us," I mean my family: me, my mother, and my little sister. And now I will glorify it and teach my little sister to do the same. I am the rose that grew from the concrete, hitting obstacles and boundaries, but I am still growing beautifully and healthily. I am what you can call beauty within struggle.

Ten
CREDITS

by KAREN MARTINEZ

"YOU ARE NEVER going to make it to college" were the words of my mom when I was beginning to dream my own dream. She didn't understand, but I dreamed of becoming a scientist, a scientist who enjoys her job and does not just do it as a routine. A scientist who will prove many people wrong, one of them being my mom. I had always known that my mom was the type of person who would say something without thinking and wouldn't care if she hurt your feelings or not. My mom thought of it as a way to make me stronger. When I heard those words from my mom, I felt my whole world coming down on top of me, with me not being able to stop it.

Many people used to say I was never going to make it through high school. I used to not care what other people said to me. Then one day in the beginning of the school year, I had a probability project to present. At that moment, it was the most important thing in my life. I only had thirty minutes to finish it before my mom picked me up. The truth is that I took fifty minutes, almost an hour. I walked outside and thought to myself, *Mom probably left*, but as soon I was out of the building, I saw the car and thought, *I am in trouble.* When I got to the car and opened the door, the only thing I saw was those huge brown eyes throwing fire at me. When we finally got home, my mom said, "Go to your room, we need to talk." She was really mad, but she tried calming down and taking a big breath. Then she asked, "Why did you take so long?"

From my bed, I replied, "I was finishing my project. It is really important for me and for my grade in that class."

She was breathing really hard as she crossed the room, until she was right in my face, screaming, "Nobody made it to college in my family! Why should you make it? You are not special or different, you are just like your brother and you're going to end up like him, in a year or two you're going to drop out." I felt bad when I heard this from my mom. I could have heard it from anybody else and it would not have caused me as much damage as hearing it from my own mother.

I remembered my step-dad saying the same thing to my brother Jose when he came in late one night. Jose was lying down on my bed, covering his ears and singing to himself, trying to block my step-dad out, but he just kept going on with the same thing. My brother's words that impacted me the most were, "That's what everybody expects me to do, might as well do as they say."

A few days later, I found out that he was not going to school anymore. He had dropped out. Remembering this, I stood up to my mom and said "NO! I am not ending up like you guys!" She replied, "We will see about that." My mom saying this to me really hurt me, but it also helped me hold on to the inspiration of going to college.

That was a time when I was moving around a lot. I went from being in Oakland for eight years of my life to moving to Ontario, Oregon. I didn't like talking to people I didn't know. I was in a new high school and had no friends. Girls came up to me, trying to punk me. The girls would wait for me outside health class and yell nasty things as I went to lunch. I ended up getting into four or five fights. I got sent to court each time and had to do community service.

Eventually I got kicked out of that high school and got sent to an alternative school where the girls with kids go. I always thought to myself, *Why didn't my family ask me if I wanted to come here? I am part of the family, too.* I felt like everything was out of my control. I wanted to run away. Then I realized that if I wanted to go to college, first I had to graduate from high school. But by the looks of it, the girls I was thrown in with were not on a path toward college.

I hadn't finished my freshman year at the alternative school when my mom told me that we were moving back to Oakland. I was so excited about seeing my friends again that I forgot about all the hard work I had done, and started doing stuff I now regret. I began drinking again and trying new things. When I would come home, my eyes would be red, and I would be walking while falling asleep. My mom would look at me and laugh and let me go to sleep. With the fights and the alternative school, I screwed up my whole freshman year.

At the end of the year, I reflected and decided to finish high school. I'd found myself doing something I didn't want to do: following in the steps of my family and ending up like my brother. I had two choices: either I would end up back at an alternative school where you can't do your work because of the babies' loud crying, or I would work hard and finish what I had started.

I decided to move in with my dad in San Francisco. We stayed on Silver Avenue, near a park where I spent most of my time. I would hang out by myself on the swings and think about what I was going to do with my future. The only examples I had been shown were my brother, who ended up on the streets, and my mom, who was a housewife with a lot of kids. My dad told me, "I don't care if you drop out of high school as long as you keep looking for God." I love God and I understand that He has been the only one there for me, but I felt that there wasn't the support I needed from my dad.

I was going to start high school again in San Francisco and I was really nervous and excited.

When I went into the counseling office, I met with Ms. Burgos and she told me that I only had .5 credits. I thought that it was not fair that I had been in school for a year and had nothing to show for it. I was really annoyed, but I felt I had no way out.

When I was going through all this, I found myself with this person I hadn't noticed, but who was always there, helping me out. Her name is Maritza. Since I was little, when my mom had problems, Maritza would give her advice, so when I started getting in trouble, Maritza gave me advice as well. When my mom used to tell me that I wasn't going to graduate, Maritza would tell me, "It takes hard work to actually be somebody in life." When my dad would tell me that I could drop out of high school and he really wouldn't care, she would tell me, "You have the chance to work hard and graduate. We had it too and did not take advantage of it! You don't want to end up like us."

As time went by, I got closer to Maritza, and she ended up being my guardian. The only condition was that I go to school, get good grades, graduate, and go to college. That was exactly what I needed: someone to push me. I said yes. Maritza looked at me as if she doubted my word and said, "I don't want anybody who drinks, smokes, or does any type of drug in my house." It's been two years now since I drank or intoxicated my body in any way.

I had to go to night school after regular school and, during summer vacation, I had to go to summer school and summer night school. The first day of summer school, when I came out of school I was about to walk down this hill that took me to the bus. I remember this guy standing right next to me and he had a gun in his hand shooting straight ahead. Everybody else dropped to the floor, but I just froze. I was really scared. The next day I didn't want to go back, but I had no choice. I had to finish summer school in order to get my credits, and that was the most important thing for me at that moment. My dream is to go to college, and without those credits I would not be able to graduate, and that would be the end of my dream.

Currently I am a junior. I earned ten credits in summer school. It sounds like very little, but I like thinking about it as *I almost got myself killed over ten credits*. The thing is that once you have the credits, no one can take them away from you. I earned sixty credits from night school, and, by passing all my classes my sophomore year, I got enough credits to officially be a junior. I see myself finally on the right path toward graduating from high school and going to college.

Many of my teachers from last year tell me that I'm different this year, that I'm always smiling now and they see me happier and looking like I'm enjoying what I'm doing. My French teacher told me that last year I was just one of those students that he has in his classroom and doesn't notice that they are there, but this year he notices me more and he knows who I am.

The truth is that I am really happy. I look back on my memories and think about my brothers and sisters and wish I was with them, but I also remember the words of my pastor: "You are being a role model, and showing them that if you can do it, so can they!"

I think about all that I have been through and of my dream to go to college and be someone important. I also think about this verse from the

Bible that has helped me a lot: "Have I not commanded you? Be strong and courageous. Do not be terrified; do not be discouraged, for the Lord your God will be with you wherever you go" (Joshua 1:9). This verse tells me that I'm not alone and to be brave and persevere. In the end, I want to be the first one in my family to graduate from high school and go to college, and to set a good example for my younger brothers and sisters. If they could see me succeeding with a PhD, starting a career as a scientist with my lab coat, my clipboard, and my goggles, maybe they could have faith in their dreams too.

Horace Mann Is a
TOUGH
SCHOOL

by DAVID E. FLORES

ON AUGUST 25TH, 2004, I got accepted to a school called Horace Mann Middle School. I stepped in the schoolyard, nervous of what would happen, like every kid that goes to a school for the first time. When I was going to my first class, in the hallway I saw a lot of bullies, wearing their pants at their knees, acting tough, and fighting with the smaller kids. In my opinion, this was a bad example to the new kids, because that would be the first thing they would see in this school, and they would want to leave right away! After a long day at a rough school, I knew this school would be tough for me. I had a feeling that I would end up confronting those "wannabe gangsters" who thought they were the best.

After many weeks of school, I finally found a good friend. We would talk and laugh; his name was Anthony Escobar, my first friend in middle school. I met him in third period where we sat next to each other at the table and started talking—saying our names, where we live, and our hobbies.

Every lunch, we were always together because there really was not much to do around lunch, so we just talked. The problem was that there were those savages lurking and finding targets to demolish! Many times they picked on us because we were small, and they liked to push us down like animals. I wished I could defend myself from those savages, but I could get in trouble with them, and I was too scared. I felt that this school's culture was like a survival camp, where the bullies were like teachers. They would scream at you, push you, and punch you to basically make you "tougher." It was not the school, but the negative culture that was vile; some people were trying to make you tougher, make you join their group and wear wannabe clothes and become a "gangster." Then again, there was also the minority of kids who actually wanted to pass middle school, then high school, and go off to college!

After many months in this horrifying school, I got a scholarship of $1,300 from the district for having As and Bs in all of my classes! I felt really happy that I received this money from the government to save for my future college. Also, I felt that it was a personal accomplishment, because not every kid gets that kind of money. My mom was happy with me and invited me and my dad to a restaurant for my achievement. During that time, my mom and dad talked about how to approach the next year of school, seventh grade. My mom told me, "David, be more careful this time. I know that this school is really bad, and you know we're here for you. If you need help inside the school, talk to the counselors or teachers who will help you." I listened to those words really well, because I knew I would need all the help I could get!

On August 25th, 2005, I entered the school, scared, looking out at the bullies I knew. When I was walking in the yard to the cafeteria, I met a kid that looked like me but was Japanese. His name was Jeffry Kondo. He had the same classes as me, so we started being friends in the classes we went to. We talked about the games that we liked, and we played a lot. It was destiny that we became friends, and this made our lives much better. It was a coincidence when I said, "I am bored, I will draw some *StarCraft* characters!" Amused, Jeffry stated, "You play *StarCraft* too; my username is E)xc-raider!" I responded, "Mine's Destro99!" I was shocked that someone actually played *StarCraft* in my area; it was really hard to find someone in San Francisco who played! We both were really excited to get home and to play together and have a lot of fun. After that, I introduced Jeffry to Anthony, and the three of us became friends. We liked the jokes that we told each other, and we laughed a lot.

The negative side was that we provoked new enemies. They started to see us as small kids, and they just wanted to bully us! But our friendship could never be broken, and over time we became the Three Musketeers. We were never apart because we always stuck together in any situation.

In November, we started to get pushed a lot by three guys who we called the Three Gangsters. We called them that because of how they looked tough and how they acted like they were the bosses of the school. After many weeks of getting bullied, being scared, and just wanting to leave school, it was time to confront the Three Gangsters.

It was December, right before winter break. When lunch started, we looked for the gangsters, instead of them looking for us. We had our hands tight for a good punch. When we saw them, we went up to them and they approached us. "What you want, little kids?" asked the first gangster. "Hahaha," laughed the others.

Afterward, we felt triumphant, powerful, ready to stop anyone that came our way, because we took down a small gang that was strong, but too cowardly to fight. After that heroic day, we noticed that during lunch the gangsters didn't bother us again. We were happy that we could live our lives in peace for the next year, eighth grade.

The summer after seventh grade, Jeffry called my house and said, "David, something bad happened, Anthony moved away from San Francisco, to a town named Novato!" I was shocked that our third friend had moved away, and only Jeffry and I were left. When Jeffry and I were playing *StarCraft*, we typed about what we would do when eighth grade came, where we would meet, where we would hang out. We didn't want to make new enemies out of nowhere!

Eighth grade would come, our final year, the last year before freedom from such an epically hurtful school, where I thought no one would want to go. We wanted that year to be real good, and to enjoy it before we moved on from middle school. We would try not to bug anyone or to provoke anyone so that we could have an enjoyable lunch. We typed a lot of what we would do, and the things that we were not willing to do: when you see a bully that has a look on you, turn away to not cause trouble, don't start a fight that will just get attention, ask teachers to help you with your troubles when bullies are bothering you. These are just a few of the items that were on the list. I memorized these items, and I was prepared.

On August 25th, 2006, I started my eighth grade year, the year that would end it all! End all of the torture from those "wannabe gangsters." The first few months started out superb because Jeffry and I already knew everyone.

A kid named Marco came into our lives. He was in all of my classes. When I said hopefully we don't provoke new enemies, and have an exceptional year, I was wrong. Even if you don't provoke enemies, they still come to you. Marco started to bug me, and then Jeffry too, when he saw us together at lunch and in classes. He bugged us because we were small! When he was bugging me I defended myself, not with punches, but instead with pushes and some "snitching" because I was tired of it! He always stated, "What a snitcher!" in a weird way to me. Why should I care? I was tired of his picking on me for no good reason! I felt protected by the teachers because they were like juvenile police: if they caught you, you were finished! This tactic was on the list that Jeffry and I created, and it was effective because I didn't get hurt. Jeffry was less bugged by Marco because he never had his classes, and he knew Marco was not smart.

I remembered my mom's advice when seventh grade was about to start, and I knew what I needed to do. In April, I went to my counselor to have a meeting about Marco, to say that he was bugging me too much. Marco was nervous about what would happen to him. It was about a thirty-minute meeting: only me, my mom, Marco, and the counselor. We agreed that Marco couldn't get close to me until I got out of middle school. I was happy that I wouldn't be bothered again and could enjoy my last months. I was not worried at all when I walked the halls of the school, because I knew we had conquered all of the evil that stepped on the doorstep to our future.

May 24th, the school had a graduation party at Golden Gate Park before we went on stage. Jeffry and I, and my other friends, had tons of entertainment. We played ball, ran, and played. After the amusing party, a friend of my mom did a favor and drove my mom and I downtown, where my uncle picked us up to take us home. When we arrived downtown, Jeffry said, "David, why don't we go to my house? It's like three blocks away!" and my mom agreed to go. For the first time in two and a half years of being friends, I went to my best friend's house. After having a blast those days, we went to our graduation ceremony, got our diplomas, and screamed "YES, FREEDOM!" After our epic scream, I said goodbye to Jeffry, he said bye to me, and bye to the school where I would never go again.

What I believe is, for every dream you want to achieve and live, you have to pass through any obstacles that stand in your way. I went through many horrible situations, and I made it. Now it is high school, then college, and then a job. My experience gives me a better understanding of how people from Mexico, Central America, and even South America struggle to reach the United States and to reach their own dreams. The border patrol are bullies who stop Latinos from entering the United States. When they deport them, they treat them like animals, pushing, punching, and more aggressive things. If immigrants reach the United States, it's hard for them to get a job. Also getting the money they need is hard, because basically they start at zero dollars. Just like when a freshman who starts high school doesn't know where to go, where the rooms are, or where to find friends; it's tough at the beginning, so you're lost. These immigrants should get an opportunity to live their own dreams, and maybe have the chance to live them in the United States. Hopefully they get chances for jobs, education, health care, and insurance. I believe that this is a free country and people have the ability to choose what their own dream is, as long they're willing to confront their obstacles. So, are you ready to overcome your obstacles?

Small Heart with
BIG DREAMS

by KARLA HERNANDEZ

IVAN MIRANDA, ALSO KNOWN AS "Lil Mijo": friend, brother, homie, family—born as a soldier and died as one. He meant everything to me, to the mains, to the homies, and, more importantly, to his family. Ivan was there every time I needed him, and I was there for every little thing he needed.

I remember back when I was a freshman and Ivan was in the eighth grade, we had long phone conversations about how he was in love. I always had his back and approved of everything he wanted to do. For me, he is still alive in every single one of my dreams and prayers. I have memories of us talking about our problems. My heart went under pressure when my homie died and I couldn't do anything about it. My *osito*, my teddy bear. I remember the first time I called him that. I was sitting down on my bed with all my teddy bears around me and I was talking to him on the phone, laughing and joking. I told him I loved teddy bears because they are soft and cute. I decided to ask him, "Do you want to be my *osito*? I could name one of them Ivan, like you." Ivan laughed about how I wanted him to be my teddy bear, but he said yes.

Back in Everett Middle School, he was just a little kid to me, my best friend's boyfriend. He became my friend and we always talked on the phone. He said to me, "*Ay niña, ya portate bien, loquita.*" Hey little girl, you need to start behaving better, crazy baby girl. He helped me, and I helped him. I would always listen to his advice, but at one point I just decided to not care. I became a bad person, someone who didn't really care about life. Later, looking at his face in the "ugly box," I felt lost. A fourteen-year-old stabbed? It was a horror to me. After his death, his words came back to my mind. I decided to change not only for him, but for myself too. I listen to him more now that he isn't with me. Even though he is not here, I feel like his advice is still alive. I loved him and will always love him. Ivan was a good younger brother.

At 1:30 a.m. Ivan got stabbed, and the cops passed and didn't help him. He could've survived, but justice is not always right. I heard the news: "*Ivan Miranda fue encontrado muerto a la 1:30 de la madrugada. Se dice que trató de defender a su amiga que estaba embarazada.*" Ivan Miranda was found dead at 1:30 a.m., they say that he tried to defend his friend who was pregnant. If cops had seen him on the floor, why did they not stop and check what was wrong? This made me cry. How come life is this unfair? The youngest kid killed in San Francisco. I couldn't believe it. Looking at his dead body gave me hope, sadness, and also happiness because I knew that he was in a better place. Paradise is where he stays, and in my heart is where he will always be.

Later, I saw stories in the newspapers about how the police got two of the boys that killed him. The two people that the police arrested are eighteen and twenty-one years old. One of the killers said hurtful words about him that made me want to take action. People say revenge is sweet, but if I had done something, maybe it wouldn't have been that great.

Seeing Ivan's body with his long hair and pretty face in the box made me cry a lot. Going to the church and seeing everyone cry and seated in front of him, I never thought it was going to be this hard. I re-member how Mama Maria sang to him in that box and said, "*¿Por qué mi hijo, por qué él?*" Why my son, why him? I also remember his dad saying, "*Si lo mataron, es porque le tenían envidia, porque mi hijo era mejor que ellos, mucho mejor.*" If they killed him, it was because they were jealous. Yes, jealous that he was better than them. Everyone was crying and *el padre*, the father, was talking, telling us, "*Si Ivan estuviera aquí, el no quisiera que ustedes se vengaran por su muerte sino que aprendieran de esta lección.*" If Ivan was here, he would not like you guys thinking about revenge, he would like you guys to learn from this lesson.

Ivan's death changed my way of thinking about the American Dream. I had a job. I was doing it not because I liked it; I did it because of the money. With the money that I made, I always used it for bad things. I was being a selfish human being. But when I heard the terrible news about Ivan, I went into denial and sadness. I couldn't believe that he was gone. This is when my goals changed. It was never going to be about having money and "tripping" about everything like people say. Ivan's death opened my eyes to a new dream of justice. The American Dream shouldn't be about finding money and living life to the fullest; it should be about health and happiness. My dream is a lifetime promise of making those four young kids pay for what they did to Ivan. Getting the people that killed my friend locked up is never going to bring him back, but I know that at least life is going to be better for a lot of people when they know four criminals are in jail.

My dream has to do with my life but in a different way. I say "a different way" because I want to work and find ways of happiness for people that mean a lot to me. Maybe this is a reason why I want to be a psychologist, because if someone like me goes through all this pain, I know I could always truthfully say that I know what pain they are feeling. Since I was five years old I wanted to be one of those people that help you with your problems—those were my words for the term *psychologist*. I know that the reason this is my long-term goal is because in my seventeen years of life I feel like I have had ups and downs. Family problems, school, and other problems got me into a lot of things that, at my age, I shouldn't be doing. I know that when I grow up, kids are going to be facing the same problems but in different ways, and I want to be there to support them. Being a psychologist is going to turn my life around for the best.

Health and love is my life. Life isn't easy, but me and my community fight to make it work. When a person shoots someone else at night, that doesn't mean everyone that lives in that area is always going to act like that. I changed because of the way I have suffered, but I still have a dream and I know I can achieve it.

I also want to show people that Latinos can achieve what they want to achieve. Sometimes the government helps us in a lot of things. But, if we think about it, the government has a bad side too. Ivan was seen on the ground with blood on his clothes by cops, but the cops didn't stop and check on him. He was close to the corner of Persia Avenue and Madrid Street. Natalie, the pregnant girl who was with him, pulled him to the corner so the cops could see that she and Ivan needed help. "I pulled Ivan over when I seen cops pass by, but they kept going so I called

911," Natalie said. Natalie could do nothing but pray. This shows that the government is not always fair with everyone. The cops could've thought differently about Ivan, but if we think about it, maybe they just didn't stop because of his race. Ivan was Latino, and maybe the cops did not see him as the victim, maybe they saw him as the criminal. Ivan wasn't helped until hours after he was stabbed. If the cops that passed would have helped, he could still be alive. This is why I think that the government doesn't help everyone at the same level. Justice is not the same for everyone. I'm seventeen years old living in a world that maybe I didn't choose, but it's mine. Things happen because they have to happen, and if Ivan had to die it's because it was his time.

I always wonder what Ivan's dream was. Maybe it was to see every one of his friends together. Maybe his dream was to see that his family was good. He always cared a lot about his friends and family. Maybe this is why a lot of people remember him with love and sadness in their hearts. Life is not all about justice and revenge, but is about friendship. Friendship is the most important thing in my life. The love that I have for my friends is bigger than someone could ever think. I always say if one goes down, we all go down. I know that for me to say that Ivan is resting in peace, I need to see all his homies happy while the people that killed him are behind bars. Ivan was my brother and friend, and he was a human being who died for reasons that don't even exist.

"Ivan Miranda, fourteen-year-old boy, killed"—those are the last words I heard from the news, but I know that sooner or later I'm going to hear the good news that Ivan Miranda's killers are paying for the death of the youngest kid killed in San Francisco. Then I know *my* words for this are going to be: "The American Dream exists, and mine has been achieved!"

Mapping Out
A DREAM

by RECA AVERILLA

ON TOP OF THESE life stories and struggles, we all have a main goal in our lives that I call the American Dream. The struggles in my life have created drama for me. I have lived half of my life in the Philippines and half of it here in the United States. I have moved three times from America to the Philippines and back again. I'm the youngest daughter in the family, with two older brothers and one older sister; being the youngest was never easy. They rely on me for all the household responsibilities they once had. I do this because I know that these experiences will help me to achieve independence.

I lived in America until I was in the fifth grade. I had best friends and freedom to go out after school and during weekends. However, this changed. When I was thirteen years old, my parents sent me back to the Philippines to finish my studies there. They feared I might get distracted by friends, as that happens to teenagers now and keeps them from graduating.

I enjoyed the first two years of high school in the Philippines. I was very much influenced by friends, and by influenced I mean they magnetized me to the emancipated world of our generation. Prior to this, I believed that girls were to be home before dark and were not to be with the opposite sex alone or in public, unless with a crowd. Though I don't recall who taught me this, I have always assumed that this matter was a fact until I actually opened my mind to being socially active with both the same and the opposite sex. This changed me a lot from the way

I dress, talk, think, act, and pretty much everything else about me. I became more liberated when I got to high school.

In the Philippines I had to stay with my aunt and my grandparents. My family supposed that I would be better in the Philippines than in the United States since none of my siblings graduated from high school because they were distracted. One of the best things I liked about staying in the Philippines is that I lived like a princess. I didn't have to worry about anything but my own belongings. I had to keep track of my own personal life and my own money, which helped me improve my financial independence.

I was extremely aware of the efforts my parents had made to fulfill my needs while I was away. They once had a dream, but for financial reasons did not achieve it. I honestly don't have any idea if my parents actually believe in their dreams anymore, but I am familiar with what they have in mind as parents: for their children to have a better life than they had. They don't want us to go through what they had to go through. They want us to have a fine job and a blissful family with a peaceful life. The reality of their lives has shown them that the American Dream is for certain people only; however, they still hold on to the idea that if you work hard enough you can achieve your dream.

Because my aunt took care of me since birth, I recognize her as a mother. She took care of me until I was in the first grade, when I had to go to the United States. When my parents sent me back to the Philippines to finish elementary and high school, my aunt took care of me, but that only lasted for two years. She was really strict. I had to be home thirty minutes after school was over, with just enough time to wait for a ride and walk home. When I got home I had to do homework and then go to sleep early for school the next day.

After those two years, my aunt got married and had a baby. She decided to move out and make her family her priority. My mom had to look for someone who could move into the house my family owned to watch over me, so my uncle agreed to move in his family to take care of me. That was when my freedom broke loose. I started going home later than before. I hung out with friends after school and joined school activities, such as plays and helping out with posters. I was free to go out on the weekends. My family saw this as negative because I spent less time studying than before, which worried my uncle that I might start to fail my classes. Spending time with friends, however, gave me the chance to explore how other people's lives work and how they had to work hard for their needs, as well as saving their own money to get what they wanted. This made me appreciate all the fine belongings I have and how lucky I am that I have parents who work hard to fulfill my needs. I learned to appreciate the blessings that were given to me. I learned from these experiences. I will keep them with me because I know these lessons will help me appreciate every little thing I achieve.

After a few months, my uncle decided to move out along with his family, so my mom's youngest brother took care of me, together with his family. This was when I finally came out of my shell. On the one hand, the positive side of this coming out was that I made so many friends. On the other hand, this was negative because I made choices that took me further away from my goals, as well as my parents' hopes for me. I had to divide my study time for my friends and for other activities, which caused me to lose focus on my main goals of having good grades, graduating from high school, achieving independence, and gaining trust from my parents.

Before realizing my mistakes, I started to get bad grades. This was awful for me as well as for my family, but I was also surprised by all the things I realized about myself. I realized I had skills and talents that really amazed me. One of the new skills I developed was being a better communicator, for I used to be a really shy person. I also became a better person because I learned from the different life stories of my friends. I cultivated an appreciation not just for my belongings, but also for the people around me and the efforts they made for me, particularly my aunt and uncles. This makes me proud of myself for learning a lot of things, not only about me but about life. By this process, I grew.

The bad grades I earned disappointed me and my parents. I am the last one my parents can count on to achieve the American Dream they had for all of us: to graduate from high school. Because they supposed that they could watch over me more than my uncle could, my parents didn't hesitate to bring me back to the United States. When I found out about their decision I was disappointed, because this meant I had to adjust again. I had to adopt a whole new environment, as well as the lack of freedom with my parents.

When I got back to the United States, I had to adjust right away because school would soon start. I was put into the eleventh grade and had a really hard time. It seemed like I was in a different world where I didn't belong. I had to learn a whole new grading system, in addition to the new people around me, which was really hard. I tried to build a good relationship with my teachers the soonest I could, because I felt it would help me more. After a few months, I finally got used to my teachers and the school's surroundings but not the grading system. I had to settle in, but everything was satisfactory.

I also had to get used to living with my parents again. Unfortunately, I had a hard time. I was sixteen and yet they were treating me as if I was nine years old. I had to catch up with the rules they made: I couldn't go out or hang out with my friends after school or on weekends; I had to go home right after school; if I felt like going to the mall, I had to go with them. My life totally changed in a blink of an eye. I felt like yesterday I was free, then the following day I was in jail. I was living in a small world, not being able to explore things on my own, not being able to learn on my own. They told me what to do and what not to do, which didn't help me grow at all. From this, I learned that you can't push a person to be independent and to grow. Let the process of life bring you there, and you'll learn and grow from the consequences attached to every decision you make.

Every day after school when I get home, besides doing my homework, I am also responsible for all the household chores. I also have to take care of my niece. I have to feed her and sometimes give her a bath. My mom constantly says I have nothing else to do but to get my life straight, which I think is not true because I have the chores to do. Although this pulls me, there are also times where it helps me pursue my dream because of my desire to prove I am a better person than they think I am.

Every day that passes constantly pressures me. There are times where I am compared by my parents to my siblings. In addition, I have the desire of proving that I am extremely serious about graduating and going to college. Despite all the pressures, I am proud of myself that I am now four months away from graduating high school with good grades. This means I am another step closer to my dream.

I understand why my parents are awfully strict to me. All they ever wanted was for us to have a better life than they did. Now they're giving me a chance to fulfill that dream, but without the support I need with decision making. Although I am not receiving or feeling all the support I need and want, I am still on the right path and doing fine as a result of my eagerness to make them proud. I want to prove that I am a person they can be proud of and that I have a dream that I am eager to achieve. I can picture myself having a stable job working in an office and being on my own.

If I learned something really important in my high school years, it was to think not just twice about my decisions, but ten times. Challenges may have brought me down, but they made me a better and stronger person. Even though I have a lot of responsibilities to overcome, I've learned to inspire and motivate myself to achieve my goals. In doing this, I'm not only making my parents proud, but I'm also making myself proud.

BEYOND
the
FLAMES

by RONALDO PEREZ

POUND! POUND! It was the sound that woke me that early November morning, eyes bloodshot, dizzy with the shock that I had woken up. As my father cried, "Fire! Fire!" my mind became clear and alert as a school bell. My heart pounded with adrenaline, fear, and excitement. I noticed my window: the dark shadow that I had fallen asleep to was now a blazing inferno from Hell. I ran out of the door of my room with one goal in mind: to figure out which house was on fire, if it was our house or the one next door. With my front door open I ran out of our house like a prisoner during a jailbreak.

I noticed the dark night and the neighbor's house on fire, disturbing it. I examined my father, with a garden hose in his hand and fear on his mind. He kept his distance from the burning house, making sure the fire would not pass over onto ours. The house, clear as day, continued to burn. I felt my breath as if I was underwater, drowning and disrupted. The loud roar and crackle sprang like fireworks into the night sky. Glass broke, paint faded, water meters ran like a spinning roulette, and metal glowed red as lava.

I ran back inside my home through the hallways, the darkest place I'd been all night. I got used to the adrenaline burning through me passionately, as a wild wolf on the hunt. As I saw the glass door, which led to the backyard, I could see the red vibrant color that my dad woke to. My mind was so preoccupied by the fire that I forgot to breathe for a while. As my nose and mouth inhaled the fumes of the poisonous air, I saw the crackling flames that engulfed the house some couple of hours ago. It was unexpected to see my mom there in the backyard, for I thought she was still in our house sound asleep with my sister in their room. I could feel my heart beating against my chest like a drum. I was outside, my body cold as an ocean rock and my face as hot as if I had a fever.

I felt hopeless with nothing to put the fire out, so I told my mom that I would climb the ladder onto the roof to see if I could find the center of this blaze. She thought I was insane. I could see the expression on her face and I knew she could see I was serious so she handed me the garden hose, and with all my strength I lifted the gray rusty ladder that weighed more than fifteen pounds to see if I could locate the core of the flames. I kept hitting the rain pipes because it was dark. I felt the ladder as soft as a feather, the adrenaline that flowed through my veins still burning with passion as great as the fire itself. After I put the ladder in place and climbed the slippery steps, about to fall off, holding on with both hands, I pulled myself up and managed to plant my bare feet on the hot graveled roof.

I could feel scratches that the roof had left on the soles of my feet like jagged knives going through every step I took. I felt the flames in the wind like a heat wave in the middle of a bright, droughtful summer. I tasted the fumes that went through my nose. For once a feeling that I haven't felt before came over me: I could not control my body, my body controlled me. I heard an explosion and at the same time my body told me, "Drop down!" I could feel this pressure pulling me onto the rugged roof, and for a moment I closed my eyes and could feel the flames surging past me. I opened my eyes and saw the fire on top of me in a perfect ball, and as fast as it came, it faded into the night sky.

I quickly stood up on the blacktopped roof to insure my mother of my safety. I stared at the bright flame and was having a previous memory of a fire that happened in my childhood: I remember my mother had grabbed me with my bright yellow blanket and stormed down the stairs of the two-story building. The smell of garbage on the steps was rotting my lungs. I peeked out of my blanket and felt warmer than before. I could see people in the street, scared and confused. I saw a couple of fire trucks, and the firemen, big and strong, surged into the unforgiving fire. I felt helpless. I was a mere child, weak and defenseless, but I also gazed at the normal men, the ones with no gear, as scared as I was. I saw my dad talking to the brave, self-sacrificing hero to make sure our home was going to be fine. The fire ended a few minutes later, and everyone had exited unharmed. I was strong now, I knew what I had to do, I was not the little helpless five-year-old stuck in a blanket, I was the unchained boy putting this fire out nine years later. I realized now, standing on this roof, that I was the fireman for the house burning next to mine. I feel that I have not experienced this sense of heroism and the power of this adrenaline before. I liked what I felt: the intensity, the rush. I have never felt so alive, even when death or severe injury was just one leap away on the roof.

I quickly snapped back into reality and pointed the hose into the fire. After a few more minutes I could see the flashing lights of the fire trucks that I remembered from so long ago and felt that I should've been in there instead of where I was at the moment. I felt I had to get off the roof at this point unless I wanted to get yelled at by the people I adored so much. The truck arrived a moment after I saw them. By the time I got down, I felt tired and told myself that I was lifted of this burden I put upon myself. I walked toward the front once more and they were getting everything ready, from jackets, to boots, to oxygen tanks. All the equipment was there. Some prepared the tanks of mass water, and some with axes prepared to go inside. I closed my eyes for a moment and felt a cool breeze of a mix of water and air. I noticed the other houses and felt it was a ghost town. There was no one outside and all the lights were off. I turned to the house that was on fire and took a sigh of relief, and told myself, "My work here is done."

The morning that I woke up, I walked outside, and I saw a giant gash on the roof of the burnt house. The walls were black-colored wood with white strikes; windows were broken from axes and extreme heat. The police were inspecting the house of what the fire had left behind. Bits and pieces of the burnt wood had fallen on our roof. I was still confused about what had happened. I feel like it was a crazy dream, but it wasn't. I knew I lived this dream. I knew this could happen any time, anywhere, and I always know there will be everyday people helping to put fires out, helping to save lives and prevent this from happening, maybe encouraging another kid somewhere to become a firefighter, just like they encouraged me the night of this fire. My parents spoke to their friend about this incident, no details, just what happened in general.

It was nothing but a story to tell, and we never really talked about it among ourselves because it didn't really concern us. We just cared that everyone was alive, and laughed at death and how it couldn't take us that night.

I want to be a role model to the community, to put my life on the line and prove that it takes real courage to do the job I was meant to do. The American Dream is to do whatever you would like to do and not let anything hold you back. It is to love doing what you're doing. It is to feel the rush you are looking for, and take charge even when death is in your face. My dream is to feel free and to respect the rights our forefathers gave us so many years ago. It's to make a change in your life that completes you.

Firemen risk their lives every day, like many other Americans, working on machines and dangerous equipment that many people wouldn't consider to take as a career. The firemen work together against a powerful force that may seem undefeatable for one single person, but when they work as a team they can achieve something far greater than themselves. They aren't afraid of what might happen, but they know the risks if they don't take charge. Like the firefighters before us that have died for freedom, they weren't selfish at all and fought to achieve the greater good. For me, the fireman is a strong symbol of heroism, and the risks that they take mean that they sacrifice themselves for the American people.

Homeward
BOUND

by JAMON BALBERAN

THE AMERICAN DREAM has influenced the minds and lives of both Americans and people abroad. I am one of those Americans. It was not the first thing on my mind last school year. That's because I dropped out of school, and I was living the American Nightmare.

I was not sitting at home all day grubbing on Lay's. I was mostly out on the street wondering where I was going to sleep that night. Most of the time I wouldn't have a place, and that called for roofs and parks. Hours merged into days, days merged into weeks, and then finally they merged into months. Half of the time I didn't even know what day it was, I just needed to survive. I was living the life of the American bum. All that changed when my uncle brought me back to reality. Being on the streets is a tough life for anyone, especially for a teenage boy. My uncle saw this, so he offered to take me in for a couple weeks. From there, every day, we just went over what I really wanted in life. That included school, parents, my social and personal life, health, and my future. As we built up these ideas, my motivation built up too. From that point on I was happy, keeping a good diet, helping around his house, and hyped up for school.

Everything was happening so fast for me. From getting kicked out to surviving on my own for three months, then trying to get my life back together. My life got jump-started when my uncle took me in. It was actually a total coincidence, because he literally ran into me. I was visiting Gateway, my old high school, and he lives right across the street, so it was only a matter of time before I saw him. I was walking, then I turned around to talk to a friend, and there he was. He noticed me right away and immediately gave me a lung-crushing hug, then took me to his house. I felt so much care and respect for my uncle. It seemed like there was this positive aura that surrounded him. Just being in his house made me stand a little bit taller.

My uncle is a guy who loves to make plans. His plan was to keep me off the streets, keep me safe, and help me develop my own life plan. So as I stayed there, day by day we developed a legit plan. The plan involved my family problems, school, and my social and personal life. Obviously my family and I were not getting along at that time. We had to find a way to bring the peace back into my house. One thing I had to do was apologize to my parents for all the rude things that I had done to them. Likewise, my parents had to apologize to me for getting carried away in certain situations. Another category in my plan was school. My uncle knew that it would be hard to pass the new school year because I dropped out for a couple months. He basically told me not to take it quarter by quarter, more like week by week. I realized that was a much easier process because it felt like less of a load on my shoulders.

Finally, there was my social and personal life. My uncle wasn't this serious guy all the time; he liked to joke around too. We would talk about girls and upcoming parties. This part of the plan is where I really got to know him as a person. He did all the same things I did when he was in high school. As we headed toward talking about my personal life, we got to my diet.

When you live outside, there's no guarantee that you'll eat every day. I would eat probably every two days, and it would be only a bag of chips, or some fruit from a grocery store. After eating like that for a while, you get used to it, and you don't get hungry that often. That had a bad effect on me because I was getting really tired and skinny. Another effect is that it doesn't give your body the nutrients it needs, so I would get sick like every two weeks. So the plan was to boost my eating habits, and we concluded that my diet affected the way I felt. My uncle determined that I was depressed, and that's why I had an abnormal diet. However, being at my uncle's made me happy, so I was slowly recovering from depression.

It also helped me to not hide things from him. I could tell him that I was going to a party and probably wouldn't be back until one or two in the morning. All he would say is, "call me if you need a ride or anything." It was less stressful because I didn't have to build up this ball of lies like I did with my parents. I didn't have to sneak out to go to a party. I could just ask him. That taught me how to be more upfront and honest with my parents.

My uncle has helped me out so much. Although, I'm just one of the many kids he's helped out. My uncle founded an organization called R.A.P., an activist group that helps kids and adults with serious problems like gang life, abuse, and family conflicts. He's helped out so many people. He's known throughout my family as the guy who gets everyone jobs.

In fact, he got me an internship over the summer at CYMC (Conscious Youth Media Crew). He co-founded this organization that's involved in movie- and beat-making. Even though I interned for only a month, I learned a lot about movie cameras and how to make movies. He also made a film that was on PBS. It's called *The Family*, and it had to do with my family living in the Mission District. It was about how we lived our lives: the struggles, the happy times, and also the sad moments. According to my uncle, it was the first reality show ever aired. I don't know what's so interesting about my family, but something must have been.

Like a lot of Americans, I want to go to college. However, most teens my age don't even know what they're going to major in. For a while I wanted to major in biology, but there is the other option of movie-making. I honestly don't know what I'm going to do yet, because I feel like I'm not experienced enough yet to get into movie-making. That's why I was considering going back to CYMC this summer. That would be really beneficial for me because I'll be making money, and I will get that key knowledge that the program provides. If I do go back, I want to work on filming major events, like protests, concerts, elections, things like that. I was tired of doing the same thing every day: wake up, go chill with my friends, come home, eat, then go to sleep, wake up, and do it all over again. That's fun for a little while, but after a minute it gets old. So movie-making to me was a new and fun hobby. Even though it is hard work and takes weeks to edit, it pays off at the end because you know that you achieved something. And that feeling is what kept me going and not quitting the first day.

With the mix of staying at my uncle's house and finding this new hobby, I was doing much better than before. I was gaining weight, I wasn't getting sick as often as I was before, and my uncle told me that I was obviously happier. It was about the middle of July when my uncle sat me down for a talk. He told me that he'd seen an impressive improvement on my part, and he suggested that it was time for me to go home. When he said that, I was like, "Are you serious, dude?" I felt kind of betrayed for a couple minutes. However, I realized that I couldn't hold my uncle down like this. He had his own family to take care of, and taking in another kid doesn't go well financially. He thought it was right for me to go home because he isn't my dad, and I needed to be with mine. Also, he thought it would be adult of me to go home and apologize to my parents.

I took it into consideration and I decided that I would leave at the end of the week. As I spent my last couple days there, my uncle treated me to dinners and lunches. I really took in what a caring and nice guy he was. I woke up Friday morning kind of sad; just thinking about leaving my uncle's was hard because it was a second home to me. As I was packing my bags, my uncle came downstairs and gave me a big hug, then a handshake. As I took away my hand I saw $100 in it. I thanked him and he told me it was for the road. I heard my dad honk from outside, so I gave him another hug and hopped into the car. Seeing my dad for the first time in weeks was kind of a weird feeling. My dad seemed a little weirded out too. The car ride home wasn't very exciting; I felt the uneasy tension between us. When I walked through the front door everything seemed abnormal. There was a new TV, a giant fish tank, and my dog was twice the size she was before I left. That's when I knew that I had been gone for a long time. So immediately I went to my room, closed the door, and pondered into space.

As I look back on it, my uncle did teach me a lot of useful life skills. He taught me how to plan, and that if you have a plan you'll succeed, but if you don't you'll fail. He taught me how to do better in school by not looking at it semester-by-semester or quarter-by-quarter, but week-by-week or even day-by-day. He taught me how to be a more mature person in the conflict with my parents. Most importantly, I think he taught me how to live the American Dream. He pushed me to do better in school, which will lead to college. He talked to me about my family situation so I could have a happy family life. And he taught me that I can do anything that I put my mind to, which includes pursuing my goals. My uncle told me that he would support anything that I wanted to do.

Fortunately, my uncle caught me when I was falling, and taught me the steps of how to achieve my goals. From him and living on my own, I learned how to be more mature and responsible. After all of this, I feel more grown-up and capable of doing anything I set my mind to.

Wave at me out the window
when you see me speeding by

THE JOKE
of the
CITY

by TAKEYA SMITH

I am Takeya Smith.
I am a woman, an activist.
I fight
for what I believe in.
I strive for excellence.
I am a poet,
writing is my life, my escape,
my breakaway from kids.

WHAT MADE ME WANT to play baseball? The reason why I even like baseball is because in third grade one of my YMCA counselors, Marcos, was in love with baseball. Almost every day he had the SF Giants' logo everywhere when I saw him. He was my favorite counselor out of the entire staff. He told me all about the Giants and the Red Sox and a whole bunch of other teams. I got really into it and expected a story about a baseball game every day after school.

One Thursday afternoon, Marcos didn't show up. When he wasn't there an hour past his clock-in time, I knew he wasn't coming. At 5 p.m. the YMCA was closing down, so I waited patiently outside for my mom with my sister. When she came, the YMCA director, Maureen, took my mom aside and talked with her for a few minutes. I ran by them and tried to listen, but I couldn't hear what they were saying.

When they finished talking, my mom gathered my sister and me into the car and we drove away. She stopped the car as soon as we were off of school grounds.

"Takeya, it might be hard for you to understand, but I have some news."

I honestly thought I was getting a present or something. I had a big smile on my face, the kind where your eyes nearly close, one of those smiles. I quickly lost the smile when her eyes got watery.

"You were going to find out eventually, so Maureen thought it would be easier if I told you myself. Marcos got into a car accident on the Golden Gate Bridge. He was in the back of a truck sleeping and fell out the back when the car crashed. Marcos passed away yesterday, Takeya. I'm sorry. I know you two were close."

For one, I didn't know how to respond to that, and two, I just couldn't believe it—I was talking to him just yesterday! How could he be gone the same day I saw him?

Till this day I still tune in to a baseball game every now and then and wear the Giants shirt that Marcos gave me. And when I play, I feel like he is with me, guiding me through the game.

Me as myself?
I am funny,
confident, but also shy.
Once you get to know me
I am completely different.
I suffer six different phobias,
and I am fine with that.

In seventh grade, I was still really into sports. I loved basketball, track, volleyball, baseball, and football. I tried to play as many sports as I could, despite my grades. A year later, I tried out for the boys' baseball team. We didn't have a girls' team because not enough girls had joined. So my only option was the boys' team.

I told all my friends that I was trying out. I was prepared and everything. I waited patiently for Mr. Lee, the coach and my P.E. teacher, surrounded by my friends. I was nervous. He stepped out of the gym, walked toward the baseball field, and approached all the guys who had already lined up. I walked to the line. Mr. Lee pulled me out of line.

"Takeya, why are you here? We don't need cheerleaders."

"I'm here to try out for the team, Mr. Lee."

He just laughed as I explained that since there was no girls' team, the boys' team was my only option. He just laughed and turned bright red—almost the same color as the perfect apples you only see on TV. His eyes squeezed shut as he laughed a little harder. I was shocked he didn't choke.

I felt foolish to have even showed up at the boys' practice. I was frustrated that I was just a mere joke to him. I was obviously serious. I mean, I had a glove and cleats, for crying out loud. I wanted to cry, but I held back my tears because I wanted to show that I was serious. So I stood my ground. My friends were gazing at me through the fence.

"Mr. Lee, can I try out?" I asked.

"A girl on the boys' baseball team?"

I knew I was getting nowhere with him. I turned and walked away as he remained, shouting his comments at me.

"We would be a joke to other middle schools in the city!"

I felt frustration, sadness, and jealousy. I was angry at the fact that I was not allowed to try out, only because of my gender. The frustration and confusion hit me even stronger when I realized that at thirteen, I was already a victim of discrimination. I was sad that I couldn't play and jealous that the guys could. Why was I born a girl?

I do not think I am crazy,
just because you see me
different.
I am a risk
even if something is completely wrong.

Since I was born I have always been just a girl, nothing more, nothing less, just a girl. I had no dad to tell me how to do or be anything. My mom never told me that I couldn't do or be whatever I wanted to be, but she also never said what I *could* be. I had no older sister by my side to tell me about future bumps along the road. I kind of obtained knowledge on my own.

When people think I can't do something, I usually want to prove them wrong. I think that the American Dream shouldn't revolve so much around money and fame, but be about achieving greatness and bettering myself and standing up for my own beliefs. Throughout history, gender discrimination has affected many women. You never hear about it, but many women are told what to be or what to do instead of asked.

People think differently of me—that I will grow up to be a drug addict, a dropout, even a Hooters waitress. Since I was young, people have told me things like, "You're not good enough." "With your bad grades, you're lucky if I let you live here when you're supposed to be in college." "You're just a girl, you're lucky if you don't get pregnant by sixteen." "Why play sports when you can be a doctor? I'll tell you why, you're just a girl." I still haven't figured out a way to deal with it. It's not like I am the only one. Many ladies of my generation and before have dealt with this specific type of discrimination.

I feel unappreciated because I know I can do way more things than what people expect of me. I have been that way my whole life. I can do anything a guy can, if not a little better. It makes me want to write a book because I know I can be successful and do something I want to do, not just what others expect me to do.

When I grow up, I want to learn all I can about psychology. I want to write a book to help people learn about themselves: their emotions, personalities, relationships, reverse psychology. I think by writing a book instead of becoming a counselor, I would be of more help by giving step-by-step guidelines for the proper understanding of oneself. By writing that book, I would achieve my dream by bettering not only myself but others as well.

Being American is having the freedom to express myself any way I want without being judged. *I am Takeya Smith. I am a woman, an activist.* I am an individual. I don't live for anybody but myself. Mr. Lee didn't trust me to be a good enough baseball player for the guys' team because I am a woman. It's not right. I can't change who I am. I won't. I deserve respect as a free woman of America.

I am an overachiever breaking out of my shell. I am overwhelmed. I know how I am as a person. I know I am strong even when I break down and cry. I know what I want to achieve. I know that I will almost achieve it, and then a roadblock will come along at the very last minute. Trying to prove myself to others is the biggest challenge I have ever faced and still face. I know that once I am older and have my head on straighter, I will be a powerful multi-racial woman and men will ask me for things instead of the other way around.

I am Takeya Smith. I'm a Siberian Tiger. A Toucan. A Mango. L.A. Vegas. I'm a Dolphin. I am what I want to be, and no one else.

The
ORANGE
BASS

by NICOLAS X. NAVAL-MORA

I LOVE THE BASS GUITAR. I love the way it sounds—its deep growl. When I play bass it lifts me off my feet, it takes me to a different place. I love the feel of the long heavy neck, the texture of the smooth maple wood in my hands. The fingerboard is made out of rose wood. The bass scales 32" and has humbucking pickups. The neck has a design of dot art, and when the light hits the design it shines like a pearl and reminds me of my family.

My dream is to get my own bass and have fun playing with a garage band or even be a rock star. If I get to be a rock star, I don't want fame or money, I just want to be well known, like Jimi Hendrix, Metallica, Aerosmith, Judas Priest, or Rise Against. They all have great history, and that is my dream to obtain.

Every day I work hard to get my desired bass, but there are obstacles I must conquer first. One of those obstacles is money. And then, where will I keep the bass, and how will I use it? How do you read music sheets? And if it gets damaged, where do I get it fixed? How will I have time to achieve this great goal?

What first inspired me to play the bass was one fabulous song called "Master of Puppets" by Metallica. It has a fast and complex bass riff.

The first time I ever played or even held a bass was in my friend's dusty and dark garage. When I first held the bass, it was very heavy and confusing. But after messing around with it for a while, I felt like it was my job to play the bass.

Every day after school I go to Guitar Center near Fisherman's Wharf to see the bass that I have always wanted: an Ibanez Gio GSR200FM bass guitar. I walk into the store, check my bag at the front counter, and go past the pay counter, through the guitar section, directly to the bass section. The people that work there already know me as I walk in with my friends, and they are very enthusiastic about us playing the instruments that we like. I see the glossy amber Ibanez hanging on the wall, with its four thick nickel strings running down its neck and a $300 price tag tied around the pick guard.

I always play the bass every time I go see that marvelous instrument at Guitar Center. I am too short to grab the bass down, so I always ask them to get it down for me. It is very heavy. The body is so glossy and smooth. When I play it I just use my fingers, but some of the other bassists use a pick. When I play the strings on the bass, it feels so light and weightless. The amp is small but way louder than you would think

I never had the money to buy the Ibanez, but I am trying. As my grandpa says, "Work comes first and you will achieve." At first I didn't understand what he meant. One day my grandfather came up to me and asked if I wanted a job helping him at the antique show. At first I didn't know what the heck the antique show was, but I went along with it because if I get money I can buy things I want for myself. The antique show is like a flea market that only sells antiques, like old grandfather clocks.

"Yes, I would love to help out, Grandpa," I said. My grandfather is a man of wisdom and toughness. He has been through war and many challenges. My grandfather was born in Los Angeles and lived there until he was twenty, then moved to San Francisco. Then he worked at a printing shop that dealt with big machinery. He is about 5'9", has a buzz cut, and wears glasses—the big U-shaped ones. His skin tone is light bronze. He wears little hoop earrings, has a mustache, and his hair color was black, but now it's mostly white.

I was nine years old when I helped him at the antique show. It was my first job. I still work there to this day. It is at an old naval base and half of an airstrip in Alameda. My grandfather and I always get there at 4:30 in the morning and I sleep in the truck until five, when we start unloading the truck. Setting up and moving the antiques is hard work, but we always get the job done; it takes about one hour at most. I remember when we had to pull out a water heater from the truck. It was old and heavy and a real pain to move—just by touching it, my hands were covered in grease. After everything is done, we sit and relax. I ended up selling a water heater. It was the biggest achievement to sell it, and it also meant less antiques to take home. By about 3:30 p.m. we start putting everything back in the truck, but by then we are tired and it is twice as hard. We leave at about 4:00 or 4:30 in the afternoon. But I have learned what he meant when he said to me, "Work comes first and you will achieve." It is that you have to work in order to get what you want; it is not going to just be handed to you on a silver platter.

Once we are done with packing up all the antiques, my grandfather goes and sits in the truck for a while until the car heats up and is ready to go. I always sit at the end of the truck. Grandfather leaves me sitting in the back until we are at the gate, and I stare at the sky and say to myself: "There is no limit to anything. The only limit is the sky." That is what my grandfather says.

"I can't reach my goal."

"Why not?"

"I am restricted from doing the things I want to do."

"Well, don't think that! The only limit you have is the sky, son."

"It seems impossible to do what I want to do."

"Keep trying, do not give up."

"Okay, Grandpa."

When I was eleven, I started working for my grandpa's cleaning service, Dickie's Cleaning Service. I was nervous on my first day cleaning houses, but it was fun, even though my grandpa always yelled at me at some point in the day. He taught me how to clean everything and even let me have my own job at an auto shop, where every Friday I go in and clean the offices and the bathroom. It's good pay just to go in and clean a bathroom and an office—$40 is good weekend money, something for me to put in my pocket.

Once we are done, we go out to grab a sandwich and talk. He gives me different advice each time we do a house-cleaning job. One time he told me, "Save money and you can buy great things that you want." I thought to myself, "Yeah, maybe I can get a bass if I save up."

My grandfather is very artistic, and my sister and I always help him out with his art projects. There was one project that took us six months to do: it was a giant shelter that was as big as two car tails. It was very heavy to lift into the truck. The whole thing was made out of fabric, and we used bamboo to hold it up. We used at least eight bamboo poles and about six tent stakes. They were rusted and old, but thick, weighed about six to ten pounds, and had the word "Aztec" on the top of them. It was perfect for the trip to Burning Man, which would be later in the year.

Seeing this magnificent project has empowered me to start on my own road. The dream cannot be handed to you; you must earn what you want in life. I am earning my way by working and saving up to buy the Ibanez. My grandfather taught me how to save my money and to work hard for my earnings. The Ibanez gave me the dream to play because of its shape, sound, color, and the desire to play the song "The Day That Never Comes" by Metallica, with their amazing riffs. My passion burns like the fire of a million suns. I imagine myself on a glorious stage with an awesome bass and millions of shouting fans, with the bright lights shining down on me, with the big tall amps pointing toward the crowd, as they scream for an encore.

K-ROXZ SPOT

by KATHIA RAMOS

OPEN THE DOOR to my lime green room and you can usually find me there, drawing letters or whatever comes to mind. These type of letters people talk about as graffiti, but many people see them as art or freedom of expression. With the music loud, blocking out my surroundings, and the door closed, I use drawing as a get-away. Everything else that goes on in my life disappears with the feeling of drawing the letters. My emotions are being poured out on the paper. Everything that stresses me is all gone when I touch the paper with my pen.

There are times when I drop the pen, though, and just think about everything that's going on. At home, it's always problem after problem. At school, they want you to solve that problem, and to grade you. But when I'm drawing, I think of my dream to become a fashion designer, start my own clothing line and store, and have a good relationship with my family. Drawing makes me feel that my dream might come true one day. Graffiti opened my eyes to art. Trying it on my own was like freedom for me, since it's hard to have a place to express myself. It also opened my eyes to clothing and gave me hope that I could be an artist one day.

To understand it clearly, you have to know my story. Learning how to draw these letters wasn't easy. Looking back to seventh grade where it all started, I remember sitting on the couch with my older cousin Matt, watching him smoothly draw cool-looking letters into a name. At first I couldn't figure out what it said, but as I watched him fill the letters in with colors, I saw letter structures forming. It was the coolest thing I'd ever seen. One day I picked up a blank piece of paper, a pencil, and an eraser and tried drawing the letters myself. I struggled with it for days; it looked nothing like his. I always felt like giving up, but I soon realized that I was just a beginner and that only practice makes perfect.

Soon after that, my English class went on a field trip to the Red Vic Movie House to see *Piece by Piece*, a film based on graffiti writers in San Francisco. Watching this film was an inspiration. This film made me see very clearly the beauty of graffiti, not just the vandalism everyone criticizes. It was art, not just something illegal that you see on the streets. The beauty I would always see in it was that anyone could do it if they would put their mind to it. It was also good seeing that this was not something only guys could do, because there were female writers in the film, too. Actually, some of the best writers were girls. Coming out of the theater, the letters reminded me of things that wouldn't come to mind, until I walked into my grandma's house and saw Matt sketching for the first time.

That upcoming weekend, I asked Matt, "Aye, can you teach me how to draw those letters?" So I got started learning the styles. We took a seat on my bed. I thought we'd start with something simple, but BAM! We started with his favorite: the crazy, wild-style letters that are so chaotic, with arrows and all kinds of things in them. Then we moved on to the simple straight letters, where it looks like drawing a bunch of sticks or rectangles, but once you fill it in you can see the letters. Next it was a flowing style that looked like cursive: the letters connect and when you write it, your hand has a flow and your wrist feels the movement.

It was already so much to absorb, I thought we were done but BOOM! I would have to develop a hand style on my own. Your hand style is unique, like your signature. From styles to color, you make sure your colors look good, as the colors are just as important as the letters. In the beginning I liked using purple, blue, red, pink, and white, with a bit of silver or gold to give it some flavor. Then we continued to picking a name; you don't want to write your own name because of the consequences. It wasn't all about fun. When I heard the consequences, I felt a little scared, but I knew I wouldn't get out of hand with it. I just figured that I would try it and move on to different things. During this time, I never thought art would lead me to a career. I was just twelve years old, hanging around with my cousin and his friends. But even as I started to grow into the art, I never thought it would lead me to where I am now.

From that day on, I didn't stop writing. As soon as I was done with my homework, I would quickly pull out a folder filled with white paper, take one out, and just flow away. My mom was always on my case, like, "Kathia, why do you draw so much?" and I responded, "Because I want to!" So she started to cool off, and actually started supplying me. She would come home with fat stacks of stickers from the post office or the ones you see on stop signs or poles with the "Hello my name is." The only thing she said when she handed them to me was, "Split them with Matt, okay?" While we were panicking that she knew our secret, she supported us and still continued to supply us. With markers, sometimes you had to be eighteen to buy them at stores (I was only twelve, and Matt was fifteen), but all I had to do was tell her the color, and she'd buy it for me.

I never was about writing on buses or on the streets. I always like to keep it on paper, mostly on stickers. I loved graffiti by that time already, but enough to know my boundaries and what I wanted to do with it. I was a little scared, but I would tag along with my cousins. They would go to the yards, usually abandoned buildings, but inside were walls filled with layers of paint. A lot of times you can find writers there. You meet and greet, and if you see each other around again, then you're friends. The writers are all ages, men and women, some are friendly and some cocky. If you were lucky you would catch the ones that you hear about the most because their tags are all over the city. The art on the walls is really a sight to see, because there's graffiti everywhere: from the floor to the ceiling, support poles to stairs. When I first saw the walls, I was just like, "WOW!" It's so nice, the colors here and there, feeling inspired. I wished I could be as good as other writers and come back and do something on a wall myself. But you had to be careful: there were cops snooping around sometimes, waiting to catch writers off guard.

One day, the tables turned. On our way downtown my cousin and his friends hit up a flow on the bus and the wrong people saw. When we got off the J at Powell Station, Matt told me to speed up with them, so I did. Almost at the exit, the cops were right behind us, saying "HOLD IT! STOP!" as my cousin said, "Go, keep walking!" I didn't know what to do or where to go, because I had to continue as if I wasn't with them. I was stuck downtown by myself and I couldn't call my mom because I didn't want to be the snitch. I was feeling very scared. I didn't know what to do for Matt and his friends. I was scared that my mom was going to yell at me for being with them. But I went back home after a while. Walking to my grandma's house, I saw a cop car parked in front, and inside everyone yelling at Matt and so angry with him. That's when it hit me: I wanted to write, but not like this. I never wanted that to happen to me.

It hasn't, but I still have never dropped the pen, just got better through the years. When you first start writing you're called a "toy" because you're new and have no skills. Being a girl, boys thought I had no flow, but they were surprised when they'd ask what I'd write and I'd show them. They'd back off because I was better than them and they knew it. They would still pick on me, but then they'd ask me to help them get better.

As for Matt, he continued getting arrested and stopped caring about everything, especially school. It was the least of his worries; all he wanted to do was write. He was super-talented and I couldn't blame him for not going to school. He saw that school would always be there, but now it was his time to develop his writing. But hearing so many speeches from his mom and her sisters telling him to get back on track, he finally did. He started drawing characters and cartoons, and different letters—more the type you see in video games. He started making his art something that would provide for him. Since he was still in school, he took advantage of the art class he had and was super-dedicated. Before he graduated, he received a full scholarship to the Academy of Arts. He graduated from high school with good grades, proving the family wrong.

During this time, graffiti was very important to me, but I wasn't serious like Matt. But seeing how graffiti made an impact for him and that his skills ended up paying off gave me hope that graffiti could do the same for me. Since he started the Academy of Arts, I didn't see him around as much, but when I did at my grandma's house, we caught up and he told me, "Don't listen to anyone. Do something you want, not what others want for you." That stuck with me forever. I didn't know what to say but shook my head and kept talking while it kept replaying in my head; it was so powerful and useful to me.

I started to notice that I had a more distinguished taste for fashion. I was into the more urban style, something original and artistic that took time to make. I always liked to be the one that stood out, even if it was just a color that was bright and caught your eye: a cool scarf or a bracelet.

Freshman year of high school, my older cousin Vanessa took me to stores like True, Kidrobot, Upper Playground, and many others with an urban twist. One day while at True, I saw a really cool design on a hat. It was a bomb with eyes and a face that looked surprised or scared. I finally found out the clothing brand was called The Hundreds. One day, by surprise, my mom took me to that store. From the outside all you see is a black store that looks closed, but the doors automatically opened. It was dark and there were only lights on the products. It was the coolest store I have ever walked into.

I actually got to meet the guy who started it all, Bobby Hundreds. I went to a sale and Bobby Hundreds was just hanging around like a customer. I told him he was my inspiration, and he said, "YOU'RE MY INSPIRATION!" I started drawing again, not only letters but also designs or characters. Sketch, sketch, sketch is all I would do, and my friends said, "Dude! You're getting good. Make it a shirt!" I thought, "This is what I want to do!"

I was still sketching until things started to get bad at home. My parents were always fussing and fighting because they were splitting up. I couldn't even talk to my sister because she was like a piece of glass: sensitive. My grades were dropping because of all the stress. I just wanted to be in my lime green room, with the music blocking everything. I would be sitting on my bed, with my sketchbook on the left corner. I would push it away and just blast the music louder. I tried to draw, but nothing would come to me. I tried doing my homework, but it wasn't any easier than drawing.

But slowly, I started picking myself up. With so much negativity surrounding me, I started drawing more and more. Fashion was what I wanted to do, but what was going on around me was a reality check. How can I possibly focus and have the space to draw when I can barely think? My mom started off supportive, but she thought it was a phase. My parents wanted me to be a doctor. Their American Dream was to be successful with a lot of money. Every time they tell me something about being a doctor, what Matt told me comes up. I remember that their dream is not mine, and I have to go for mine.

I started drawing again, regaining my confidence in achieving my goals. Always in my lime green room, envisioning my future. I can see ten years ahead, counting the money in the register, making everything spick and span, turning off the lights and locking up, looking in and thinking, "This is all I really wanted, and I got it!" Looking up and seeing the big "K-Roxz Spot" sign above me, hoping my family still loves me. I want them to be proud of my accomplishments by finding a way to support myself and be myself at the same time.

Seeing everything going on around me, I didn't see my dream happening. But I soon came to realize I couldn't do any of that by lying around. Now I'm drawing a lot and keeping up with my schoolwork! Keeping up with my grades will bring me closer to getting into a good art school, which could be the next step to my future. I will hopefully soon be taking fashion classes over the summer at Academy of Art. I've seen Matt go from being arrested for tagging to finishing up a short film on animation. Bobby Hundreds dropped out of law school to follow his dream. Why can't I? I'll just keep dreaming. Wait, scratch that: I will work hard, and be dedicated, and make it come true. I will have my own store one day and have people just like you drop by. Look for it: K-Roxz Spot!

THE STAIRS
that Never End

by VERONICA SILIEZAR

MY MOM ONCE TOLD ME that life is like a flight of stairs. Once you get to the top, you see a door by the hall, and to open the door you need a key. And that key is an education. I remember the day she told me this: I was in the seventh grade and she had just looked at my spring progress report from my second semester. My grades were not the best, a B with a few Cs and Ds. So my mom decided that she needed to talk to me about my grades.

When I came in through the door she called out my name, not angry but in a weird "I need to talk to you" tone, the one that makes me wonder what's going on. I remember it was typical cloudy, foggy, and gloomy San Francisco day, just the way I love the weather. So I responded to her and she said, "Come on, let's go out to the stairs." She left the report card in the kitchen.

So I said "Okay?" in a confused tone on my way out of the kitchen. Then we went out to the stairs with a white handrail on the right side, where it smelled like my mom's delicious home-cooked spaghetti.

Then she made me follow her all the way down the stairs. She waited there and said, "Okay now go back up the stairs and come back down." I just looked at her and said, "Okay?" I was so confused; I didn't know why she wanted me to go up and down the stairs. So when I got back down the stairs she looked at me and said, "Now go back up but try skipping a stair." I looked at her and said, "Why?" She said, "You'll know in a minute." I said "Okay?" again, while skipping the stair, and all I kept saying was, "Okay?"

Then she said, "Okay now skip two stairs." I tried to skip the two stairs; it was now difficult to do but I was able to skip the stairs thanks to my good balance and long legs.

She said, "Now try skipping three stairs." I said, "Okay? That's more difficult. What's this all about? Are you trying to get me into pilates or something? Gosh I'm going to break a sweat here if I keep doing this. What's this all about? I'm lost." She said, "Alright so I got your report card with not-so-good grades. They're decent grades, but I know you can do better." I said, "Yeah, I know I don't have the best grades. Gosh, that's what this is all about? I was getting worried you lost a screw. I thought you were going to make me want to join some pilates class with you or something." Then she said, "No, crazy! This is about your grades, and no! I didn't lose a screw, silly. I'm trying to prove a point about how life is like stairs. Don't try to waste your time on going up the stairs very slow, but don't try to rush going up stairs because you can end up missing a step or getting to the top but missing things you need to learn in life. It's better to take it at a good pace and work hard physically and mentally while going up to reach your goals. Once you have reached the top, what do you need to get in the house or anywhere?"

I said, "A key?" She said, "Yeah, so education is your key and it opens the door to anything you want in life. Without the key you can't get into your car, or your house." She explained to me that education is everything and it helps you achieve things in life. It helps you have a good job—your dream job. We kept talking about what she was saying. To be honest I kind of thought it was silly and weird at first because I didn't get how she wanted to compare life and education to stairs and a key. But later I heard the stories from people that come to our school, telling us how education takes you where you want to go in life and how you can basically achieve the so-called "American Dream." With an education you can have a good life with a nice job, one where you get good pay and benefits. You don't want a job you're miserable working for, a job that requires hard labor and that ends up killing your body, a job with no health benefits, Social Security benefits, or any other benefits people are supposed to have.

For each of us, the American Dream can come true, or it can just be an illusion that fades away after waking up. For that dream to become reality you need to work, which is not an easy thing to do, especially when you have obstacles in your way such as not having enough money or not taking advantage of the education that is available. If you don't take advantage of your opportunities and work hard to overcome obstacles, your dreams can become illusions.

It took me about three years to understand the importance of an education. In my sophomore year of high school I saw the news about how many people were losing their jobs. I could see how having an education could help these people find new jobs, and I understood how a diploma would give them a better chance of being hired.

I appreciate that, living in the United States, I don't have as many obstacles to overcome as my mother did growing up in El Salvador. The Salvadorian Civil War broke out at the time she was going to college. She was studying to become a nurse and had only one year left before graduation. Since the war broke out, she had to leave everything behind for her safety, because so many people were dying due to the war. My grandma decided to send her here to the United States. Yes, today the United States is at war too, but that war is not being fought on U.S soil. Even though we are affected economically, we don't live in fear that one day our neighbor's house will be destroyed or that something can happen to us on our way to school. That's why my mom couldn't reach her goals in El Salvador, but her struggles continued here in the United States.

When my mom came to San Francisco after my grandma sent her here, she was living with her brothers and sisters. She did go to school for a while to learn English, but she didn't continue going because she hadn't settled in yet. Then, a few years later, in 1993, she had me and she was working hard and had a busy schedule and didn't have time to go to school. Then when I was five years old, my dad moved out of the house. My mom would work hard and take care of me in the afternoons because she could only afford a babysitter for the mornings, and she couldn't go to school in the afternoons or at night.

She has been such a hard-working single mom, and I admire that about her. She has been able to support both of us without any help from anyone throughout these years, even through this tough economy. I love my mom for that, and I thank her for being such a hard worker. Now that I'm older, I tell her that she should try to go back to school because now she doesn't have to worry about having to afford a babysitter or anything like that. I want her to be able to accomplish her dream, just as I want to accomplish my dream in the future.

I think that the same way my mom worked hard to support us, I have to work hard to accomplish my dreams, taking life at a good pace and not trying to race through it, but not slacking off. I think that my mom told me her story and metaphor so I can go up the stairs and get the key, which is education. She was very close to getting her own key, but there were a few obstacles in the way, like the war in El Salvador and that my dad left. I'm fortunate that I don't have those obstacles and also that I don't live in a place that has sexist beliefs, or a place that doesn't allow women to get an education. I am thankful that I only have one obstacle and that is a money problem, but I will try to overcome that obstacle.

Take the
FIRST STEP

by ELIZABETH ALVARADO

"THIS IS THE HORACE MANN Middle School's Class of 2006." Cheers filled the theater as I stood, cheering along. I was filled with disappointment, happiness, and pride for the graduates and my friends.

"What happened? Where's your cap and gown?" said Erina.

"I didn't cross the stage."

"Here, you can keep my cap," she said, giving me her cap.

I felt the pity in her words, but I accepted the cap anyway.

Bing! The bell rang and I came back from memory lane. I realized I was in summer school with the rest of the students who didn't graduate. I felt regret that I didn't try my best to succeed.

"This is a waste of time," I told Jessica, also a Horace Mann student who failed. "I could have been sleeping late, could have gone to Mexico if I wanted to, could have been out all summer."

"Yeah, this be feeling like a jail. It's hella nice outside and we locked in here for five hours."

That summer, I figured out what I had to do to graduate. I learned about credits and requirements. I promised to be on top of my stuff. The whole experience had me aiming for my high school diploma to make my mamma proud. Most of my teachers and school staff think of me so negatively, but they don't know my story.

They don't know that in elementary school, I loved school, I did my homework, I learned, and I wanted to be in school. But in the third grade, things changed.

"See this?" my third grade teacher would point to the side of her neck, "You did this to me. You kids always have me screaming." She had a big ball that looked like a tumor at the side of her neck.

I would just put my head down, ignoring her accusations, what she had to say, and what she had to teach. I mean, what eight-year-old wants to hear her teacher blaming her students for her sickness, her stress, and her problems? Putting my head down brought my teacher's attention, and she arranged a meeting with my mom.

"Are there problems at home?"

"No," my mom said, confused.

"Elizabeth is a smart girl." Teachers always seem to get the parents on their side with this line. "I think it's very unhealthy for a child to be tired all the time. She comes to class, puts her head down, and doesn't do homework. She needs more sugar in her blood. You should give her chocolate."

My mom looked at her, confused.

"Oh no. Just a little bit of chocolate." Okay, Ms. Doctor was trying to prescribe me some chocolate. Chocolate was going to make me crash afterward. Where did she get her PhD? Candyland or the Willy Wonka factory?

This showed me that teachers weren't as nice as I had expected. When the teacher asked if I did my homework or my classwork, I didn't care. I felt really small next to her because she was demanding. I didn't know when she was being mean and when she was actually being nice; to me, she was always evil! She thought I was a bad child, when all my previous teachers always said I was good and intelligent.

In middle school, my peers always thought of me as a quiet, very shy, and a goody-goody, and I wanted to change that. I thought it was more about appearances than intelligence. Every year I changed friends, changed my attitude, and paid less attention in class. In sixth grade I had more intelligent friends who went to the computer lab at lunch and did not even socialize. In seventh grade I found a group of girls we call "chunts," people who like salsa and/or meringue, speak Spanish all the time, and don't care what people think of them. In eighth grade, I went back to my elementary school friends, and it seemed like they hadn't changed. Roxana was smart and imaginative, and Kennia was hyper, realistic, and talkative. They were two smart girls and I felt like the ignorant one in the group. School was like a kick-it spot where I met new people. School was something I had to get through. I just sat in six different classes, five days a week. I cared more about the gossip.

When teachers asked me which class I liked most, I would say lunch. When they asked me about my favorite activity, I would say kicking it with my friends. I didn't even bother remembering the principal's name. I didn't even know my counselor until the last few weeks of eighth grade, when she told me I was at risk of not graduating. I knew if I failed three classes I couldn't cross the stage. Still, I didn't show up to school until third period. I thought it was too late to try to do well in school. The teacher thought my friends and I were disruptive, lazy, and ignorant, so she gave up, put all of us together, and gave us an F. We even called our table the rejected table.

In my freshman year of high school, the teachers gave us a "Freshman 411" booklet that explained the history of the school and the high school requirements. I learned that I had to earn credits and not wait until the last semester to get good grades. High school is about how well you do in all four years. At the beginning of each semester I would go to my counselor to talk about my classes. One time, I noticed that my classes were all wrong so I headed straight to the counselor's office to see Ms. Lightfoot. She was too busy, so I kept bugging her until she fixed it. Or I would go to Ms. Burgos, who was always happy to help. With my transcripts, I had proof of what classes I had passed and which ones I had to retake. I would always have backup plans: free periods, summer school, cyber class, and night school. I would always beat my counselor to the punch when it came to getting my classes together. She wasn't the one looking for me; I was the one looking for her.

I found subjects that motivated me. In ninth grade I loved art. I took it seriously and took my time creating my drawings because they had to be perfect. In tenth grade I had a tough P.E. teacher. "No pain, no gain!" she screamed as we ran faster. She always had us running like our pants were on fire. We played football and the whole class enjoyed it; even the people who didn't like running participated. She was tough, but I could tell she was proud of me when I pushed myself over my limits in her final. I ran sprints more times than I ever had, and she passed me without a doubt. Although I looked forward to P.E., I still wanted to take a break from time to time. I had a group of friends who would skip. I would see them on my way to school.

"Where you going?" I would ask.

"Over there." They pointed in a different direction away from school.

"But school is this way." I pointed in the direction of school. "Well, I already missed a class, it wouldn't hurt to not go to school."

But, in my junior year, I realized I didn't want to go through that again.

"C'mon! Let's go late to class!" one friend would say.

"Nah, I'm good. I need to go to class," I replied, grabbing my notebook from my locker and getting to class before the bell rang.

In eleventh grade, my motivation was tenth-grade English because I had a teacher who would speak the truth. He had that Raza power.

"It's Mr. Villacaña, with the 'y' sound and a little flying thing on top of the 'n.' No, not Vilacana. *Villacaña!*" he would tell the class when he introduced himself.

He had pride for his culture. He would give us assignments that would make us think. In the second semester, I looked forward to algebra and French. Math was my favorite subject and French was interesting to learn. Senior year, my favorite class was finite math. This class makes it easier to understand life's mathematical problems, like debt, mortgages, and taxes.

"Finally, something that is useful in life," I thought to myself.

I'm not a school person, you know, the preppy, smart, big-bag-full-of-books type of person. But I'm trying my best and pushing myself. I don't want to be known as a failure. I don't want to be known as a statistic. I want to succeed. I want to be known as independent. I want to cross that stage and I don't want to be another person in the audience while my friends graduate. I don't want to feel like I am less of a person. I don't want people bragging about their diplomas while I'm empty-handed. I want to finish high school, period; nothing else after that. I just want to go straight to work, because if I struggle in high school, how will I make it in college? Now that I'm in my senior year, I'm struggling to find something that I'm good at, because life in America is hard without a degree. I want the money, the cars, the clothes, and I want to build a house for my mom in Mexico. I just want to be successful. And the first step is the high school diploma.

FREEDOM
on the
ROAD

by CCARLOS GONZALEZ

WHEN I WAS TEN YEARS OLD, the Chevy Avalanche was released. My family was impressed by how nice it was. At the time, we had a green Plymouth Breeze, which was cool, but my siblings and I were getting older, and we needed more space. My dad was working as a welder and my mom as a teacher at Hesperia Junior High School in southern California. With both my parents working, we were able to save up to get a bigger car. We saved up for about a year, enough to exchange our good old reliable Breeze and get the new car.

It was around March, and we turned a couple of corners in Victorville to get to the Mark Shultz Chevrolet dealership. The place was sick; it had all kinds of nice cars, like Hummers and Escalades. My brother, sister, and I were running around like baby chickens, while my mom and dad filled out the monstrous amount of paperwork. The staff treated us well, with complimentary drinks and food, and the dealership even had a mini-golf platform, which kept us busy. A few hours went by and finally we were allowed to leave with the car. We were so excited. The Avalanche was massive inside, the seats were so comfy, and I loved that new-car smell.

Now we had all the space we needed. Plus we could fit our vicious pup Wheizzer in the car with us. Being blessed with a new car and transportation was fantastic. It really showed me that if you work hard, you can get what you want.

The freedom of owning a car is being able to go anywhere, anytime, and do whatever you want with it. To go wherever you want is fantastic because you make your own rules and routes. Having a car is more than just going places. It's about working hard for that car. It shows you can have freedom at any time.

My dream car is an original Hummer because they look like a beast of a vehicle. They are used by the U.S. army, so you know they're tough, and they have a lot of room inside. I first saw one when I was five. I was dazzled. That car looked tight—like a Suburban on steroids. If I had a choice of color, it would be desert sand color like the original ones. It would smell like Windex and Armor All because I would keep that mess clean. The car would be automatic because I don't know how to drive stick. It is obsolete to drive stick; most modern cars do not require it.

The car gives us freedom to drive anywhere. The car takes me to my favorite destinations, like the skate park. We drive the car with the music blasting all day. I like having the windows down so I can enjoy the cool, relaxing breeze and the sights of San Francisco: all the huge buildings, the bridges, and Alcatraz. It's always nice to drive on the Bay Bridge, listening to music and talking to my mom. I live in Oakland with my mom and we cross the Bay Bridge twice a day. There's a lot to see. I love driving into San Francisco every day. I love the view, the ocean, and the city. While on the road, we listen to a lot of music.

Music is great. It makes everything better because it calms you and pumps you up. My mom lets me listen to anything. We take turns playing her iPod and mine. My mom usually plays her music in the morning, and I play mine after school. Ahhh, I hate my mom's music: all this Mariah Carey junk, a lot of Spanish music, and bad rap. My mom and I are always laughing at the most random things, like what is on the road, the other drivers, or other cars. We always hope the Bay Bridge doesn't collapse under us. Traffic is *no bueno*, just sit and wait.

On these drives, we not only have fun, but we also talk about serious things. One time we talked about my mom's parents, who immigrated from Zacatecas, Mexico, for a better life. After my mom finished high school, they wanted her to get a job instead of going to college. She chose her own path of going to school because she thought she would have a better life for herself and her future family. She went to UCLA and graduated. Then she became a teacher. Today she is a principal. I am happy she went to college. This inspires our whole family to want to go to college, and it gave me more freedom. Maybe I could succeed just like my mother.

My dad, who is from Santa Ana, had a tough life as an ex-gang-banger but came through and became a welder. He joined the gang when he was young, in either middle school or the beginning of high school, because everyone in his neighborhood was in it, his friends and family were in it. He didn't really have a choice, but still he enjoyed being with his friends and family. He was a problem-solver, someone who would be told by a boss to threaten and beat up others. He is a big, buff Mexican and not scared of anything.

However, he became a Christian and started drifting away from the gang. My dad began painting cars and lowriders, and that became his job. He left the gang to become a welder. His job made him move to Apple Valley, seventy miles from where we lived. My dad tells me to follow my dreams and work hard; if I love something, follow it and put my whole self into it. His life experience has helped me learn from his mistakes. Now he is retired and working for his teaching credentials. I think he will be a good teacher and no one will disrespect him. Soon both my parents will be in the education field. My younger brother Slaytr is a beast of a child. He grew up always wanting to fight. Slaytr has always been a tough kid, and he is an insane wrestler. He is built like my dad and is clam-quiet. He should never be underestimated. My sister Vanezza is cool because we have a lot in common. She is a crazy person to talk to. She always has something funny or dumb to say. Vanezza tells her stories loudly. She is also very artistic. She wants to study to become a hairstylist at Aveda. I'm glad to have two great siblings who relate to me and will be with me forever.

When I was younger, I always sat in the back behind the driver on family trips. My family always has their regular seats: my dad drives, mom sits in the passenger seat, Slaytr sits in the middle, and Vanezza sits behind the passenger seat. My brother and I always bring our skateboards. Usually the drives are chill, just friendly talk and whatever is on the radio. It's peaceful.

My favorite family trip was when my brother, dad, my friend Max, and I went to Las Vegas, Phoenix, and southern Arizona when I was fifteen. We drove from Hesperia to Las Vegas to spend the night, eat, and skate. We stayed at the Imperial Palace and ate at Carnegie Delicatessen. I got a fat pastrami sandwich; it was the best meal ever. After we ate, we went to a skate park on the outskirts of Vegas. Then we went walking around. We saw all the big hotels with lights everywhere. The place reeked of cigars and alcohol. We fell asleep ready for a long drive across the state to Arizona.

In the middle of the day, we stopped at the Grand Canyon. It was so big; finally seeing it was amazing. It was orange-colored, with layers upon layers of brown dirt. I wondered if you could see the canyon from space and how long it is. Above the dirt were trees, green in the middle of summer, and at the top were a lot of tourists with cameras around their necks, sunscreen on their faces, and strange hats like Indiana Jones would wear. People were taking pictures everywhere.

It was fantastic and nice to have the freedom to drive to one of the world's biggest, most famous natural landmarks. I felt relieved that I had finally seen it. I felt small compared to its giant size.

When we left, I was excited because we were going to Phoenix to bed down for the night and eat a lot. The long drive to Phoenix was hot and boring. There wasn't a lot to see other than funky gas stations and desert: cactus, rocks, dirt, and a couple of coyotes. We went swimming after a long of day of driving for three hundred miles. Max and I were bored, so we went around the hotel and took the "do not disturb" signs off every door. We ran around, laughing, and had a good time. We went to bed exhausted and ready to drive another hundred miles the next day to Sierra Vista, in southern Arizona near Mexico, to visit my grandmother.

There are tons of deserts where my grandma lives. They are surrounded by mountains, some of which had snow at the top even in summer. I was happy to see my grandma, and she was happy to see us.

My grandma lives in a giant seven-bedroom, four-acre home. In Arizona, I got to see family whom I've never met before, and they were very cool, especially my cousins Matt and Junior, who are from Santa Ana but moved to Arizona because they had gotten in trouble. They are really nice people, and I was happy to finally meet them. Having freedom is not being limited, just following your dreams. My parents wanted a nice, durable, safe car, not just to drive us around, but also to allow us to experience freedom.

RAGS
to
RICHES

by OSCAR PINEDA

EIGHT YEARS AGO, I remember living in a small room with other families. It was a sad time for my family; we didn't have a lot of money and my parents didn't have good jobs. My dad was a construction worker and my mom was a babysitter. I couldn't get the things I wanted for Christmas. What I really wanted was a TV, but I couldn't get it because my mom told me she couldn't spend money on a TV.

Every Saturday my father would take us to Reno so he could try to win some money in the slot machines. If we were lucky we could sleep in a hotel, but that wasn't likely; usually we would have to sleep in our 1967 Toyota Corolla. Every time we slept in the car, I would have to sleep in the backseat with my older brother, while my dad would sleep in the driver's seat and my mom would sleep in the passenger seat. The car was a two-door and it was really small, so we were all cramped in there. It was really hard for me to go to sleep because it was cold inside the car and because there were crazy people yelling outside in the streets.

A couple years later my mom's boss gave my dad a job working for the recycling company. My dad made a lot of money that year, and we moved into an apartment. I finally had a room, but I had to share it with my older brother. My dad bought us a laptop, a 20-inch TV for the living room, and he bought me a PlayStation. After my dad got his job, we bought so much stuff that we had to cut back on the spending.

When he was a little kid in El Salvador, my dad wanted to do judo, but my grandma didn't have the money for it. Now that we had money in America, my dad had me practice judo. At first I didn't want to do it, but I kept going anyway. After a year of practicing, I received my yellow belt, and my dad put me in tournaments so I could compete with other people and represent my judo club. After placing in all the tournaments I went to, people from all over California knew me. My dad wanted me to become really good at judo, so he put me in camps and clinics. After two years of judo, I was promoted to a purple belt. I took state my first year, but my second year I lost in the finals, taking second. There was a tournament in Texas called the Junior Olympics, and some of my teammates and I went. It was cool taking a plane for the first time in my life. It was a very different environment; it was very hot, and when it rained it was still hot.

The day of the tournament I was very nervous about my upcoming matches. On my first match I was completely out of it; I had no idea what was going on. So after that I put my head back in the game. I did a hip toss move and my opponent went flying into the air and landed flat on his back, winning me my first match. I was so happy because it was my first time beating someone from out of state. My next opponent was from Florida. The match started and about twenty seconds into it he flipped me upside down and I landed on my back and lost. I was pretty mad that I lost, but I focused on my next match coming up against a guy from Washington, which I won in fewer than ten seconds. At the end of the day I won three and lost two, and took third place. People I didn't know congratulated me, and I thought that I'd achieved fame for judo. I was ranked fourth in the nation, and my dad was proud of me.

A year later my dad bought our family a house. I finally had my own room and a backyard. Now that we had space in our new house, my brother wanted to teach me wrestling. At first I didn't want to, but again, I kept at it anyway. My freshman year was pretty decent; I had a season record of 14–2. Losing in the finals in the San Francisco section league was the worst day in my life, because I was undefeated in my section but when it came to the last tournament to go to state, I lost. After the match ended, the crowd went crazy for the person who beat me. Summer came and my dad sent me to three wrestling camps, which cost over one thousand dollars.

My sophomore year my record was 10–2, and I was in the finals again to go to state. The stadium was packed. I was nervous because the crowd was so loud and because my parents were watching. I was also nervous because my opponent was a senior. However, all the coaches assumed that I was going to win this time. They finally called my name, and I got even more nervous. When the match started I took him down first. By the third round, I was leading 8–3, but somehow in the last second he beat me by one point. The buzzer went off and the crowd went wild, and I felt so sad that I had lost twice in the finals. After my match, I saw my opponent being interviewed by Comcast and awarded Most Outstanding Lightweight, which made me even more upset, since that could have been me. I never got to achieve fame for wrestling.

Now that wrestling season is over, I can think about what I want to do. Here's my dream: I want to become a doctor after I graduate from college. One summer I went to a wrestling tournament at UC Davis and I thought the campus looked cool. So I want to go to UC Davis, but I'm pretty sure I'll never make it there because I'm really not that smart. Since I know that it's not possible for me to become a doctor, I'll study business in school so I can open a pizzeria. It would probably be a restaurant for kids and near a school so they could come in at lunch. I want it to be somewhere safe and where there are a lot of people.

I also want to go on Major League Gaming with some of my friends for the game *Halo*. We know that there are many gamers that are better than our team, but we still try to get better each day. We want to get paid for playing a game. I think in a few years this dream could happen, but in the meantime I'll stick with wrestling and try to get a scholarship to go to the school I want to go to, and see if I can do what I want to do. If any of this happens I could achieve my dreams of having money and getting a good education. I think money is a big thing because without money you can't get the things you want and therefore you won't be happy. And if you have a good education, you can get a good job, which can get you a lot of money.

My dad always wanted a black belt, but he couldn't even start judo at all. He is proud of me because I'm very good at it, and he likes the medals I bring him every time I win at the tournaments. Even though I don't like this sport, I do it to make him happy. He came to America because he wanted to get a better life and a better job, which makes me think my dad and I have a similar dream: we both want money. He has achieved his American Dream of having money, going from being really poor to being above middle class. I believe my dad and I are happy with our lives because we don't have to worry about not having money. And my dad is happy because I am good at sports and I'm happy because my dad has money and gets me anything I want. I believe that because we are happy.

The Bunny and
THE DESIRE

by KIMBERLY SOLARES

THE OBJECT THAT IS MOST special to me is my plush toy bunny. He is one of a kind, and he has floppy ears. He is a light shade of yellow and holds a carrot. The carrot has a few stitches that I made on the leaf. I made two hearts, and in between them I stitched an initial, an *M*. The *M* stands for the first letter of the bunny's name, Moisescito, after my dad's name, Moises. The bunny is small and has a rattle inside him. My dad bought him when I was four at Westlake Plaza in Daly City. There were a bunch of teddy bears, plush puppies, and kittens. Moisescito was the only bunny there, so I picked him. I guess the reason I picked him is because everyone gets teddy bears, puppies, or kittens. I hardly ever see bunnies. Plus, each year for my birthday I would get a giant teddy bear from one of my uncles. The bunny was the only one that I have ever seen. I have never seen one like him, so I think it's pretty neat that I'm the only one who has him; it makes him special. I used to take Moisescito everywhere with me. He always had to be with me. I would take him to church, to the mall, to sleepovers, and on trips. Until this day, I still have him. He sits on top of my pillow.

When I went to visit Guatemala for the first time, I was eight and the bunny had to come with me. There were no questions asked, the bunny had to come. My dad would go off to do family business and I would get stuck on the ranch with my cousins or with a family member that I barely knew. The bunny would remind me of my dad. When I came back to the United States, I searched through my bags but couldn't find him. I accidentally forgot him in Guatemala!

When I found out, I started to cry and cry. My dad told my grand-mother to mail it to me within a week, but I begged for him to come back sooner. My grandmother told me that his eye got poked out by a chicken. I just started to cry even more, but she told me that she would be able to sew it back on. After my grandmother sewed it back on, she mailed him back to me. When I got him back, I was so happy!

I may sound insane for saying this, but sometimes I would talk to my bunny. I used to take him to the roof of my dad's apartment building and just gaze at the view of San Francisco. I could see the Bay Bridge and downtown. I would talk to him up there where it was just me and him, and my dad didn't think I was insane. Sometimes I still talk to my bunny, when I feel frustrated and I know no one will understand me. He never talks back and is quite a good listener. I guess, since I am my dad's only child, I got lonely. Like for instance, if my bunny couldn't come with me somewhere, I would tell him all about it later. He couldn't go to swimming lessons. When I got back home, I would tell him about the new dive that I learned. I was very excited to learn new dives and swims because I was one of the few Latinas there in the pool. I felt proud of myself because I learned to do tricks and dives, and I would teach them to my friends. I learned horseback riding and I would tell him how exciting it was, how big and tall the horses were.

My bunny has always been a safe zone for me, the only thing in my life that has stayed the same. The reason he is a safe zone for me is because when I am with him I feel comforted and encouraged. He may not talk or respond, but in a weird way he helps me. He brings the good and bad memories of what I have had so far, all the things that I have ac-complished in my life, all the hardships and trials that have been thrown at me so far in my life. He helped me get through it when my two best friends left. One moved to New Jersey to finish school and the other one went to college in L.A. He will always be in my life. I can't imagine myself without him. I may not be so attached to him now, but I don't think I will ever really outgrow him. I grew up with him and he has always been there for me. He's the one object that represents all my memories.

The bunny mostly reminds me of my dad. I think the reason is be-cause one of my earliest memories is of my dad buying him. Also, when my dad would go and do laundry, he would take me. He would wash the bunny, and while the bunny was drying I would just sit on top of the washer and watch him tumble around and around inside the dryer. Whenever my dad went to work his night shift and leave me with my babysitter or nanny (he worked at night in a big hotel around the north side of downtown), he always made sure I had the bunny. My dad knew how much the bunny meant to me.

My dad has played an important role in my life since he and my mom split up when I was one year old. Ever since, he and I have become closer. I am daddy's little girl in a way. When I was younger, my dad was always there for me. We only had each other. We would cook, clean, go for bike rides, and go camping together. He put me in private schools, even though they are expensive, and made sure I got good grades. He would pay for my lessons and take me out to have fun. For example, we went to the movies, theme parks, and restaurants. Sometimes I would go with my best friend and my dad would go with her dad while we were together. My dad always wanted the best for me and still does. He always told me to study and read books. Now I like to read for fun. Yeah, I know it sounds weird. Not that many kids like to read for fun, but I do. It's fun to read stories and books and imagine them in your head like a little movie. I guess since my dad would let me go to the library and let me pick books to read, it stuck with me. I'm glad for that.

My dad wants me to have a good career. He doesn't want me to be in the situation that he and my mom are in right now and have always been in. They are always working and having to pay bills. He wants me to be successful in life. He wants me to do well in school and get a good career. He wants me to go to a good college and to make the right choices. He wants me to finish school (high school and college). My parents don't want me to be in the same situation as they are in now. They have always had big dreams for me. We may not agree on the same career that I should have, but as long as I know what I want to do, they're okay with it. They both encourage me to pursue my career.

As a little girl, I always wanted to become a veterinarian. My parents aren't animal lovers like I am. But they support me in my choice. When I was younger, my dad got me my first hamster. I don't remember what age I was, probably seven or eight. I was excited to have one. I had never seen a hamster before I had that one. After that, my dad got me more pet hamsters. I adored those little guys, so small and furry. Those were the main pets I had when I was growing up with my dad, plus a few fish for a couple of months. At my mom's, I had a bird, bunnies, kittens, and a puppy. I was always curious about animals. I wanted to learn more about them, so I knew what I wanted to be when I was older.

When people asked me what I wanted to be, I would tell them, "a vet." They would tell me to check out UC Davis. It is in northern California. I have heard of it, but haven't really checked it out. I heard it's supposed to be the best veterinarian college in California. I'm trying to build my experience in the animal science field by working in animal hospitals or volunteering. I believe by having more experience in the animal field I have a better chance of doing the thing I love the most, which is to help and work with animals. I guess in a way, the bunny started my love for animals. Having all those pets increased my love for them as well. I'm not completely sure how I want to help them. I want to work with domestic pets or exotics ones. To help and work with animals is my dream. My bunny has helped me in life and will always be with me. The American Dream for others is having money, cars, or a big house, but for me it is having privileges and opportunities. For example, having the opportunity to learn new things, doing the things you love in life, to travel each year, to have a big family, to grow up in a nice calm neighborhood. To have the career you love to do, or to have a job you love. Not many people have the chance to horseback ride every week or travel out of the country every other year. Some of my friends and family members can't leave the country to visit their homelands. They can't see their grandparents or family that they haven't seen in years. I don't take it for granted.

The
BRITISH
COIN

by ROBERTO "POTATO" HERNANDEZ

IT WAS A MONDAY MORNING in 1997 at Cleveland Elementary School. As I walked to school, I wasn't feeling good. I had a bad headache; it made me feel like I was upside down and almost made me vomit. I had to go to school, but first I went to the store to buy some chips and a soda. It was 8:30 a.m. and the corner store was full of kids. There was a line of about ten kids in front of me, like animals, monkeys, waiting to get in. Twenty minutes passed, and I was still not in the store. It was 8:55 a.m. already, and I had five minutes to get to school. The guy let me in and I bought some chips. I ran to school with one minute left. I was late by a few seconds and the teacher screamed at me, "Why are you late? And why do you have bad food in your hands?" She took my chips and soda away and put them in her desk.

I sat at my desk and we started reading a book called *Alien Parents*. *Alien Parents* is about aliens coming to Earth and adopting a kid. As the kid grows up, they keep their secret from him. Half of the book happened in the house where they lived. I was really into the book and didn't know two hours had passed. I saw myself as the kid in the book, because I think I was adopted, but not by aliens (I hope!). I don't feel close to my family because almost everyone in my family likes Mexican music, and I am the only one who likes rock. Also, I have a different last name than my parents.

Soon it was lunch time. I put my things away and walked down the stairs to the lunchroom. As I was walking down, I glanced back at my teacher and saw her taking out my chips and cola! And she started eating them! I almost wanted to scream at her for eating what I bought with my money. But I didn't do anything because I would have gotten expelled. When I got to the lunch line, the lady serving the disgusting food they had gave me the one thing that I can't eat. She gave me beef. I almost vomited on the table, because I don't like beef. I told my teacher I didn't like beef and she said, "I don't care. You better eat that or you won't go to recess." I was just sitting there with my hands in my pockets, and I felt something rough. I took it out, and I saw it was a British coin. And when I saw it, I had a daydream about going to a different country. That day made me think that I want to travel when I get older. I would like to travel because I want to get away from all the bad things that have happened to me. To me, it's like the opportunity to travel is my American Dream: to be free, to be able to go anywhere and without curfews.

I have gone to different places with my family. I have been to Reno, Nevada, and when I go to Reno I feel like I want to live there forever. I have gone to the casinos. My mom is friends with the manager for Circus Circus casino. We get invited twice a month, but we rarely go. I have also been to Las Vegas, where we had a good time. I was amazed by all the bright lights and the casinos on every corner, people walking and taking pictures of the beautiful things, like the MGM, with the big lion at the entrance. Also, there was this really big skyscraper with a roller-coaster on the very top of the building.

When I went to Vegas for the second time, I went to a car show where I saw two different Ferraris. One of them was red with a convertible top and 20-inch rims. I also liked the design it had. It looked like there was a rip on the door where a purple tiger was jumping out of the door. The second Ferrari was black with a nice racing body and a very nice design all over the body. The design was a rip on the hood where a clown with red eyes was popping out of the hood saying, "I'm coming back and winning this time." I also saw other nice cars, like a black BMW with a racing body and a Rockstar sticker with all the other racing companies' stickers. I also saw a Porsche 911 with a racing body, and I fell in love with the design on it. It was a werewolf on a hill howling to the moon. The moon was behind the edge of the hill and the moon was almost covered with fog. I also saw a hot rod show. The street was full of old 1970 Chevrolets and almost all of them had headers sticking out of the hood. There were old 1987 Mustangs, too. But there was one I liked the most out of all of them. It was a 1987 custom Mustang built from scratch, with a custom convertible top, custom rims (32-inch rims), and a custom hood that would come up with a push of a button. I liked the doors especially because they would go straight up, like butterfly wings. It had custom seats from the Apex Racing company that were specially made for the owner. I also saw a black hot rod with headers sticking out of the hood and painted flames. It was cool.

I also saw the water show. At the water they played a special song called "Time to Say Goodbye," and the water moved to the beat of the music. The water would go really high and change colors. I enjoyed it a lot. If we ever go back to Vegas, I would like to see the show again.

I have also traveled to Los Angeles. I like L.A. because it looks like a fun place to live. I have family in L.A., and we go visit them once a year. I have also visited family in Fresno, and it gets really hot over there. My cousin has a really big house; it has five rooms, three bathrooms, and one really big kitchen.

The other place I have visited is Mexico, where I have family. I like to visit Mexico because I have a lot of family and friends there. My friends and I go to the forest and shoot at lizards with a slingshot. Where I stayed was weird; my house was in between a desert and a forest. On the desert side, it was always hot. I remember my friends and I went to the desert side, and we would play a game called "Changie." We made up this game. To play this game you need two bricks and a broom, and you would cut the broom into three pieces. One piece was half the broom and the other half would be cut in the middle, and you would put the short piece on the bricks and whack it off, up to the sky, and then you had to catch it. I lost a lot of pounds playing that game all day in the desert! The desert was really dry and really hot. On the other side, the forest was always raining and cold. My friends and I would go to the forest and get wet.

My family would like me to visit Mexico at least twice a year, going for a month. I think that my family in Mexico would say the American Dream is coming to California and making a lot of money so they can also send money to their folks in Mexico. My family here is big, too. I have family all over: San Francisco, Daly City, San Bruno, San Pablo, and Sacramento. But I don't visit them a lot, because they are boring, always talking about stuff in Spanish. I don't even understand Spanish! I always talk to them in English.

I would like to visit Russia, Germany, and France. I want to visit Russia because I want to see the art in their museums and hear the types of music that they listen to. I want to learn to speak Russian because I have a Russian friend who has inspired me to learn Russian, and maybe we could talk in Russian. I would also like to visit Germany because I have seen a beautiful picture of Germany's mountains with the snow falling on them. And I have heard that Germany has good art schools and good museums. I would like to visit France because I would like to see the Eiffel Tower and go up to the top to see all of France. I've heard that the driver sits on the other side of the car over there, and drives on the other side of the road, too.

Traveling is my American Dream.

BEHIND
the
WHEEL

by DORIS MEDRANO

EVERY TIME I RIDE THE BUS, I have a bad experience. I get in, and if it's not packed, I try to find a seat. When I do sit down, I listen to my iPod and look around. The buses usually look the same. There is graffiti all over the back area of the bus: on the ground, on the sides, on the panels, and carved in and on the windows. Often, the bus is filled with creepy, annoying, or nasty people. I catch myself noticing that people never really look at anybody else on the bus. They stare out onto the street from the windows. A lot of times the bus smells bad, either like pee or throw-up or even alcohol coming from the drunk person next to you. Sometimes I see little kids on the bus alone and think to myself, "Why on earth would their parents let their kids out at such a young age?" I usually hear people's iPods when they are listening to their music too loud, and people screaming "Back door!" until the bus driver opens it. It's times like these that I wish I had my own car, so that I could go about my activities in a comfortable and safe way. For me, the American Dream means having my own car to go where I want, when I want.

My parents came to the United States for their own American Dream. My dad came here from Mexico when he was only fifteen years old. He eventually got a job and worked his way up to build and support his family. My mom also came to the United States to live a better life. She immigrated here from El Salvador. The fact that both of my parents immigrated to the United States to create a better life shows their bravery. Their courage to come here and achieve their dream makes it possible for me to accomplish mine, and a big part of my dream is to leave public transportation behind.

Have you ever felt unsafe riding the bus around the city? I have. About three months ago, my friends Ticia, Alexa, and I wanted to go to Serramonte to go shopping. Since none of us drive, we had to take one Muni bus and one SamTrans. We walked up to 24th and Mission St., and as we were getting there, so was the 14 bus. We hopped on, and none of us sat down since it was so packed. The bus rode for about ten minutes and then broke down on Cortland Street. Everybody had to hop off and wait for it at the next stop. We all got really irritated because there were so many people at the bus stop. The next 14 came, but since there were too many people at the bus stop and too many people on the bus itself, it passed by us without picking anybody up. Ticia, Alexa, and I thought about the situation and walked back a block to the stop before to wait for the bus there. That way, when the bus got to Cortland, we wouldn't have to hop on with everybody there. We soon got on the bus and it took us past Geneva, almost to Daly City. We got off in front of a laundromat and waited there for about twenty minutes for the next SamTrans. It finally came and we got on. We rode for twenty minutes and got off in front of the food court at Serramonte.

By the time we left Serramonte, it was freezing and dark outside. We waited for a few minutes for the SamTrans and hopped on. It dropped us off at the same stop where we got on. The 14 took forever to get there. We got on and sat in the back. A few stops later, a bum-looking guy got on the bus and sat directly in front of us in the four-seaters. Ticia, Alexa, and I looked at each other all weird because he was looking at us in a really strange way. We started to get a little bit scared. I looked away because I was creeped out.

All of a sudden, Alexa hit my leg and whispered to me, "Look! Look at the guy!" I looked up and saw the guy cover his lips with his hand as if he was signaling for us to shut up and not say anything. We looked at the seat in which he was sitting and noticed something weird coming from under his leg. Ticia told us that it was blood. I guess we were the only ones that noticed, until the guy to his side looked and changed seats. The guy was just sitting there, not worried about the fact that he was bleeding. All three of us were still staring at him, and we saw him look around and move his leg. We wanted to tell somebody or ask him if he needed help, but we were too scared.

He soon got up and got off at the next stop. Everybody that was sitting in the back of the bus watched him leave and saw that he had a hole in his pants. We all looked down at the seat and saw that it *had* been blood. It was the most disgusting and creepy thing I have ever seen. Next thing you know, another guy got on the bus and sat on the same exact seat! We all looked at him, speechless. I felt bad for not letting him know, but it was already too late. From that day on I never wanted to ride a bus again, especially not a 14. Every time I get on a 14, I still make sure I don't sit in any of the four-seaters. A major reason that I want to learn how to drive and get my own car is so I can drive anyplace I want in a comfortable space.

Avoiding public transportation isn't really an option when you don't know how to drive, but it's not easy for everybody to own a car. You have to get somebody to teach you how to drive. You also have to work hard and study, take the test and actually pass it. It doesn't end there. After going through the process of learning how to drive and passing the test, you have to work for the car. Many people don't have the money to just buy a car, so they have no choice left but to work for it.

In my case, my dad has told my sister and me that whoever learns how to drive first can get the BMW he has in the garage. Learning how to drive before my sister wouldn't be the only problem: the BMW is a stick shift, meaning I would have to learn how to drive an automatic first and then move up to stick shift. Most people barely know how to drive automatic; imagine driving stick! Therefore, I'm not sure about getting that BMW.

Another obstacle I would have to face in order to learn how to drive would be my fear of driving. I'm scared to learn for many reasons. If I were to learn and become a good driver, I would still face the risk of getting into an accident with a bad driver—anybody who is under the influence or just not paying attention to the road. Accidents can happen anytime, anywhere.

One of the scariest and most dangerous places to drive would be on the freeway. I know because I have been in an accident before. About two years ago, on April Fool's Day of all days, my family and I decided we wanted to go have dinner at Sizzler. We got ready and hopped on the freeway. While my dad was driving, my sister, my brother, and I were in the backseat, chilling. On one side of the freeway, there was a wall about the same size as the car. I was sitting in the seat behind my mom, next to the window. I looked to my right, and all of a sudden, I saw an orange and black car coming straight toward me. At that moment, I didn't know what to think, and I panicked. A few seconds later, I felt the car crash into us and saw my dad start to struggle with the wheel. I looked at my sister and brother. We were all screaming. On impact, the car twirled. My dad stopped it just before it hit the wall. After this, my dad never drove with his family on the freeway again. Now, instead, he always takes side streets.

I'm also scared of passing the driving test. In order for me to pass the test, I would have to study a lot, since I don't know much about driving. If I put my all into the test and didn't pass it, I would feel pretty disappointed and frustrated in knowing I failed. However, my fear of failing wouldn't stop me, and I would just keep trying until I accomplished my goal because driving is part of becoming a responsible adult.

My dad is the only one in my family who knows how to drive. My mom has always wanted to learn, but she never got the chance. In my eyes, the fact that my older sister, who is nineteen years old, can't drive is pretty sad. She's stuck riding on the bus and depending on others. She goes to school at City College, all the way on Ocean Ave. We live in the Mission District, so every day she spends almost an hour on the bus. By the time I'm in college, I want to drive there; I don't want to be riding the bus. Having a car would also help me become more punctual. I'm not a morning person, and I'm always late to school. A car would help me get to school on time. Also, if I were to get a job, a car would make it possible for me to be there on time and not get fired.

Overall, my American Dream is a way for me to feel free, comfortable, and safe. Driving my own car would be a great accomplishment. Not everybody can say they're capable of driving their own car, although this doesn't mean they aren't able to achieve it. Obstacles are a part of everyday life; you just have to learn to go through them. Somewhere in between the creepy dude and the hour-long bus rides, I realized how much I dislike public transportation. Wave at me out the window when you see me speeding by.

$\mathcal{M}y$ $\mathcal{O}bstacle:$
RACISM

by HORACIO CAMPOS

WHEN I WAS SIX YEARS OLD, I came to the United States with my family, looking for a better life. I was born in a small city in Jalisco, Mexico, called Encarnación de Díaz. In the 1990s, my mother had traveled back and forth between the United States and Mexico until ultimately deciding to move to the United States permanently. My mother influenced my belief in the American Dream: achieving success and being emotionally and economically established and stable. But there are always obstacles between you and your life goals.

At some point in life, everyone experiences racism. It probably will happen early, in a social setting, and it can make you feel less than you are, but it's only a small obstacle on the way to something greater. There are few places in the world in which people from different social classes and races meet and may socialize with each other; the bus is one of them.

On a nice Saturday afternoon, my friends and I were waiting for the bus to go down to the Mission District to hang out. The Muni was all tagged up—it was full of a variety of colors that ranged from bright purple to deep black. It was loud and stopped in front of me. When I got on the bus, I noticed two men sitting in the same row of seats with a gap separating them. One of the men was checking his BlackBerry phone, wearing a suit, and carrying a briefcase. The other man was talking to himself aloud. I could not understand all he was saying because of his thick accent, but he did mention Jesus and God several times.

On a bus there is less space and it's more crowded than the street. It is easier to bump into people. On the bus everyone is more like a union of people with great diversity. You would think that it would be easier to be a victim of racism on the bus because of the more complex environment. You might think there would be more of a chance that you would experience prejudice. The fact is, there is less chance for people to be prejudiced on the bus, because most of the passengers are very respectful, even though there are a few exceptions.

We got off the bus on 24th Street and Mission Street. The Mission District is where a lot of people of all ages, races, and social classes hang out. You could say that the Mission District is one of the most diverse places in the world. Walking down the street, I accidentally bumped into a bitter, mean, old white guy.

I said, "My bad," and kept walking. As I walked away, he started to yell racial slurs and insulting comments.

"Dirty Mexican! Damn wetback!" he said. He was wearing a sweater vest and was so wrinkly that his neck looked like a bunch of skin hanging and got red like a tomato from all the rage inside that he was letting out on me. As I walked away, I heard what he was screaming and I cussed him out. After I was done, we started to laugh and talk of what had happened because in a sense it was funny; it was unexpected and a foolish act on my part, because I could have avoided the incident if I had been paying attention to what was in front of me while walking.

It is very unusual to see an outburst of racism in the middle of the streets here in San Francisco, because most people are open-minded when it comes to interacting with people of other races. People in San Francisco are used to seeing and doing things with people of different races; therefore, everyone gets along without being intentionally racist. I feel very unhappy that the first outburst of racism I witnessed in person involved me as the victim, and what's worse is that it happened all because of a little bump with the wrong person. I guess it's true that people can be at the wrong place at the wrong time.

After walking for a while, my friends and I were getting thirsty, so we decided to go buy refreshments from the liquor store. We walked into the liquor store, which was run by an Asian man. As we entered the store, I noticed the worker get up from his seat and start to examine us with a mean look on his face. We walked to the back of the store, where they keep the cold drinks. As we went, I felt a cold stare from the owner, so my first instinct was to look over my shoulder. Then I noticed he was following us as though we were going to rob the store. So I looked at him with a serious face, because what he was doing was insulting to my friends and me.

"Is there a problem?" I asked.

"I'm just doing my job and taking care of my inventory," he responded.

Then I stated, "Well, you don't have to worry about us stealing, because we don't do that, so stop following us."

With a mean expression on his face, he clearly stated, "I know you're not going to steal from me because I'm watching you."

Without anything else to say to the man, I shrugged my shoulders and I said, "Okay then." After a while had passed with us not deciding what to buy, the owner got impatient and ended up kicking us out of the store.

After the day was over, I started thinking of how racism is going to affect me and what I will be able to achieve in life. I don't think I'm going to be able to achieve what I want if I don't overcome the obstacle that is racism, because I can't help it that my superiors may be racist against who I am, where I'm from, or what I stand for or believe in. It's also the case that without knowing it, I might make a comment that may offend my superiors. After thinking a while on the subject, I came to the conclusion that racism will never go away, and the best way to overcome it would have to be to walk away from situations that involve racism. I would also try to avoid making racist comments and to never refer to others by their race or their skin color.

BROKEN BONES
with a
SOLID SOUL

by NESTOR JAVIER MUÑOZ

BIG CARS, BIG HOUSES, and a lot of money: many of us see these on TV shows like *Cribs* and *Rags to Riches*. It seems like people on those shows have reached their American Dream. I have a simpler dream. My goals are to graduate from high school and go on to get a well-paying job as a doctor.

I want to graduate because I want the feeling of accomplishment and because of my brother. My brother encourages me and pushes me so that I can graduate and have something he never had. I want to have the accomplishment of graduating in front of my friends and family. Once I get my diploma, I can go off to college and major in pre-med. One of the greatest feelings I ever had was being able to cross the stage and graduate from elementary and middle school. It felt good seeing my family and how proud they were to see me in that cap and gown, but the most important reason was that I felt as though I had accomplished something.

I can remember my elementary school graduation as if it was yesterday. I don't remember the day, but the year was 2004. My friends and I had been talking about graduation for the past week. My class and my friend's class had been rehearsing for the graduation for about two weeks. About a month before our graduation, one of my classmates wrote a letter to Superintendent Arlene Ackerman, asking her to please attend our school's graduation. A few days before the ceremony, our school got a call from the superintendent saying that it would be her honor to be at our graduation. The first thing that happened on graduation day was that the superintendent gave us a speech about how proud she was to see us graduate. She was wearing a piece of clothing that looked like a cape, and at the end of her speech she told us it was very valuable to her and important to her. She chose a student to wear it for the rest of the ceremony. Then there was one student who gave a speech for each class. We also danced and sang to Whitney Houston's "Greatest Love of All" remix. We put on a great show for our parents.

My middle school graduation happened in 2007. That was the longest graduation I have ever been to. It took two hours to give all of the students their diplomas. We had our school choir sing Vitamins C's "Graduation (Friends Forever)." Once the ceremony was over, we had time to take pictures with our friends, family, and teachers. My mom and brother were so proud to see me at my middle school graduation.

My brother is a big reason, if not *the* reason, why I have not stopped going to school. Many people see my brother as a bad role model because he did not finish high school. I, like most little brothers, have always looked up to my older brother. My brother is most likely to be seen carrying or riding a skateboard. He's about three inches taller than me and he looks just like me, except with a ponytail down to the middle of his back and a thin beard with a goatee. He has always been like a father to me. I can remember when I was little we had a routine. Usually my dad and mom had already left for work. So my brother would wake me up and I would get up to put on the clothes my mom had left out the night before. My brother would give me something to eat, usually cereal. Once we were ready to go, my brother would walk me to school. My school was about a five to ten minute walk. On the way to school my brother and I would talk a lot. We would talk about life and how sometimes life isn't fair, but it just is what it is.

The first thing people see when they walk into my room is a giant mural painted by my brother. My brother is really into art. His style is really unique. It has a sort of street influence and a graffiti style to it. He painted "SF" in big letters on the wall, with the Bay Bridge in the background, car lights, and buildings. He has never made any murals other than the one in our room. When I see the mural, I imagine all of the famous places in San Francisco, such as the Golden Gate Bridge, the Bay Bridge, Pier 39, and Fort Mason.

There are a couple of words that my brother has said to me and I will never in my whole life forget. He said, "Don't be a screw-up like me."

Even though he did not graduate, he wants the best for me. He wants me to graduate high school and become something in life. Thinking of my brother and remembering all the fun at my past two graduations always makes me not want to quit. I want to be able to graduate along with my friends and have my family there. I want to make my family happy by being the first in our family to graduate from high school, and I want to shove my diploma in the face of the people who doubted me and said I would never graduate and would be a no one.

I remember a day back in middle school when I turned in a book report late, and my teacher ended up calling my dad. When I saw my dad, we had a big talk about doing my work and turning it in. My cousin was with us at the time. When he heard about what happened, he told me that I was going to be a nobody in life, just a lazy bum, not graduate and not get a job. I didn't like it when my cousin said this because he was referring to my brother, in a way. This really got me mad. I didn't say anything to him, but if I could have, I would have told him off and told him that life as a teenager isn't that easy here in the Mission. Once my graduation ceremony is over with, I can't wait to see my cousin to show him my diploma and prove him wrong. Once I have graduated, I am planning to get a job and go to college and major in something that has to do with being a doctor.

Back in eighth grade I broke my ankle, and I had to go to the hospital. I was playing soccer with my friends when a couple of older-looking guys said, "You guys want to have a game?"

We said yes, so we started playing. I was playing defense, so a guy was rushing toward me, but I managed to take the ball away from him, and as I started to run, he came from behind and tripped me. After I felt his foot hit mine all I heard was a crack and a pop. The pain was horrible.

A week passed before I went to the hospital. My dad and I didn't expect it to be broken, but we were wrong. Once I got to the hospital, all the doctors were really nice and very friendly. They really helped me relax because I was really afraid of being in there. I am not sure what it's called, but I want to be the doctor who puts casts on. I really liked how the doctors saw it as a piece of art, and not just something they were putting on your leg to protect it. The doctor put the cast on me, but he just didn't like the way it was, so he started over. He did it a second time, and like the first time, he raised my leg and checked to make sure my ankle was in the correct position, so that it would heal in the correct way.

Just recently, I cracked my rib in a wrestling match. I got an X-ray and I was able to see my rib, which was cracked and swollen. Radiology is another area of medicine that interests me. It fascinates me to be able to see the inside of our bodies and to see if there's something wrong, such as a broken bone. Just like the time I broke my ankle, the doctor was really nice to me and explained to me how to read the X-ray.

High school is one of the many stops on the path to achieving my dreams. All I have is one last year in high school, yet I can see my graduation already: me and all of my friends in our caps and gowns up on a stage with our parents in the audience. I can see the happiness in the faces of my mom, dad, and brother. Finally, after fourteen years of being in school, I will get the diploma that I have worked and struggled for, with my name, NESTOR JAVIER MUÑOZ, on it.

Once I graduate from high school, I am planning to go to college. I want to go to San Francisco State because it's in the city and close to my house so I don't have to pay for a room at the school, and so I can always be here with my friends and family. Once I am done at San Francisco State, I want to go to medical school and get into radiology or orthopedics. It is very important for me to stay here in the Bay Area because I want to be close to my family and friends, especially my brother, who is like my backbone.

Whether we think about it now or we don't, deep down we all have an American Dream. Some of us will one day reach our goal, and some of us won't. Hopefully, I can go on and fulfill my dreams.

Playing
BALL

by MARC CESISTA

I REMEMBER WHEN I had my first basketball. I was about four years old. I always played basketball, even before that, but having my own orange Wilson ball was special and made me so happy. My dad was the one who gave me that ball. There wasn't a birthday or any occasion coming up, so I was surprised. I had asked for a ball for my birthday, but I didn't expect to get it out of nowhere. My dad doesn't usually give me things that I like, but with this, he got it right.

Back then, I wanted to be tall so I could play in the NBA. I would be watching NBA games and be so amazed with their athleticism and skill. The players would be dunking with ease and making threes like it's automatic. Basketball meant a lot to me, and all I could do was dream. I didn't really play any other sports when I was a little kid. I wasn't that interested in football, baseball, or soccer. I was just focused on basketball.

Sometimes I would practice on my game, but I never got better. I thought I wasn't playing right, and that's why I wasn't improving. I didn't have a coach or trainer to teach me how to play the right way. I tried to learn to play by myself, and that's what kept me occupied and busy. I couldn't shoot threes back then, the ball just wouldn't reach the basket at all. But when I did make a basket, it put a smile on my face and I pictured myself shooting in the NBA.

I remember playing under the sun on a hot day. This one guy kneed me on my left thigh. I had a bruise from that, and every time I moved, it hurt. It caused me pain but not that much. My mom didn't like me to play basketball because she kept saying that I would get hurt or injure myself. I understood why she said that—because she cared. But I still played ball, and I couldn't help it.

Watching NBA games got me thinking of how the NBA players got where they are. I was jealous of them. I don't know how much money they make, but I know once you get in the NBA, you're rich. I wanted to be in the NBA, to be rich. As I grew up I realized that there is more than playing basketball and getting rich in the NBA. Just because you're rich doesn't mean you're invincible. You can still be miserable and rich. A lot of NBA players today have a lot of personal problems of their own outside the court. I used to just think that once you were rich you wouldn't have any more major problems. I was only a kid and only wanted material things. In order to get to those things, I needed money. I used to think money could buy happiness and I still do, but now only in some situations.

When I play pickup games, I always want to win, no matter what it takes and who we are playing. I do moves that I practiced: jump shots, fade-aways, bounce passes, and lay-ups. It feels great when I do the moves I practiced successfully. It feels like I'm improving and making myself look good to others. There are still a lot of things I can't do, but I'm taking my time to practice them. It's not easy to practice and perfect the moves and get the timing right in the game. I watch NBA games, and I see the players complaining too much these days. They try to make excuses for every foul they get called on. I do my best not to make excuses and just play with it. If they call a foul on me, I respect it and keep playing. Because later, if I get fouled, they'll have to do the same thing. When I play pickup games, I try to make plays for others, so they can score. I do my best for my teammates by playing the right way. I sometimes imitate the moves I see on TV.

I also watch games to understand what not to do. It's alright to make mistakes, everybody makes mistakes, but what matters is how many mistakes you make. Basketball is all about making the least mistakes. If you make less mistakes than the other team, that gives your team a better chance of winning, because you're playing the game the right way. Mistakes will happen from time to time. I still try not to be nervous about making mistakes, because that can keep me from doing what I do best. Basketball is a metaphor for life. It is the same approach I take to everything in my life.

Just like real life, you need to understand what's going on in the game and be mature enough to take responsibilities for yourself and your team. Basketball helped me become a team player. One person can't do it all by himself; he'll always need people to back him up or step up in the game. I like playing ball, but it's not my first priority, school is. I only play in my extra time now, not like before. I wish I didn't have to do anything, so I could play ball as much as I want. Basketball has become a part of my life and I will still play even when I get old, and I will teach my kids how to play basketball the right way. Though I'm not playing as much, I'm still taking these values from basketball in everyday life.

Even though my dream of playing in the NBA most likely won't come true, I still play basketball and have fun playing. It's just a dream, and it's no big deal, I'm still good in life. I don't hate basketball because I'm not in the NBA. I just don't make it my first priority, because there are more important things to do. I think everyone has dreams. For some that don't think they have dreams, they just haven't realized that they do yet. Some dreams are achievable and some are more difficult to accomplish. I think there's no dream that can't come true. All dreams are achievable, if you really work hard for it. I guess I didn't work on basketball enough to achieve my dream.

You have to work for everything. It's not a steady road to achieving your dreams. You'll have times when you'll feel like Superman and times you'll fall on your face. The important part is getting up higher than before. The American Dream can be a distraction sometimes. People depend too much on it and it affects their reality. You don't sleep to get closer to your dreams. I do my best not to fall for that. I have a lot of dreams in life, and I think that's good. Some are little and some are huge, but every one of them counts. Being an NBA player was one of my big dreams, and it still is. I'm still young and there are more things I could do. All of this is good, but dreams are dreams, and reality is waking up.

The GIFT

by JASMINE ANTONE

"I never thought this could happen, this rappin' stuff. I was too used to packin' gats and stuff."

IN ENGLISH CLASS we were handed lyrics and told to listen to a song. Even though I had heard the song plenty of times, I'd never just sat down and listened to what was being said. In the song "Juicy" by Notorious B.I.G., he talks about how he has overcome some of his struggles through hard work and dedication. Biggie talks about how he had to sell drugs on the corner just so he could help feed his daughter. He also says that there were a lot of people who didn't believe in him, and how he didn't have any support and encouragement. However, Biggie says in the end of his song, "I like the life I live 'cause I went from negative to positive."

Growing up, I experienced struggle and was not always able to get the same as others. As a child I remember my parents not having the best jobs with great pay. We had to make do with what we had. Soon my dad lost his job, and then we had to start living off of my mother's income, which wasn't that much. Eventually my parents separated. However, even though my parents' relationship was over, they continued to be good parents to me. Times were difficult, but my parents tried their hardest not to let it show and still give me things that I wanted. I never felt that I was deprived because my parents always kept me busy. My parents would take me on bike rides, my dad and I knew practically every playground in San Francisco, and I was loved. Many people might say that I was not living the American Dream, but what is the dream?

I asked my mom what her American Dream was. She said that when she found out she was pregnant with me she promised to do right by me and show me good values and how to make correct choices. My mom also said she wanted to show me a better life than she'd had and to teach me the lesson that there are struggles in life but people always get through them.

Growing up, my mom didn't have such a great life. My mom went from house to house, living first with my grandma, then with my great-grandma, then even staying with her friends. When my mom was small she shared a three-room house on Florida Street with ten other people. She told me how she and her sisters fought over who would go to the corner store next with food stamps to buy milk or whatever was needed. My mom expressed to me how even though our family doesn't have a lot now, I still have it good compared to her childhood.

One day I was in the car with my mom and I told her about something that really bothered me. In our school we have palm trees in the hallways where people are encouraged to write their wishes and attach them to a tree. Earlier that week my friend wrote on a wish paper that he had gotten from the school, "I wish for food." I was so shocked, because out of all the things in the world, my friend wished for food. It was heartbreaking to know that my friend wasn't getting food. To me, food is something that every child should have; every parent should provide. After I told my mom the story she said that she used to be like that. She told me that as a girl my grandma really never cooked. She and her sisters were just lucky to even get ground beef. My mom even told me about something I'd never heard about: "government cheese," large boxes of dried cheese and dried milk made available for people on welfare. My mother hated that.

That's why even though we all have struggles, I know what my mom means when she says we can get through them. My mom is a perfect example of someone who had a very hard life but never gave up. Today my mother has a great job working as an underwriter; she is in a very good relationship with a nice man; we live in a lovely apartment in lower Pacific Heights. She has certainly given me a better life than she had, and she continues to teach me to make good choices.

I asked my dad what his American Dream is, and he said that he wants to be a better father than his father was to him. He also said he wants to see me make something of my life; he wishes to see me achieve my dreams and to be anything I want to be. My dad also said that he wants to make a difference, no matter how big or small, just make a difference.

My dad's mom came from an Indian reservation. Her parents died when she was a young child, and she grew up with her grandparents. She married my grandfather when she came to San Francisco, but he became an alcoholic. My father was one of five children, and life was never easy for his family. But my father has realized his American Dream. He is a very happy person with a great sense of humor. As a dad, he calls me repeatedly to make sure I'm okay.

I don't live in a huge house. I can't buy expensive clothing. I don't go skiing for winter break. For some, I have definitely not achieved the American Dream. However, I have so many riches in my life. I have two parents who really care for me. I am smart, and I am working hard at school. I have great friends. My dream is to be able to enjoy life to the fullest. I want to be proud of who I am, I want to be able to do things that I enjoy and just be me. Also, I want to make something of my life. I would like to go to college, and be able to get a career, not just a job. I want to be able to wake up and be happy to go to work. I want to help people make a difference in their lives. I want to give back to the community. I want to be able to help the children like I was helped when I was a small child.

"I like the life I live 'cause I went from negative to positive."

Biggie expressed the simplest thing in his song; he went from a world of drugs and gangs to living his dream as a rap star, and he was very proud of it. Biggie succeeded and felt pleased about his achievements, so in the end Biggie achieved his dreams. A dream doesn't have to be big; it just has to be something that makes you happy or makes you feel accomplished. My parents have shown me that with determination everyone can achieve their dreams. I thank my parents for that gift.

The Way to
BEING
SUCCESSFUL

by HELDA PONCE

I STILL REMEMBER the graduation ceremony. I wore a white dress, white shoes, and my blue cap and gown. I was so excited and jumpy. When they called my name I was really nervous, but when I held my diploma in my hands it felt good because I had graduated from a school for the first time. My parents were very proud that I was another step closer to the American Dream that had gotten cut off for them. They hope that I will make our family proud by achieving my dreams.

In Mexico, my mother and my father only got to the sixth grade. My mother was really good at math, but unfortunately she had to say good-bye to school because she had to start working to help her family with the bills. My mother started working at a shoe factory. She would go into work around 6:30 a.m. and leave around 2:00 p.m. My parents felt bad about having to leave school. They could have been doctors, lawyers, or whatever they wanted to be in life. Both my parents had hopes and dreams of graduating and having important jobs that would make a lot of money for the family they would have. When my father pulled some money together, he and my mother left for the United States. They still had hopes of having a nice family, a good home, good jobs, and money.

Today my family is made up of me, my parents, my older sister, her two-year-old daughter, and my two older brothers. My sister graduated from high school in 2005 but didn't go to college. She just started working, and about two years later she had her baby girl. My sister felt sad because she wanted to go to college. Now she has a difficult job, and that is a challenge for her. I had to take care of my niece after school and I would do my homework in the night. At first it was stressful for me, but I love my niece with my whole life.

My older brother graduated from high school and he didn't end up going to college. He didn't go to college because he started working. He needed the money to help out my parents with the house bills. He was disappointed at himself for not trying harder to work from 5:30 a.m. to 12:00 p.m. and still accomplish his goal of going to college. I hope one day he goes to college. My second oldest brother is going to graduate this year from John O'Connell High School and hopes to be the first one in our family to graduate from college.

I went to Alvarado Elementary School, and there I made the best memories of my life. One time, me and my friends went out to the store through the little gate on the side of the school and bought chips and soda. We felt such a rush thinking we were going to get caught, but no one ever found out and that's our secret to keep. In school, I just wanted to have fun. I didn't have much enthusiasm in class, I would never pay attention, and I would talk back to the teacher. It got worse when I got to the fifth grade. I always got phone calls home. My dad or mom had to come down to the school and talk with my teacher about my behavior in class. But my teacher made me change my act; he told me, "If you don't get your act straight, you will fail the class." I wanted to graduate, so I started to do all my classwork and all my homework. In that school I met new friends, and to this day I keep in contact with some of them. And the day I graduated and got my diploma in my hands, I felt so good about what I had accomplished.

Then I went to James Lick Middle School and met friends there. I went through the sixth to eighth grade at that school and got good grades. At first, I had a lot of fun with my friends in class. I was always joking around or getting into problems with other kids at school. I soon changed all that. I thought to myself, "Why am I going to not pay attention in class when I could do my work?" The day I graduated I felt sad because I thought I might not see some of my friends anymore, but I also felt happy because I got a step closer to my goal. My grades are going to get me somewhere in life. This means being successful, having my own money, having a good job, graduating from high school and college, and having all my diplomas in my hand. Independence means being able to do things myself, like getting my own job, and also buying my own things with my own money. It means having to do things on my own and feeling proud that I did them on my own.

I have attended John O'Connell High School since 2007 and am going to graduate in 2011. At first I got good grades. Then I got bad grades because of all the pressure I was under. It's hard because I don't have a place in my house where I can study quietly, away from the constant yelling back and forth between my siblings and parents. However, I know that not everything is my family's fault, because I also got lazy and wouldn't do any homework. My mom would say, "I want you to do better; I don't want you to end up like me, cleaning houses, and earning more money to save up, and not have a better job. That's why I want you to do better in school and graduate and get a good job." Those words pushed me. I have changed and improved my grades and I pay more attention in class now. I work harder because I want my mom to be proud of me and see that I am succeeding in school. I still want to graduate and I still want to go to college.

My diplomas are symbolic of me becoming a better person and reaching my goal. Right now, I am indecisive about what I want to do in my life, but I know for sure that I want to go to college and graduate. There are three careers I would like. I would like to be the type of lawyer that helps immigrants fight for their rights, because I like to argue and fight for what I believe in. I would also like to be a cook because I really like to cook and watch the Food Network, which is where I get ideas. I also get ideas from watching my mom cook American and Mexican food. Most of all, I would like to do photography for my career because I like taking pictures of people when they are caught off-guard and of random things. Those picture may seem pointless to some, but I think that sometimes those are the best pictures anyone could take.

So now it is my turn to pass my American Dream down to the kids I will have in the future. It doesn't really matter what dream you have; the best feeling is knowing how you got it. Look back at the road that got you to college, the education that got you to where you are now, and the hard work it took in school learning what you know now. It's not what you have, but what you know!

Now Playing:
THE AMERICAN DREAM

by JEFFRY KONDO

MY PARENTS HAD A HARD TIME providing for our family when we lived in the Philippines. They had many different jobs, such as running a convenience store or being a taxi driver, but those jobs did not satisfy my parents' financial goals, so they saved up money to move our family to America. To my parents back then, America was "a place where jobs are given easily, and money is not a problem." Their idea of the American Dream was to start a business, one that would be famous worldwide, one that would be remembered throughout the generations, and, my favorite, "one that would be featured in many commercials." What this business would be, exactly, was a mystery even to my parents.

In 1997, when I was four years old, my family moved to Oklahoma with hopes of finding better jobs and starting the business my parents dreamed of. They found restaurant and hotel work, which offered decent pay and housed our family. To this very day, they are still working hard just to be able to house us all. They still believe that America is a "land that is full of opportunities," but my parents did not want to take the risk of losing everything my family had, so they declined pursuing more desirable jobs, which would have required taking extra classes.

My family's life has improved since moving from the Philippines. So far, my parents say that we have completely transitioned into America, as we have followed American ways and have accepted them. My family can support me and not have to worry too much about our economic status. My parents have met many friends and have grown to like America. Even though they didn't get what they wanted, my parents say they like it here. They expected a big house with a colorful lawn and a garden for their hard work. Instead, we live in a small studio in a bad neighborhood where cars honk every night. But I like it here because living in America has given me goals and a future to think about, like studying a career that suits me. These opportunities might not have been possible anywhere else, so I thank my parents everyday for moving here.

Now I see America as a place of hope, but this was not always true. In middle school, my life was a living hell. I was bullied constantly because I was short and vulnerable. It was so bad that I almost stopped going to school and became a delinquent. The classwork and homework were too hard, which made me ignore all work completely. The idea of going to school and having each and every day be the same was too much for me. I really believed that nothing special was going to happen to me in America and that it was a mistake to have come here in the first place.

There was no way I could have a positive outlook on my future and goals when all I could do was question why school was necessary and what was available to me. Middle school offered nothing but the cold, hard truth about life in America: that nothing is handed to you unless you work very hard for it. That truth was very hard to believe, as I came from an elementary school that only talked about letters, words, and numbers, with the occasional "I want to become a successful person!" speech from visitors. I was desperate for motivation, anything that would give me hope for my future. I began to feel like there was something wrong with me. I began to think there was a reason why I was falling behind my peers, or why I had a terrible outlook on life.

My life became worse my freshman year of high school, when I was diagnosed with agoraphobia and was thought to have Asperger's syndrome, which makes people socially inept. After that, I believed that there wasn't anything possible for me anymore, that the only door open for me was the door to absolute failure. I realized my fear of going outside and social interaction with people when I was thirteen years old. I was told to run an errand that required me to go outside. I suddenly felt like going outside would only lead to humiliation and defeat. But I forced myself to leave the house. I felt like I was going to freeze on the spot when I realized I was in a crowd of people. My heart was racing and my mind was hopelessly searching for a way out. I felt as if I could read people's minds, and that they were thinking:

"What is this boy doing here?"

"What a disgusting kid! Get him out of here!"

"That boy is an eyesore."

This may not have been what people were thinking, but I believed all of it: that I was disgusting and annoying. I ran back home as fast as I could, and I've been scared of being outside and of social interactions ever since. At the time, it was impossible for me to establish eye-contact with strangers or have decent conversations, and I lost hope in making friends after I discovered my phobia. I felt that there was no point in progressing in my life.

The idea that my dreams were unattainable goals stuck with me until eleventh grade. Then, one summer day, I started to think about my future: the goals I could reach, the goals I should reach, and the goals I wanted to reach. I remember the day vividly. It was a weekend, and I was bored out of my mind. I was in my room, sitting on my floor with nothing to do. Suddenly, a thought appeared in my head that made me question myself and what I was going to do with my life. I asked myself, "Where am I going to go in life?" I looked at my life, full of sadness and pain, and thought of how promising and auspicious life could be.

Since I myself did not know the answer, I called my friends and asked them what they were planning for the future. I discussed different ideas with my parents, and they gave me very good advice, such as which jobs might work for me, and what careers they wanted me to strive for. Billions of possible ideas and thoughts surged through my brain—everything from being a janitor to being CEO of Microsoft—and I realized that it would actually be possible to find a career I wanted and that would be best for me.

With the help of my family and friends, the future became very fun to think about. Even daily tasks, like taxes, bills, resumes, and jobs, became interesting to think about. I even began to think about how I would deal with my phobia to reach my goals, such as seeking help from professionals who might help me get more used to being outside. My view of the future had suddenly changed from enduring despair and sadness to an exciting future full of opportunity and hard work.

It's become so much easier to imagine myself living a better, richer, and happier life. I can imagine myself becoming successful at many different careers. Careers such as animation and engineering excite me the most, as I would be surrounded by many forms of art and electronics. A career isn't the only fun part of the future; I also think that personal life, away from work, is very interesting as well. With the money I earn, I will be able to buy many things, such as a car, paintings, or antiques. I could give back to my parents, and if I have enough money, I could buy a huge house for them to live in. Because of my newfound devotion to living my dreams, planning the future and setting goals has become a hobby for me.

Now I feel like I can do anything. Even if the obstacles that block me from my goals are problematic and scary, I am sure that I will be able to surpass them with my fighting spirit and the help of my family and friends. The American Dream suddenly feels like a game to me. It's like a movie playing in my head, with many challenges and puzzles to solve, and this has strengthened my resolve to progress onward toward my goals.

I am aware that things may go wrong and I may end up in places where I don't want to be, but I am ready for the challenge. There are many risks I will have to take, many obstacles I will have to overcome, but I have already taken some risks. For example, I have agoraphobia, but I have joined a video game club to meet friends and become better at speaking with people.

I've learned that even if life seems dark and hopeless, sometimes all it takes to move forward is simply thinking about the future. It is a goal you have to work hard for—it is never guaranteed—but if you have high hopes and diligence, it is possible. With the many doors open to me, I can aim for any career and hopefully live a better, richer, and happier life. I aim to show my parents, who have sacrificed so much for my well-being, that the dreams that brought them to America might not have worked out in the beginning, but will work for all of us in the end.

Garcia's
SUCCESS

by ELIZABETH GARCIA

HOUSES AREN'T JUST a place of shelter but also a place of memories. My family has moved so many times, has memories in so many different houses, and to us our houses show how we have improved and succeeded in life.

My family's first home was in East L.A. They had just come from Mexico to the United States. They wanted to experience life here like my mom's sister did. Even though they had a house and things in Mexico, they wanted to come to the United States and better their lives because my mother's sister made it seem so glamorous. They came with big smiles and big suitcases filled with clothes. When they first came to the United States, they went to L.A. They lived in a small room they had rented in my dad's aunty's house. It was a very cramped room for my mom, dad, and brother, even though they didn't own much except the basics: a mattress on the floor, a TV, clothes, shoes, diapers, and a microwave to make their food. The reason they used the microwave was because my dad's aunty did not like them touching her things or using them without asking. When they did ask, she would say no and rarely said yes, and when she did, she wasn't so happy about it. She really didn't like them in the house so she only allowed them to go from their room to the bathroom and the kitchen, and otherwise they had to be out of the house. I don't know why she didn't want them there, but it was difficult for my family to live with someone who didn't really want them around, someone who was kind of forced to take them in because they were considered family.

It was also stressful because she and my parents never seemed to see eye-to-eye. The conditions weren't fair, and after a while they got tired of it and decided to move. By moving they hoped to move to a better place with more space and with better people.

The second home my family had was in San Francisco, and this was where I was born. Because I was born, our family needed more room. We moved into a house on 23rd and Folsom. The house was a peach pink color, with a metal gate and a narrow passage that you had to walk down because our house was behind another house. We lived with family again. It was a bigger place because there were a lot of us: my dad, his three brothers, a cousin, my two aunties, my mom, my brother, and me. Even though it was bigger, more comfortable, and with family, it was still hard to live there because we all had to share rooms. No one had their own room, so no one had their own things or any privacy.

Since we are family, it was easier for us to fight and argue than to get along. There was always someone arguing with someone else about taking their things. Or they argued because they wouldn't let them sleep or just because they wouldn't get out of the bathroom. I didn't see what the big deal was. There were never any clean towels, there was always spit with people's leftover toothpaste, and no one even opened the next box of toothpaste or threw the old one away. Also, there were other people's combs, brushes, and clothes on the floor. "I bet rich people don't have to deal with this," I thought. Another reason there was fighting in the house was one person or another was constantly walking in and out of the house. Every time that happened you would feel annoyed and never at peace because someone was always on the move. We also never ate together because there were a lot of us, so if you were hungry you would have to go out and eat, and no one ever brought anything for someone else. Everyone just seemed to care for themselves and not take anyone else into consideration.

My parents didn't feel right about us growing up in a packed house where no one cared about anyone but themselves. When my dad would work or my mom was busy and they asked someone in the house to take care of me or my brother, no one ever did because they didn't feel like they needed to. Since there were so many of us, everyone figured someone else would do it. My parents got fed up after awhile and decided to move once again.

The third house we moved into was on 26th and Folsom, in a gray apartment which people seemed to consider "the projects" because it was around a very diverse location. The apartment had two rooms, a living room, half a kitchen, and a balcony. The whole apartment was a basic grayish white color. It wasn't the biggest place we moved into, but it was better than the rest of the homes we had lived in. The living situations were also getting better. We didn't have many people living in the house anymore like we used to. The only people that came with us were my dad's brother and his wife with my cousin. So we split the rooms. One room was for my parents, my brother and I, and the other room was my uncle's, aunt's, and cousin's. We all seemed to get along, and both my dad and his brother had jobs at a taqueria. My mom and my aunty would stay home and take care of the kids.

It was easy to get along because we didn't have any reason to argue. My dad and his brother got along, my mom and aunty got along, and my brother and cousin and I were around the same age, so there was no fighting.

Then my auntie got pregnant, and that's where the problems began. My auntie started with the mood swings. My uncle would be stressed and very protective of his pregnant wife. He didn't want anyone bothering her or arguing with her or anything. Everything had to be her way, or my uncle would get mad, and it would start arguments in the house. Once she started getting bigger, so did the problems. We didn't seem to see eye-to-eye anymore. My uncle felt like because his wife was pregnant, my mom had to take care of her and cater to her when he wasn't around. My mom felt like she wasn't a maid and didn't have to wait on her hand and foot. My mom had her own responsibilities and priorities with her own kids and her own chores. She would help her once in a while, but not always because my aunt was able to do things on her own. She was pregnant, not disabled. This caused tension between my mom and uncle, and they couldn't seem to get along, and then strong words started to flow out of his mouth. My mom was so hurt by them she couldn't live there anymore. So she took matters in to her own hands searched for an apartment. She came back home with the keys in her hand and told my dad we were moving. She showed him the keys and we left.

The fourth place we moved to as a family (just me, my mom, dad, and brother) was on 26th and Folsom; same street, different building. My uncle and his family stayed in the old apartment, so when I would look out my balcony I would see my little cousins playing on their balcony in the building right next to mine. I would see my little cousin Lizeth in her pink outfit playing with her Dora ball. She would look up, smile, and wave hi. My aunty or cousins would come out on their balcony, and we would start to talk. People would walk back and forth in the parking lot while we had our conversations. People we knew from the buildings joined our conversations. It was funny to have many conversations with people below, the other people in the parking lot looking up at us while we talked. Hearing the cars and other people's conversations, so many people, it was like our apartment was our own little city.

Things were finally good. We had a place of our own and had something to call our own and not share with anyone. My brother and I shared a room, and our parents had their own room. My parents had a bed and not just a mattress. They had a TV, drawers, clothes, plenty of room, and enough privacy. My brother and I had toys, a TV, and little things to keep us entertained. We had bunk beds to save room in order to have a place to play. This house felt at peace, and it felt good to be in it. It was in a good environment, not the best, but better than the past houses. After a while we got used to living in that home. We loved living there. We didn't think we would ever move, but then my brother and I started getting older and that caused problems. There wasn't enough room anymore, but since we didn't have money to move and didn't know where we would go because we had been living there for so long, we just decided to stay.

Since I was the youngest, the closet became my room and my brother had the bedroom. My parents thought it wasn't that bad living in a closet, but I didn't feel like it was fair that since I was the smallest and the youngest, I got stuck in there. But I got used to it. When I turned twelve the closet wasn't big enough, so my parents decided it was time to move. They looked for houses everywhere, but all of them were too expensive, so they decided to look outside the city. They found a nice house for a good price in Richmond. They bought it and we were going to move. I didn't want to and neither did my brother, because we would lose our friends and everything we had in San Francisco, but in the end we still ended up moving.

In this last place, where we live now in Richmond, we are at peace. I love living in my house, and so do my parents and my brother. The day my parents got the keys to the house, they felt a sense of accomplishment, and we were all happy that we could be the first of our family to own a home in the United States. Our house has three rooms, two bathrooms, two living rooms, a kitchen, and three floors. We also have a yard and a studio in the back of the house. The walls are a sky blue color with pictures of all our memories, like my quinceñera pictures and pictures of my grandparents and cousins at the park and in Mexico. We have TVs in every room. We actually have our own rooms however we want them, and with enough privacy. We have our own laptops, stereos, bikes, and cars. Whatever we need, we have. Everything in there is ours, and that's good to say. We came from nothing and became something. We don't worry. We don't live paycheck to paycheck. We have more than we need. We get what we please. We don't need much, but we earned a lot.

By moving to this house in Richmond, my family got closer. As a symbol of our closeness and achievements, my family went to get matching "Garcia" tattoos when we moved there. We have the house and the American Dream. I don't know what comes next, but what I do know is that I have to start to make my own life and my own family. It's not going to be easy, but in the end it will be worth it. It gives you a game plan for life, for where you are going in the future and where to go when the going gets tough.

Precious Is My PURPOSE IN LIFE

by BRIAN HIBBELER

LIKE MANY YOUNG AMERICANS, my aspiration for the future used to involve a larger-than-life idea and was completely centered around attaining recognition for myself. I knew that I wanted to take advantage of my talents, such as my abilities in written and verbal communication. Now I believe that my future should involve not just myself, but helping other people achieve their own dreams. I discovered my new dream after I watched the film *Precious*.

After casually following the film's success for several months, I decided in the early morning hours to watch the trailer. The trailer hooked me when the title character professed, "Love ain't done nothin' for me. Love beat me. Made me feel worthless." I questioned how Precious could believe that's what love truly was. My curiosity prevailed and I was determined to see this film. My parents and I went to go watch *Precious* that weekend. Before the movie started, a small group of individuals around us chattered incessantly, while I texted furiously to my friends. When the movie finally started, the audience became silent; for the next hour and fifty minutes we were immersed in a brutal tale of abuse and poverty.

Watching *Precious* was the first time I had ever gotten *lost* in a film; I experienced the film as if I was the main character, Precious, feeling the suffering that was inflicted on her. I had to find the courage to defy obstacles and unlock my own resilience, as she does at the end of the film.

When the film finished, the air was thick with emotion, as the entire audience silently wept. It was as if we all attended a mass-therapy session; everyone's personal demons painted on the silver screen for everyone else to see. As we exited the theater, the still atmosphere starkly contrasted with the buzz of conversation that had preceded the film.

Precious opened my eyes in a way no other film had ever done. It changed the way I viewed life, both mine and the diverse lives of others. It helped me understand the broader picture of how different people are. I not only understood that there were different life situations, but I understood humans more, and realized that a person's experiences can have a profound effect on who they become. I recognized that people I had liked, disliked, cared for deeply, or never noticed, did not entirely choose to be who they were, but had some "help" from their surroundings. Walking down the street to the car after the movie, every person I passed looked different. I saw each person as an individual, not as a color, religion, or any other label that the rest of society had attached to them. Each person was an individual story, completely unique from the person next to them.

The rest of the weekend I reviewed the movie in my head several times, and it began to empower me. I began to create my own path toward my new idea about my future. The film made the problems in my life seem so insignificant; I realized how blessed my life really is. The film gave me self-confidence, which was something I never had in life. I have always suffered from acne, and the many insults I heard growing up suddenly didn't matter anymore. I realized that I should no longer care what other people think or say about me, because all of the constant negativity seemed so insignificant.

I attended school that following Monday, and used this newfound confidence to my advantage. I looked at learning as a privilege, and not as a punishment; every assignment in class I saw as an opportunity to challenge myself. I looked at every detail about life at school as just one little step toward my future dream. I no longer saw a need to create conflict, or acknowledge the negativity in my school community. Ultimately, I disassociated from the ubiquitous disapprobations in my life. I used my own demeanor at school to set an example of how transcendent life could be. That week, I not only discovered self-confidence from the film, but my perception of the film changed from inspirational to a call to action.

My call to action is to help the homeless in San Francisco. I was adopted at age three by the loving individuals whom I have always known as my family. They help me remember how lucky I have it, and I have learned to be more grateful for that. However, most of the people I talk to do not know that my birth mother was homeless when she had me. She wandered Haight Street, drank liquor, and did several different drugs while I was in utero. I was born up the hill from the Haight, at UCSF, and since she was seen as unfit to take care of me, I was placed into foster care, where I lived for three years before being adopted.

Precious's dream was to raise her children, become independent, and finish her education. She strove for what she believed was impossible, and by the end of the film she had already begun accomplishing some of those dreams. At the end of the film, Precious escapes from her abusive life, but does not have the resources needed to survive.

I want to be that resource for the people in the world like Precious. I want to create an environment for the homeless to restart their lives. This space would provide all of the necessary living amenities, job training, and education for children. It would be a year-long program that would help the homeless reenter society. Even after these individuals left the program, I would stay in contact with them.

I know now that I do not want to live my entire life knowing that the only person who benefited from my actions was myself. Most people see life as a simple game of wall tennis, believing that as long as they play themselves, they will never lose. I personally believe that my purpose in life is more inclusive than that. The movie made me understand the idea of having a second chance at life—or, if not a second chance, then just a chance at life to begin with. I feel like it is my duty to help some of the people who have not gotten that second chance.

Precious was bombarded with negativity from the most important people in her life. However, she made a choice to ignore her mother and everyone else around her. She lived life the way she needed to live it. Society is always dictating how to look, what to wear, and how to survive. However, I realized that I have a choice whether or not to listen to these messages and to further fuel them for other generations to deal with. I no longer care what people say about me, whether it be students who use put-downs or adults who tell me I cannot do something.

Institutional and interpersonal oppression happen every day. From the media saying you need to be a size two or have silky straight hair, to friends saying that you cannot win something and should just not try. However, when we say, "I cannot do this because..." we have instantly taken those oppressions from other people and internalized them. I learned I need to take responsibility for that. Eleanor Roosevelt once said, "No one can make you feel inferior without your consent." Most of us still do not understand that we are responsible for limiting ourselves when we say we cannot, should not, or could not reach that certain goal we dream of achieving. We are responsible for our own lives; no one else is. If we accept the oppression of other people, then we will never change the positive outcome, let alone have a chance at living our dreams. Many influences in my life have told me "You cannot do that," or "There's no point in even trying." I learned that sometimes people have to try, because otherwise the mere possibility of that goal is eliminated. I believe you have to shoot for the impossible, or you will never know if you would have made it or not.

The ability to persevere and to strive for something beyond our comprehension is a quality we all have inside of us, though most of us have never learned to unlock this instinct, and most of us never will. This is due in large part to the negativity of our society. The media and people of power paint success as very limited, as if by chance. There is a constant flow of news about the people who are unsuccessful, especially the homeless. These individuals are perceived as hopeless, and no longer independent. It makes students and future generations feel that once people, such as the homeless, have become unsuccessful, they do not deserve another chance at the American Dream. Success becomes impossible, and furthermore creates greater divides in our society. I am not striving for the impossible simply for the wealth, fame, or fortune it brings. I am striving for a dream that includes not just my own happiness, but that of others as well.

I believe that my family, who has supported me for sixteen years, gave me a second chance at life. I could speculate as to the various ways my life could have ended up, but the one thing I can be sure of is that it would have been worse than where I am now. *Precious* inspired me to want to reach out to the homeless of San Francisco, and to help change their lives. I want to give them the second chance that I got, to pass on that message of resilience. I want the homeless to know that we have not given up on them as they wander our streets at night, and to help them deal with the listless emotional degradation and the perpetual fear of dying.

People like my family—who never give up on me—inspire me to never give up on the homeless. I must pass on the rare opportunity that I was given, and spread it among many. My personal American Dream is to simply give other people the chance at the same American Dream I have been given. If I can find opportunity in this great country, then I want to do everything in my power to ensure that as many people as possible get that same chance. Ultimately, giving the homeless a chance is like giving my birth mother a chance—and I will never give up on her.

I had never seen a
big red bridge
and couldn't imagine one

BEHIND
the
MUSIC

by ARES ALMENDARES

I'VE NEVER THOUGHT of a dream as something that can be achieved; it was just something to motivate an American mind. My parents both immigrated to the United States during childhood. My mom is a strong, Salvadorian-born woman. My father was Salvadorian and Cuban. They had five children, me being the middle of two older brothers and two younger sisters. My name is Ares Almendares. I'm seventeen, born in San Francisco, and this is my chase of the American Dream.

My dad had his own law business before he died. I didn't really get along with my father. I didn't hate him, but I stayed away a lot. My mother had a hard life. She was considered the smartest in her family because she loved school, and no one pushed her around. She was shot when she was young, during the Civil War in El Salvador. She still has nightmares, and she tells me how her kids should prosper in America. She wants her dream home where her kids don't have to fear the streets. Her dream has been on hold as her children grow up. But she's trying to fulfill it now that all the boys in the family are older and can take care of our sisters. She's a fighter. I know I would rather have her dreams come true than mine. She means the world to me.

I was sent to El Salvador when I was only six months old because my parents didn't trust any babysitter. This was the explanation they gave me, but I never believed it. My first four years, I lived in the slums of El Salvador with my relatives. The slums are the poorest places you could imagine. If people were lucky, they could make their home out of scraps. I lived by a city dump. The city trash was survival for most and useful for me. The dump was the dirtiest place. People made homes out of garbage thrown away or recycled and sold things of value they found. The smell wasn't something I got used to, and I threw up a lot. I remember a lot because I have a good memory and my relatives told me a lot, too. My parents sent me money, but my relatives spent it on their greedy needs. I always got enough food; my parents made sure of that. But all I knew of America was that my parents were there.

When I was four, I became friends with a boy whose name I can't remember, but I'll call him Niño. Niño had no family when I met him. He was brown and short. We became friends because we played at the dump a lot, picking up cans and whatnot. I met him because my grandmother took me with her to the dump as she talked to friends.

My grandmother didn't really raise me—the people at the dump and my neighbors did. This is where Niño comes into the picture. Living in poverty really teaches you the value of a friend. Niño did not have a family. A year before, his mother told him she was going to get water and told him to wait. Niño waited and waited. The next day, Niño was an abandoned ten-year-old. He was like a big brother to me. He was smart for someone who didn't really go to school. When he came to my house, he had manners and said "Thank you." This was a rare quality and surprised my grandmother. I've always wondered how he was always happy when he didn't even have a family. I know if that was me I would be depressed, because to me family is everything.

For my fourth birthday my relatives asked me what I wanted for my birthday. I said that I wanted a radio because Niño liked a song that was stuck in his head. I didn't know what I wanted, so I agreed. This is where music was really introduced to me. I remember listening to it and dancing around the dump, and I let him borrow it a lot. My uncle Tito put new batteries in it whenever he visited and wasn't busy working at a factory.

Soon after my birthday my relatives said my parents wanted me to go to the United States. I guess I was excited when my relatives told me. I remember telling Niño, and his reaction was like, "Wow!" I told him I was going to come back for him soon. After that I don't remember much. I gave him my shoes because my parents sent me new ones. He kept the radio. I gave him a down-low high five. That was the last time I saw Niño. He was a big inspiration in my life because he convinced me to get a radio and made me learn his dance.

My journey to America was by truck, and I don't remember much. I remember packing and waving to my family. One of my uncle's friends took me. I just remember stopping for gas, sleeping, and first seeing the border of America. When I arrived in Los Angeles, where my parents lived, my mother says I was shy and I ate a lot because she kept feeding me whatever I asked for that day. I had met them before, but to start living with them was different for me. Now I would wake up to a different ring in the morning and a new family. I do remember some parts of the first weeks in my new home. It was way cleaner, bigger, and just a different feel. I used to be in a home made of metal scraps and in a leaking room, and now I was in a solid home. It felt different because I spent more time inside. In El Salvador, I was always out as soon as I heard the chicken singing at six in the morning. I saw my recently born sister. I remember carrying her, or at least trying. I couldn't believe she was my first sister. I quickly got used to my two older brothers. They were hesitant to take me places but soon loved me. By the time I turned five, the first steps of my dream had begun with being here.

In first grade the teacher used to tell us what dreams to choose and what was right: It was grow up, go to college, have a good job, and raise a family. The way the teacher said it put her version of the American Dream in reach and everyone was doing it. As I grew older I started thinking about what I wanted to be when I grew up. It wasn't a cop, firefighter, or doctor. I wanted to be in music, and my uncle became my role model. He was a producer of Latino American music. I loved music. In fifth grade our teacher asked us what we wanted to be. Everyone had the same old-fashioned answer and I had an outcast one. Even then, I knew I was different than most kids in my class because I was true to myself and wasn't afraid to say it.

Over the years I got into bad behaviors. Growing up in the Mission District in San Francisco does that to a kid. Adults kept telling me, "You're never going to grow up." One time, my principal called me a "dumb little Mexican." I hated her for saying this and wanted to hurt her. I wasn't Mexican and had good grades, and my parents always taught me to not discriminate. Those who don't support us, and don't believe in a minority coming up, cast a shadow over everyone's dreams.

When I was in seventh grade, my mom sent me back to El Salvador. Without telling my friends goodbye, I was back where I started. I didn't care about my dreams any more. I just wanted material things, and I was going to give up in school. El Salvador was so violent. I couldn't even walk outside without threats. A lot of times gang members would empty a bus of people, kill the driver, and burn the bus. With things like that happening, all I wanted to do was survive. In El Salvador music was just the thing on my MP3 player. Music was important to me, always in my head with my MP3 player, or dancing, even making my own songs, playing around. The music I mostly listened to were oldies, hip-hop in Spanish and English, and a little of everything else.

My Uncle Hector was where my influence in a music career came from when I visited him in El Salvador. Born in the slums near where I was, he was a veteran of the rebels from the Civil War of El Salvador. He was the third to finish high school in his family, including my mom. I personally looked up to him because of his passion for music. A young poet, he worked with Latino hip-hop artists. His mission for his music was making young kids rich by producing music in Central America's most dangerous country. He once told me that he wanted to make it big in America by getting his music to the Latin American community of America.

I asked him how he would make this possible. He said it was his American Dream. To reach his goal, my uncle saved money. After a while he gained enough money by working small jobs to have a mini-studio in his home. He got some poets from the barrio, and with his own little business and support from a small, poor community, he started a temporary organization to keep young kids out of gangs. He worked with some big artists in Central America and ran fundraisers for El Salvador.

He was who I wanted to be when I grew up. After a while my uncle got a visa and came to America. I didn't communicate with him much during that time because it was expensive to call El Salvador and he was busy. All I knew was that his dream was that much closer. We really became close when I went back to El Salvador. My uncle was in El Salvador trying to make it to America and working in music. I don't remember how, but something happened and it changed my life.

The only motto I had then was: *How I survive is what makes me who I am.* After two months, I went back to America. My nightmare was over. I learned a lot in El Salvador. I got closer to my cousins, and they were my best friends while I was there. They always had my back when it came to fights, food, and protection. They also took me to my uncle's home safely while I was getting to know him.

When I got back to America my friends asked, "Where you been?" I kept everything to myself, and in a joking way I just said, "Don't worry. I'm here now." My friends noticed a change in me, not only in looks, but my attitude. I was more respectful and I did things differently than before.

In my sophomore year of high school, I got a letter in the mail saying my uncle was dead. The entire letter said he was killed by patrol men at the border and it was under investigation. After that we didn't hear anything from the state. When this happened it hurt me. My hero was dead, and I felt like maybe I should go on for him and carry on his name. I had an advantage because I am an American citizen and a young, hard worker.

Now that I'm a teenager, it's all about money and my future career. Without money, especially in America, you're nothing. I know morally it's not true, but mentally it is. It's all about success in business. I got hired for a job that teaches me how to be a music producer, and this gave me my highest hopes. I also have business ideas: about signing artists, starting nightclubs, and giving aid to my people in El Salvador by starting organizations. This whole idea is my version of the American Dream. Every time I miss a day of school or get a bad grade I feel achieving it gets harder. Getting good grades makes it easier because then my mom doesn't bother me and a big load of stress is gone.

I've started building my own little music studio and working for an audio program in San Francisco. I want to be a music producer and start an organization to help my people in El Salvador. That organization will serve the part of El Salvador where I grew up, and my main objective is giving shoes and building homes. I chose shoes because working in a dump there is glass, chemicals, and trash. It's very hard to not get cuts, and many people die from bacterial infections they get in the dump. Building homes is needed because leaking houses are a problem that should be solved. This is the twenty-first century and it's crazy to keep living like that. So starting an organization that does these things is a dream of mine.

Being Latino in this country means I've encountered lots of serious racism. All this makes me think maybe America isn't a place I want to be in. But the music in America got me addicted to the land. I can't leave. I'm here to stay and I'm going to do what I got to do. California is the blueprint, music is the plan, and my dream is the outcome. I'm not talking of being famous, just always having music close to me and making a difference. When I say "difference," I mean taking kids off the streets, not just in El Salvador but in America too, and sharing the love of music. Sometimes I do wish my life turned out different, that I would be different. But then again, it made me who I am now. And I'm proud of it. As long as I have music in my ear, this brings me to another world of peace. The beat just calms my mind and lets me forget everything.

My dream really is to make my mother and Niño proud and maybe even carry on my uncle's dream. I think of life as a "try situation." You are born, you try, if you don't succeed, "Oh, well." Most of my good days I feel like I'm on track.

And I have always been raised to at least try....

From
HERE
to
THERE

by FIKI MEHARI

BUS IS A GOOD WAY to get around the city. But it costs a lot of money—75¢. You can try to get on the back of the bus so that you don't have to pay, but you might get a $75 fine. For some people, that's not the problem. Their problem is the fighting and how the bus smells. A lot of people on the bus start talking and then fighting, and that distracts people. Then they have to say something, and that's how it starts. And if you are a teenager, it's really bad for you because there are a lot of people on the bus who act like somebody they're not. They want to fight over what street you're from or the color you claim. You end up fighting over some stupid stuff, and you get in trouble. That is not my main problem with the bus. My problem is that I hate to stand up for a long time, and when homeless people get on the bus, they can smell so bad that I just have to get off and walk. I end up wasting my money, and these days it's hard to get money because of the economy.

One day I didn't feel like walking.

I didn't want to be late to school. So I was sitting on the bus, and when I stood up to pull up my pants, this guy came and took my seat. I told him to get out of my seat, but he refused. And I just went off on him. I hit him in the face and we fell on the floor fighting. I got hit in the eye and was bleeding. The bus driver yelled at us to stop. I was really mad, my heart was beating fast, I felt like I did something really bad, and I felt like I was going to jail for a long time. The fight lasted for three minutes, until the bus driver stopped and called the police.

I got arrested, and the police took me to the station. While I waited, I was sweating, my mind was racing, and my whole body was shaking. The police were going to call my dad, but I told them not to because he was going to be really mad. So they called my mom and she picked me up. She was mad and disappointed in me because this is not the way to show her that I respect her for all she's done for me. It was a bad day for me, and, to top it off, I had a date that night with one pretty girl.

I was upset for not showing up for my date, but I was angrier that I got into a fight over a seat. That's why I want to get a car—so I can get anywhere I want, like a job interview, on time. I want to get home on time so I can do my homework, get good grades, and make my family happy—especially my dad, because he's been through a lot and will do anything for me. I really want to help him by getting a car so I can drive him anywhere he wants. Like if he is sick, I can take him to see a doctor, because if you really love your family you should do all you can for them. Even the small things count.

My family is from Eritrea in East Africa, My father came to America in 1999 for a better life for himself and our family. My mom, brothers, sisters, and I stayed behind until my dad could afford to bring us to America. He had a cleaning job and was going to school at the same time. He was working really hard to bring us to America.

Finally my family and I came to live in America with my dad in 2003. We were really happy to be reunited, but, at the same time, being in America was hard. We had to learn how to speak English and learn the culture. We had to stay together, watch out for each other, and make sure we didn't make mistakes or break the law. It was hard for me because if I had a question or needed help, I didn't know how to ask because I couldn't speak or write in English.

I have a big family—three brothers and two sisters. I'm the middle one. My family members love me, they really care about me, and they want me to do well in school. I want to do well in school too. We came a long way to America to have a better life and a better future. The only thing that makes me happy is my family and how they believe in me.

The people in my family who believe in me the most are my older sister, mom, and dad. They think I'm smart. They tell me they like how I talk to my little brother when he does something wrong. I always give him advice. I tell him how he can improve in life and reach his goals. My little brother is twelve, and his goal is to be an NBA player. I think he can do it because he always works hard and because he believes in himself. I told him he should have a second goal, to make sure he knows what he wants to do in case he doesn't make it in basketball. He's really smart, like my older sister. I think he can do what he wants to do if he puts his heart into it. He and I play basketball every Sunday. I try to teach him new moves and help him get better. He always thanks me. Sometimes, though, we have fights because he thinks I talk too much. But we're always tight. It's important to me to help my brother because my older family members have helped me.

My mom is my everything. She went through a lot of stuff for me, some things I won't forget. Like when I was a little kid, I used to get sick a lot, and she went back and forth with me to the hospital to make sure that I was okay. When we came to America, she left her whole family so we could have a better future.

The second most important person in my life is my older sister. Her name is Hiwet and she's twenty-three. She has her own car and is independent. She goes to school and has a job. She came to America when I did, and she was the only person in my family who spoke English. She went through a lot of stuff for my family. She always wants to help the family out; she thinks about us before herself. She always asks us if we need help with anything. She is sweet and nice. Everybody who knows her respects her, and she deserves it. I hope I can be independent like her and have my own car and help her when she needs help.

My mom always asks me why I want a car. I tell her that it's because I'm tired of paying 75 cents to stand up on the bus or walking when the bus is full. I tell her that if anybody gets sick, I can drive him or her to the doctor's office. Plus, my parents trust my brother and sister because they have cars. They can help out when my parents need rides. Plus, they are the oldest of the kids and my parents think they are good role models. I want my parents to trust me and treat me the way they treat my brother and sister. I also want a car because in this world, girls like a boy who can take care of himself and who can help his girl out. They like an independent man. If I get a car, I think I can get any girl I want. I'd be able to take girls anywhere they want. But people say gas is so expensive nowadays and the economy is bad. I understand that, but I'm not going to drive my car everywhere I go. I'm going to drive it when I need to and when it's too far to walk.

I still remember that day I got in a fight. When I got home with my mom from the police station, I wasn't worried about missing my date. I was mostly worried about how my dad was going to react. I was thinking I should have just stood up or found another seat. My mom told me to go to my room and wait for my dad to come home. I was praying in my room, hoping my dad would understand how I can get mad so fast that I can't control my hand.

My mom came to my room and told me not to worry, but I still felt really bad. I should be making him happy by getting good grades. Instead, I was fighting, giving him a hard time. On top of that, I let my date down, and she was pretty too. I really liked her and I was hoping she'd understand.

When my dad got home, he told my mom that the school had called him; he asked why I had missed school. I came out of my room and told him what happened. He was mad and said he thought I knew better than that. I told him that I want my own car so I won't get in trouble like I just did. He said that if I need a ride, I should ask my brother or sister. He said this was a bad time to talk about me getting car. Three weeks later, he told me that I will get a car next year if I do well in school and don't get in trouble on the bus again.

What I want you to know is that even though I still want the car, that's not my entire dream. The dream is not all about money. I'm not saying you don't have to have money, but money is not everything. Money is important so that you can buy your children clothes and school supplies. I'm happy with my family, not because they buy me stuff like clothes and an iPod, but because they are there when I need them and they know what kind of person I am. My parents know I always work hard and do my best in school, and they forgive me when I make a mistake. I'll reach my goals when I have my own family, my own house, and a car. I am motivated to stay on track so that one day, I can feel that I made my parents proud.

Something
OF YOUR OWN

by LISETT RODRIGUEZ

I CRIED SO MANY TIMES that day, watching it slowly go by. Five years of memories of living in the San Francisco townhouse instantly played in my head. My cousins seemed to be growing up so fast. It seemed like *I* was growing up way too fast. We've always had to move around because we don't have a home to call our own.

People always seem to dream about having their own home. Either they want to live in a mansion with luxurious furniture or a small cozy house with just enough space for themselves and their families. My family never had a house of our own, so we kept moving from apartment to apartment.

The first place we lived was small and crowded. Every time I pass by, it brings back memories. I remember playing with my family—my sister, brother, aunt, and uncle. I remember a room full of toys and running around a lot. My home was one beige building with two apartments, which my whole family rented. The apartments we lived in were in the Mission District of San Francisco, and had a small front gate and stairs leading to the front doors. I lived there until I was three or four years old, before I started kindergarten.

My dad lived with us in that apartment, but I don't remember him being there. He would stay with my mom, brother, sister, and me for a while and then would leave without warning. It frustrated me that he wasn't there for us. It made me feel like he didn't care about us. He seemed to be there more once my sister was born because she remembers more about him than I do. It felt weird to call him my dad since he wasn't there for us. He didn't want to live with so many people in that one apartment and said we'd be better off if we moved out of the city away from them.

When we left San Francisco, we moved into an apartment across the bay in Richmond. I remember the streets looking lonely all the time. Once, there was a dead rat near the street drain and no one picked it up for two or three weeks. We could smell it from a block away. Even though my mom never liked walking near where the rat was, we had to pass by it every day going to and from school.

In the new apartment, my older brother, sister, mom, dad, and I only had one room to ourselves because we moved in with a family my dad knew. Again, we didn't have a place of our own. The room was small, with two beds and a TV placed on a dresser. Even though my dad eventually left, we still stayed in Richmond. We lived there for six years and moved four times.

Finally we moved back to San Francisco, realizing the mistake we made of ever moving to Richmond. My family and I were elated to return. We rented a townhouse in the Mission. Upstairs, the townhouse had two bedrooms and a large closet that, with all the people living in the house, we used as a third bedroom. Again, there were nine people living in the house. It was all the same people, except instead of my dad, a younger cousin of mine now lived with us. We are a very close extended family; we had decided we couldn't live far apart from one another. I was excited that we wouldn't have to live with other families. We were closer to having a place of our own.

When we first moved in, the owner told us that, in five years, the rent would be raised. For now, we were to pay $1,900 every month. That was a lot of money, but we wanted any opportunity to move back.

Although we were happy, living with so many people meant no privacy at all. My cousins ran around the place screaming at the top of their lungs, bouncing off the walls while I was on the phone. There was never a room that was empty enough to escape to.

We all dreaded the end of our five years there, when the rent would be raised. My mom, grandmother, and aunt were the ones paying the rent, and they didn't know what they would do. They all waited until the last minute to find a new apartment, and we all ended up somewhere horrible.

My mom had a hard time looking for a place, but she tried not to show her frustration. It wasn't until the week before we had to move out that she found a place. My grandma and aunt are as independent as my mom. They support their children on their own, without a husband. They didn't tell us where they were going, and my mom didn't tell them where we were going, either. I felt embarrassed about where we were headed, but we never all talked about it. Later on, my aunt told me how embarrassed she felt about having to live in a hotel, too.

The day we moved out was a miserable, gloomy day. I had grown attached to this house; I was happy to go home to it every day. Everyone else was in a horrid mood, too. We weren't going to be living together anymore because being together had caused too many problems. My mom, grandma, and aunt had been arguing, and weren't talking to one another much. Every time they fought, it hurt me because I loved them all so much and didn't want them to be angry.

Seeing all the rooms so empty made me feel as hollow as the rooms sounded. I had moved into the townhouse with my family when I was ten years old and in the fifth grade. When we moved out, I was fifteen years old and in the tenth grade. I would miss seeing my family every day and inviting my friends over. I would miss all of it.

In the hours before we left, I talked with my cousin. We were sad that we would no longer see each other every day. I had watched almost every moment of him growing up, and now I was going to miss him. We had so much fun inventing games and laughing until we couldn't breathe. Reminiscing about those moments made it harder to say goodbye.

When it was time to leave, I couldn't hold in my tears. I hugged my aunt and cousin and told them that I loved them. Then I said goodbye to my uncle, and finally to my grandma. She cried, saying, "I love you, Chavelita." I would no longer get to hear her tell me "*Que la Virgencita te cuide y te acompañe*" when I left the house. It was hardest to tell her goodbye, because she looked after us and cared for us as much as my mom did. The house was full of misery. We all wished everything would go back to the way it was.

Our new home was a hotel near the Civic Center Bart. It wasn't very noticeable because it was between other buildings, but I was going to have to notice it every day. Inside the hotel, the hallway lights were dim and the other people walked around like zombies.

Our room had a bed, a dresser, some boxes my mom had brought earlier, our mattresses, and a sink with a mirror just above it. There was also a little closet with no door. The room had an emptiness I had felt earlier in the lonely townhouse. It was real, and I wasn't going to have a home until we could find a place we could afford.

The room was too small to fit three people. It looked like it had enough space for one person. The worst part of the room was that there was no bathroom. There were two bathrooms on our floor. The toilets and showers were in stalls, which disgusted me. We were also without a kitchen. There wasn't even one to share with other people. All we had to prepare food with was a microwave. Our other option was to eat fast food. Either was an unhealthy diet.

We tried to get settled in, but it just didn't seem right to be in there. We tried to forget ever having moved there. There were some mornings when I would wake up and think I was back in my old house. I'd wake up disappointed, realizing I was still in the rundown hotel. We set up our little television so we could try to take our minds off of all that was happening, but I couldn't stop thinking about it.

There was one window in our room, which was near my side of the bed. There was a post office across the street and a busy road with cars passing by. I spent most of my time looking out that window. It helped me not think about where I was.

Every time I try to talk to my mom about that experience, she says, "Liche, please don't remind me of it." She apologizes for having put us in such a situation.

Although we only stayed there for three months, the days stretched out like a class in which the teacher doesn't stop talking. But one day I came home from school and my mom had a surprise for me. She handed me a box with a key in it. I knew the key meant that we were moving out. I cried with happiness. The key was an early birthday present, and I couldn't wait to get out of there. I was so anxious that I wanted to leave right that second.

When we moved, it was into a studio in the Mission, our old neighborhood that we never want to leave again. We're much happier now. It's a big step from being in the hotel room.

My mom has been talking about moving again once the lease ends. I'm tired of moving all the time, but there seems to be nothing I can do since it's my mom who has to pay the rent every month. She would like a home for us to call our own someday. That's everyone's dream, isn't it?

FINDING MYSELF

in San Francisco

by CRISTIAN SOTO

THIS IS THE STORY of how I fell in love with San Francisco. The first time I came to San Francisco was when I was six or perhaps seven years old. I can hardly remember because I was so little.

I used to live in Nogales, Sonora, Mexico, which is a border city to Arizona. The states are so close you can practically say it *is* Arizona. Every day, my mother and I would cross the border to Arizona in about ten minutes. We would buy food, and then we would go back to Sonora. I remember those were the days my mom was starting to learn how to drive, and sometimes she would be scared to drive.

One day I heard my mom talking to my aunt on the phone. My aunt lived in San Francisco and she was telling my mom how beautiful the city was. When I heard the name of the city, it got my attention because it sounded like an interesting little town. My aunt told my mom there were trains that ran on cables and went all over the city, and that we should come visit her sometime. My mom didn't tell us anything that she had talked to my aunt about, but we had overheard the conversation, so we knew she had invited us to visit.

We were excited to visit my aunt, but there were a couple of problems. My mom didn't have any money to go, and plus my dad was hardly ever home because he worked in Tucson, Arizona. It was only on special occasions that we got to see our dad.

One day my mom told us we were going to San Francisco for the summer. I was extremely happy because my aunt was going to pay for everything. I was excited that I was going to a new place and that I would be there with both of my parents and my older brother. Ever since I was a little kid I have liked discovering new places and meeting new people. I thought San Francisco was going to be a small town with not a lot of people. When I finally got on the airplane, I was scared because it was my first time on a plane. I thought that it was going to fall into the ocean or that it was going to crash with another airplane.

When we arrived in the amazing city of San Francisco, my aunt picked us up from the airport. To my surprise, San Francisco wasn't just a little town. As soon as I got off the plane I was attracted to the place. I had never in my life seen so many people in one place. It was shocking to see so many people dressed fancier than in Arizona or Mexico. The people looked really important. They were walking fast like they were late to an appointment. While I was there, I asked myself, "What are these people doing, and where are they going?" I was curious to know and wanted to be a part of it.

After my aunt picked us up, we went to her beautiful house. One of the things I noticed about the houses in San Francisco was that they were close to each other. It wasn't like the neighborhoods in Mexico, where the houses were separate from each other. The next day I woke up and my aunt took us to the piers, which were crowded with a lot of people. It was then that I figured out that the houses were so close to each other because a lot of people lived in the city. When we were on the piers I was dazzled by the view of the bay. I couldn't stop looking at it; it was too big to be ignored. It was so blue. It appeared that the bay didn't have an end. To see something so huge as a little kid was impressive. I had no idea something of that magnitude could exist until that day.

I knew I had to come back one day, not just to that park, but to the city. The summer was reaching its end, and the last place we visited before going back to Mexico was the Golden Gate Bridge. We walked from one end to the other. I remember that the bridge was high and the weather was foggy. The cool summer air was so different from the hot weather of Mexico and Arizona. Once I crossed the bridge and got to the end, I was exhausted because the bridge was long, full of traffic, and loud. It was too much walking for a kid like me. I had lunch with my family at the end. We all had a good time, but then we had to leave. I didn't want to leave because I had fallen in love with the city. It was time for us to go back. I had to get all set and ready to go back to school. I started crying because I didn't want to leave. My mom told me that we were planning to come back and visit again one day. Sadly, I packed all my things and promised myself I would come back to San Francisco.

My dream became to live in San Francisco. The next summer we couldn't go, but the summer after that we did visit again, and we kept coming for many summers. Every time we visited, I noticed new things about the city. More than ever, I wanted to live in San Francisco. One weekend when my dad was home, I sat on their bed while my mom was cleaning and my dad was doing some paperwork. I had planned to talk to them for a while, but I couldn't find the right time or the right words. I was only ten years old. I told them that I wanted to move to San Francisco and that I wanted my dad to be with us more often. My parents listened to me and then told me that if we did something like that we were going to have to change our lifestyle and it would affect us as a family. My mom and my dad talked about it and decided to move our family to San Francisco. The first months were hard. We all had to adapt to a new style of living in a city with more people than we were used to.

As we were adapting to a new life in San Francisco, my dad had to find a job. It was hard for him to find one. A good change in my life while living in San Francisco was that all my family was together now. I got to see my dad every day. I was happy because now I had a life with my dad. Some of the greatest memories I have with my dad are finding new places in the city to eat. We also had to learn how to use public transportation, since my mom didn't have a car and my dad had not driven a car since he'd had an accident when he was young. I got lost so many times in the city. One time I stayed in an after-school program, and I got out a little late. I tried to go home, but I got lost for more than two hours. I was really scared because it was getting dark, and I didn't really know the city that well. My mom got worried, but nothing happened to me.

Although adapting to the city was difficult, we finally did it. When a dream comes true it's shocking because you never expect it. Now that I was living in the city of my dreams, I wanted to get to know it. I would ask my mom for permission to explore. She would only let me go out if my brother came with me or if I was going with a friend. But I didn't want anyone to come with me, I liked to be alone and I didn't like people to bother or distract me. Sometimes I would lie to my mom, saying that

I was going with a friend, and then I would go explore the city by myself. I would stay in places for hours and hours. People who passed by might have thought I had some kind of problem, but I didn't. I just appreciated the city and the people.

I also had a lot of good friends. I would go to Ocean Beach or the piers and look at the sky. I would see the people passing by with their dogs and I wondered where they were going, how their life was, where they came from, if they were happy or sad, and if they had any problems. I asked myself all of these questions because I was curious and wanted to know how people felt. While being in the parks and stores of San Francisco, I would question whether I was the only one who saw the city like this and if the people living in the city were just robots walking around. That's how people seemed to me.

When I graduated from middle school, my mom would let me go out more. I would go to Yerba Buena Gardens, the same park I remember visiting with my family during my first trip to San Francisco. In that park I would sit down to watch the people. I would look at the buildings and wonder who owned them and what went on inside of them. I remembered sitting in that park the first time I came to San Francisco and the promise I had made to myself, that I would come back to San Francisco. Speaking to the park and to the city, I said that I had finally kept my promise. The sky was cloudy, but suddenly the sun was shining as if the city was welcoming me, and I started crying out of happiness because I was finally living in San Francisco.

A New
COUNTRY

by CARLOS RIVAS

GETTING USED TO a new way of living in a new country can be similar to being in a desert alone with no one to possibly get help from. When I was twelve years old, my grandma told me that my mom and dad had called her. They told my grandma to tell me that I was going to be close to them in a short time. My mom decided it was time for me to head to the United States of America.

My grandmother is a really respectful person. She was always there for me when I needed her. In my life she has been the person that has cared the most for my well-being. She has eight children: four girls and four boys. Unfortunately, one of them died in the El Salvador Civil War thirty years ago. Some of them are also living in the United States. They all care for her and send her money so she can buy whatever she wants. She lives in Sonsonate, El Salvador, a city close to the capital, San Salvador.

I was going to leave all the beautiful places that I knew in my city. For example, there were really good pools to swim in, and also there were parks to play soccer, basketball, tennis, etc. But mostly, I cared that I was going to see my parents again after eight years.

My grandma was sad and I was shaking because there were many difficulties ahead. I was scared and happy at the same time. She told me, "Don't worry, son, everything is going to be okay, and finally you are going to be with your mom and dad." I said, "I will miss you, grandma, but promise you are going to visit me once in a while."

My family and I are from El Salvador, and it's a long way to get to the United States. Life in my country is hard because there are no jobs, and people have little resources to live on. Many people leave the country to go in search of a better life. Some were fleeing because of civil wars that were happening in my country. My mom and dad were thinking about new opportunities for me and my future. That's why they wanted to bring me with them. Opportunities are more available in new countries, but it's also a hard life.

My mom and dad are two great people. I'm glad they are my parents. They were born in extremely bad conditions. People in El Salvador didn't have a childhood. When my parents were young, they had to work to help their parents and didn't have the time to go to school. My mother went to school, but she only went until seventh grade, and my father didn't go because he was always busy helping my grandpa in his work. Though he didn't have a school education, my father is very active and smart. He works at the San Francisco Airport as a chef in a restaurant. He is thirty-four years old now and is a hard worker. My mother works at a McDonald's. She also is a hard worker and cares a lot about me. She is one year older than my father and she has four children: me and my three brothers. My siblings are younger than me, and one of them was born here in the United States. My parents and all of my family are very important in my life.

Life in El Salvador is really hard and there aren't many jobs. There is also a lot of violence in El Salvador. El Salvador is located in Central America along with Honduras, Nicaragua, and Guatemala. It's really small in size but has a lot of people living in it. The violence in El Salvador is really dangerous because there is this gang called MS-13, which stands for Mara Salvatrucha; this gang is known worldwide. They were always killing rival gang members from the Mara 18. It was hard to live in a place where you go out of your house and you feel insecure because of all the gangs around you. I lived with my two brothers, David and Andres, and my cousins and Aunt Maria. My grandma also lived with us, and we were all happy. I lived in a town called El Carmen. It was a little town, but all the people were friendly; the only thing that scared me was that there was a cemetery close by. Around the little town there were gang members too, so we were careful not to mess with them when we played outside. Most of them were friendly and I had some friends that were into that gang, MS-13. I left really good friends and neighbors who were good to me and my family. I had a good friend who got killed by some gang members because he was going out with one of their ex-girlfriends; R.I.P. Jorge. His parents were really sad about it and they decided to leave for Guatemala. I was sad too because of what they did to my friend. He was only twenty-three years old. It's hard to live in a place that has gang members so close, and that's one of the reasons my parents decided to bring me to the United States with them.

It was November 23, 2003 when I was preparing myself to go to the United States, along with my aunt, uncle, and two cousins, my father's siblings. We took a bus to get to Guatemala, and we then took another bus to get to Tecún Umán. This place was near the sea, and there was a beach close by. There were a lot of coconut trees and there was sand all over the place. We took a boat and sailed to Mexico. We took one day to cross the sea. In Mexico, my family and I took the bus that headed to Los Angeles. It was really exciting to see a big city in the United States. After arriving in Los Angeles we took another bus heading to San Francisco, and I started to admire the great architecture around the Bay Area, like the Bay Bridge and the Golden Gate Bridge. After we got off the bus, I saw my dad and I ran up to him and hugged him because I was really happy to see him.

After enrolling me in school, my mom took me to buy some clothes. I was sent to Everett Middle School. This made me excited and afraid at the same time, because I didn't speak English. I got my schedule and the first class up was English. In the school office, they called a kid from my class to show me the school. He was friendly and his name was Carlos just like me. He asked, "Where did you come from?" rapidly. I said, "El Salvador, and you?" He responded, "I'm from Mexico." I was happy because I had made one friend I could talk to. We arrived at class, and everyone was staring at me. I entered the room, and I sat with Carlos. The teacher was very friendly and happy. She was really pretty and also made me feel good to be in her class because she didn't toler-ate put-downs in the classroom. As time passed, I made more friends and learned more in my classes. After I passed seventh grade, I got the chance to get to know my very best friends, Adrian Alfaro and Jona-than Soto. They are both from Mexico, and when we all graduated from middle school, we decided to go to John O'Connell High School.

The first year in high school was really exciting because you get to meet more friends. Most of my friends play soccer at school. I appreciate all the friends that life has given me and hope we all can stick together after we graduate from high school. Sophomore year was really awesome because I had the best teacher in John O'Connell, Mr. Bonaccorso. I really liked him because he was always saying funny stuff and made class fun and easy. All my classes were good, but I stopped coming to school. I was absent in almost all of my classes, and because of this I only passed one. Now in senior year, I am still absent a lot. The consequence is that I won't graduate from high school because I don't have enough credits.

I still love to play soccer, and this year, my school soccer team won the final against Mission High School. We are the champions, and I hope that our school can keep winning.

I am seventeen, and I'm going to turn eighteen in August. My goals are to graduate from high school and go to college so I can become a doctor's assistant. Most of my life, my dream was to reunite with my parents and learn English, which I did. To all people that have not achieved want they really want, I say to try and make it happen.

Waking Up to
THE FUTURE

by ROBERTO HERNANDEZ

MY DAD SAID that if we came to the United States, we would have a better life. He said that if we all got together here, we would be able to have a better house, better clothes, and more stuff. He said we wouldn't have to pay for each school semester like we had to in Mexico. We also came here because we hadn't seen our dad in four years.

The first time my dad went to the United States, I felt so sad because I didn't want my family to be separated for a minute. I told my mom to convince him to stay with us, but my dad said no; he was only going to be away for one year. The day he left, I was in my room, covered up with a soft blanket, and he told me, *"Hijo, ya me voy. Quiero que cuides a tu mamá y tus hermanas. Tu vas a ser el hombre de la casa, en lo que regreso de los Estados Unidos."* (Son, I have to go. I want you to take care of your mom and sisters. Now that I'm leaving for the United States, you are going to be the man of the house.) When my dad told me that, I felt so insecure because I was just barely nine. I felt like I couldn't take care of my mom and sisters, but I promised him that I was going to do my best.

My life in Mexico was fun. I got to spend all the time I wanted with my cousins. I always loved to go swimming with them. I feel like I'll always have Mexico in my heart because that's where I was born and spent most of my childhood.

But when we were in Mexico, it was hard for my mom to pay for our school. My dad sent us money to buy things we needed, like uniforms for school and school supplies. My mom couldn't find a job in Mexico, so she started to sell for Jafra, which is a company that sells makeup and things for women, similar to Avon. She paid for our school with the money she made from that.

While my dad was in the United States, I felt more grown-up and secure about myself. It was the first time I had to take care of my family. One way I helped my mom was to do chores around the house. I also bought the groceries when she didn't have time. And I started to work with my uncle—every Saturday from 6 a.m. to 9 a.m., selling food for parties, such as pork chops and taquitos. My uncle would pay me eighty pesos at the end of the day. Then I would go to the flea market next to where I worked and buy clothes and stuff for my sisters' and mom's hair. I gave the rest of the money to my mom so she could buy anything else she needed.

I had always loved to go out to the park to play soccer with my dad. After he left us, it was different because I was the only guy in the house. I couldn't play with my sisters because they would play different things, like Barbies. My life started to get boring because I didn't have anybody to play with. When I talked to my dad, he would tell me how pretty the United States was, and then he would describe the Golden Gate Bridge. He said it was big and red, and that you could walk across it. When he told me about that bridge, I was surprised. In Mexico, I had never seen a big red bridge and couldn't imagine one. I already wanted to go there and take pictures to send to my family so they could see what San Francisco looked like. He told me that there are a lot of families who go to the beach and play volleyball there. I got excited and felt like I wanted to go to the United States. But I didn't want to let him know because I knew he would tell me to go and live with him. I was very confused. I was born in Mexico, and that was where I thought I wanted to spend the rest of my life, with my family and all my friends.

I remember when my mom told me that she had talked to my dad, and he had said he wanted us to come live with him. I didn't want to go because I didn't know anybody there. I didn't have any friends. I didn't want to leave my family behind. I was afraid that I would change if I went to the United States. I thought my attitude would change, and if I ever came back to Mexico, I would feel like I didn't fit in.

My mom and I had a conversation about going to the United States. I told her that I didn't feel comfortable moving because I didn't know how to speak English. How was I supposed to communicate with other people? When my mom told me that we were moving to the United States, I couldn't sleep at night, thinking about how different my life was going to be. I was worried that people would make fun of me because I didn't speak English, or maybe because I was Mexican. There were a lot of thoughts going through my head because I didn't know what San Francisco was going to be like.

My dad had already gotten a house for us all to live in. We told my mom that we didn't want to go to the United States. She said that we had to, because what was the point of us being in Mexico if we weren't making money? My dad was a bartender, and the person he worked for let him borrow money. My dad sent my mom the money, and she brought us to San Francisco.

When it was time for us to leave Mexico, I felt so sad because I didn't want to leave my cousin, aunts, uncles, and grandmas. We packed our bags and went to my grandma's house and said goodbye to everyone. All of our family was there. My grandma made enchiladas for us to eat one last time. My little cousin Christian came up to me crying and grabbed me by the shirt, asking me not to leave him. I remember I told him I was going to come back. He gave me a small comic book to read on my way to the United States. He told me that when I came back to Mexico, he wanted to see the book in my hands.

The first time I saw my dad, I felt happy. But I felt different—because I didn't know how to speak English. I didn't know how to have a conversation with anyone. Every time we wanted to go out to eat, it was hard for us to order what we wanted.

When I first went to school in the United States, it was so different. My school in Mexico didn't have any lockers. I felt uncomfortable going to school because most of the people knew English. I felt like just going back to Mexico and living by myself. When I got to my first class, it was so weird because I didn't know anybody. I was lonely.

Time passed, and finally I started to make new friends. I took English classes at home, and it helped me a lot. Now that I know more English and go to a different school, I feel more secure about myself. I feel like my heart doesn't belong in Mexico anymore. Now that I'm here in San Francisco, I want to spend the rest of my life here. I have great friends who I want to see when I get older. I'm a different person now because I have to put more effort into anything I want or need. I know that when I finish high school, I'm going to college to become someone I'm proud of. I went through a lot of hard stuff to get here, so I can't give up, and I have to keep going on this road. I never thought that I was going to be here, or that it would change my life for the better.

MY DREAM:
Under Construction

by JAIZEL ROBLES

MY NAME IS JAIZEL, pronounced as *jay-zel,* not *jas-sel* or *gis-zel*. I am a Filipino, born in San Francisco, California, raised in Pampanga, Philippines, and now living in Daly City, California. Junior year is supposed to be the hardest year in high school because there are classes that are required for admission to a four-year college. It is a time to take school seriously, to be able to lay out the foundation for the future. Everyone has dreams; they always begin with just one thought, one word, and one goal in order to strive and reach over limits that can easily be reached. I've heard this phrase a million times: "Anything is possible." Which is true. Because anything can happen at any given time, at any given moment—but only if you take action.

We live in a world that can either make you or break you. It is all about taking possible risks to achieve that almost perfect life. Life is something imperfect, but something we see perfectly. As Forrest Gump's mama says, "Life is like a box of chocolates. You never know what you're going to get." By choosing, there is a possibility that you may love it, hate it, or maybe in between. There was a time in my life when I had no control over choices that I made. I knew dreams were meant to be pursued, but I did not know what my own dream was.

Little did I know, entering high school can change everything. Two years ago, I was enrolled at Jefferson High School. Jefferson has a really vile reputation due to all the gang violence that involved weapons and the killing of students. August 2007 was my first year in high school.

Afraid? Nervous? Totally! Of course I was. All I could think about was whether I could survive this new environment that I just stepped into.

It was exactly 7:30 (and 56 seconds) a.m. when I awoke, realizing I was going to be late for my first day of school if I didn't get out of my bed quickly. My best friend, who lives just downstairs from me, was banging on the front window of my room, screaming, "Jaizel! Best friend! Wake up, sleepy head!! Hurry! We're going to be late!!!! We're going to leave you!" I am not a morning person—period. I peeked outside and it looked so mellow, all I saw was the sun not wanting to shine, just like I was feeling. I quickly donned any clothing I could get a hold of in my hands, ran to the bathroom, brushed my teeth, washed my face in a jiffy, and did not even get a chance to look at myself in the mirror. My hair uncombed, still tangled, people would notice that I just got up from bed to rush to school. But I didn't care what anyone thought. Of course, I did at some points before—but who hasn't? I ran outside to catch up with my friends.

The school was only three blocks away from my house, meaning that it should have been impossible for me to be late; but no matter how far or close anything is, I'm always late. Some may call it Filipino time because time for Pinoys is slower than actual time. It was actually my first time not being late for school. My best friends Trina, Steph, Ana, and these two guys all walked together expressing how excited, scared, and nervous we were and so many inconsistent emotions coming out.

"I can't believe we're in high school!" Ana expressed.

"I know, right?" everyone responded.

"I wonder what it'll be like...?" Steph asked.

Our thoughts suddenly scattered all over the place. All of us wondering in silence. I began by squealing, "I'm gonna get jumped!" Everyone laughed and we lost some of our nervousness because I acted with hilarious facial expressions. I just like to be the entertainer around my friends, making life not boring but randomly interesting. We got to school and I had to line up in a long line because I didn't get my schedule on the day I was suppose to because I was running late (like always).

By the end of the day I made it through four periods. I lived, and my teachers were all wonderfully nice. I also met some okay strangers and friendly acquaintances. Being in a high school is difficult, but soon I got used to it. Every day all I could think about was my future after high school. Would my major in college change? Would I have a career that

I'd enjoy and get paid well? Would I have that dream house that I've always wanted? Before high school, I hadn't really thought about it deeply. Before I knew it, time flew by so fast that it was second semester already. Second semester of my freshman year was when I stepped into the wrong side of the world.

I was pulled into a crowd that I did not want to be pulled into. I was under the influence. I would constantly cut school just to do what "normal teenage high-schoolers" would do: live life to the fullest extent and not be limited by rules. So, I ambivalently became one of them. Shocking? I know, because I'm not really like that. I was deceiving myself. Coming from a religious family and feeling pressured by peers was really a challenge because the tainted side had won. Staying up all night, going to parties, clubs, and rebelling against parents was part of a phase, and the list can just go on and on. These actions were totally against God's will, and my parents' too. At this time I really did not care what anybody thought about me, or about my disappointing choices. I would just do what pleased me at any given opportunity. As if I had a box of chocolates, choosing one while blindfolded.

The honest truth is that I am not attracted to what some would call "normal teenage actions" because it's not appealing to *my* eyes, taste, or smell. This stage I went through was absolutely the most difficult part of being in high school because each student is expected to be in a clique. A clique that you may be invited into, forced into, or even denied. I was seen as a mischievous chick that disliked education and was too cool to be in school. What everyone did not know is that I am the complete opposite deep down. A good girl, I might say; I am respectful, responsible, metacognitive, and trustworthy. I try to be by myself for my own good.

I am the type of person who anyone could count on if they had problems. I barely like to go out, instead I prefer to read a book, sleep, eat, or write at home. You could label me as a nerd that is not intellectual, because I just wing all my report card grades by doing what I am supposed to do but not really applying it in my head. I try to study textbooks, but, eh, they're too dull. My reading level is not even where it is supposed to be. I would not mind if someone did call me a nerd, though. I would accept it as a compliment because this indicates that I am not that "cool bad chick." I would want to be seen as a nerd with glasses and point out that I am not what they think I am.

Sophomore year, I came to my senses and realized that my actions now would truly effect my future. I decided to bring my education back on track. My mindset was in a whole different perspective. I have learned that I have goals and dreams that I want to fulfill before leaving this earth. I knew my future was waiting to be reached. So I planned out my two years for my junior and senior year, knowing that it'll be totally for my own benefit to transfer out of Jefferson High School. I decided to start off new where no one knows me, where I would not get bothered or be part of a clique. I just wanted to be myself, be that outsider, the odd teenager that does not like teenage stuff. I chose .San Francisco Unified School District because it was the only district that I knew of that was near Daly City. My father and I drove to the placement center. I remember it like it was yesterday when I turned in all my papers and the lady asked which school I wanted to go to. There were so many high schools to choose from, and I finally chose John O'Connell Technology High School because it was only a few blocks from my dad's work, which meant that transportation was easy for me, and it was a public school.

Now I am a junior attending John O'Connell Technology High School, where it feels like more of a family than total strangers. This is because the majority of the students are Latinos, and it is somewhat similar to my Filipino culture. Being a part of this school is an experience that I would not forget due to the diverse surroundings that I had never been in, like those friendly students that I always saw but never actually learned their names. Having fewer students in the school gives this connection where everyone is like a family. Everyone was very friendly my first day of school, and I have already made new friends and found a cute, handsome, tall guy.

Different choices in life lead you to distinct paths. They may lead you to the right or wrong one. When I hit the wrong path it made me realize how I wanted to do things the right way. My dream is to walk onto the stage and receive that diploma and get accepted to a four-year college. Afterward, I want to have my own settled home with that settled job, enjoying my settled life.

My dream is a work in progress. Step by step, day by day, I live to move forward, to press on with the goals that I have in mind. Trying not to look back from all those barriers that tried to stop me, I still stand wonderfully strong today. If I could make it, anyone can too. Today my mind is still set on the prize of having that excellent jubilant life to live one day, somehow. Living seventeen years in this world, I've gotten through so much, like leaving my friends to move on, and I know there will be more obstacles that I need to overcome, many battles that are waiting to be faced, for me to stress about. But at the end of the day, I am still me. I am still true to myself, learning how I am aware of my choices. Still standing, even if I trip and fall I get up and still strive for what I want: that someday, I will be somewhere with that someone, doing that something that makes life perfect. The most important thing is to reach your goal once you realize what it is, because you never know what you're gonna get!

Future GREATEST

by ANGEL SANTIAGO

WHEN I WAS LITTLE, I wasn't a gifted kid. I wasn't an A+ student either. I would clown around in class. I didn't take things seriously. I didn't respect anybody, not even my parents. I took advantage of people's kindness and weakness because I wanted things my way. I was selfish. It wasn't until I started to play football that this changed.

The American Dream is whatever makes you happy. I didn't have one until I started playing football. I used to see football on TV and think it was just an okay sport. But when I caught my first pass, I fell in love. Football made me work with other people because it wasn't just about me. It was about the team. It gave me a reason to be responsible because I needed to be reliable to my teammates. It taught me about respect.

I really started to get serious about football when I played it in high school. I started the season late. I missed a few games. When I first showed up, the other players were looking at me funny. They thought I was just some Latino kid who didn't know how to play football or speak English. They thought I couldn't catch, but I showed them that I knew how to play football. Doing it major like a pager! I proved that the stereotypes aren't true.

On the day of my first game, I felt nervous. But at the same time, I felt ready to play. When it was finally time for the offense to take the field, I ran out and the crowd went crazy. They were yelling, "Go team, go team!" That was a rush. We scored on the first drive and it felt okay, but then it was time for our defense to make a stop so we could get the ball back. Unfortunately, the other team scored, and the first quarter came to an end with a tie.

At the start of the second quarter, our team had the ball. It was my time to shine! We called a trick play: When the quarterback got the ball, he tossed it to the running back. The running back stepped back to avoid tacklers, and saw me open downfield. He threw a bomb downfield. As I was running deep, I just laid out and it dropped into my arms! I was tackled immediately, just three or four yards short of a touchdown. The crowd was going NUTS! After I caught the ball, I never felt more loved in my life. The next play we scored a touchdown on a hand-off, so we were up by one touchdown. But unfortunately our defense let them score again, bringing the score to a tie at the half.

After halftime, all my teammates were pumped up and so was I. I was ready to make a play in the second half. We got to receive first. The quarterback threw an interception that the other team scored, giving them the lead. We were down by a touchdown. But on the next drive I caught two passes, giving us first downs each time. The other team recovered a fumble and took possession as the third quarter came to an end. Luckily, our star running back redeemed himself by scoring a long touchdown run that tied the game.

With only five minutes remaining in the fourth quarter, the game was tied 21–21 and we had the ball on our own 30-yard line. I thought it was time for me to step it up and make a big play for my team. With third down and eight yards to go, we took the field.

At the hike, my job was to pretend I was blocking so it would look like a running play. But when the quarterback faked the ball, I ran past the defender, leaving me wide open downfield. The quarterback threw me the ball and the next thing I knew that ball was in my arms and I was running into the end zone. The crowd went WILD! I was so happy. The crowd was cheering my name. I ran back to the sideline and my team-mates were slapping the back of my head and telling me what a good job I did. After that our defense held the other team scoreless, so we took the victory by a single touchdown: mine.

After that we didn't win another game and didn't make it to the playoffs. But I didn't care, because I was living in the moment. After that I realized football is what I want to pursue, because this is what makes me happy. When I came to school after that game, everyone knew my name, and underclassmen looked up to me. That game was the talk of the week. I even got props from the principal and all the teachers.

Later, in front of everyone at practice, my coach told me that I was the Player of the Week. When I told my parents about the game, my mother told me she was proud of me. On TV they showed highlights of the game, and my mother watched it. It felt good to see her smile and know that I was the one who made her smile. My pops said, "That's my boy!" He told everyone in the family, so everyone was calling me the athlete of the family. That game changed my life.

I'm ready to start winning, in and outside of school. Even if it means working hard every day, getting to school on time, eating healthier and meeting new people. Football made me more confident; it made me want to try new things. You can't stick to the same routine every day. You have to switch it up a little sometimes, and I realized that once football came into my life.

Football also made me do better in school because if you don't have good grades, then you can't play football. The love of the game made me want to be successful in my academics. It also made me a better person. When I play football, I don't smoke or drink. I want to stay in shape, take care of myself and my body. I want to go to college, play football, and hopefully get recruited. I have to play and do well consistently. Then the teams will start looking at me; professional recruiters will start taking note of how I play. Before football, I did want to go to college, but it wasn't as important to me as it is now.

My dream is to play professional football in the NFL. In my dream I would play wide receiver for the San Francisco 49ers. I would like to sign a major deal for the big bucks. I love money and I love playing football. Plain and simple, the dream for me is doing what I love and getting paid big money for it.

But it's not only about the money, I love the game more than the money. I see other athletes and I idolize them for what they do, both on and off the field. For example, football players give back to the community. Recently, some NFL players gave money to Haiti to aid earthquake victims. They're not selfish with their money—even if you have a lot of money, that shouldn't change you. Don't let living your dream change you, because once you're living it, you could lose it as quickly as you got it. It's important to keep your values in mind.

If I achieved my dream, it would change my life and my family's life too. I would buy my mom a big house. She brought me into this world, so the least I could do is give her what she wants. I would spoil my family with money, gold, jewelry, or whatever they would like. I love my family and they deserve to have whatever they want. I want to see them happy and I want to be the person to make them smile.

I want to be well-known, not only on TV but also in my community. I want to be known as the man who made a change in the world. I want to do this by influencing kids to stay off the streets and to stay in school. I would not only give to my family, but I would give back to my community by donating to charities and to schools in need. I would buy kids the books they need. I would also buy a football field for a poor school. I would speak in schools and tell kids to stay in school.

Whatever happens, I will always keep my values and show people respect. You have to give respect to earn it. I don't want be known as a jerk or a bad guy or a selfish person, but as a nice, sweet, gentle guy who spreads happiness and joy all around me.

I keep going to school so I can keep reaching for my dream, and I would tell kids to do the same. I would say, if I can do it, then anyone can.

LEAVING HOME
to Find Home

by JUAN VALDIVIA

MY MOM AND I never had a problem. I was a spoiled brat, but we were always close to each other. Though everything changed when she found out I was gay. It took her and my dad by surprise. At first they didn't accept me at all. I understood, because it would be hard for any parents to find out that their son/daughter had a different sexual orientation. I felt like I had disappointed them so much.

My mom looked at me with hateful eyes every time I went home. I wanted to be accepted for who I was and have nobody judge me; I wanted attention but I didn't get it. So my hate for my mother built up inside me. All I thought about was forgetting the pain and finding something to help me feel better about myself. So I started rebelling, cutting school, fighting and drinking. Every day during the summer I spent with my boyfriend. We felt we had nobody else but ourselves.

Time passed and my mother and father told me they accepted me the way I was and that they didn't care what anybody else said. I believed my mother, but still inside I felt hate for her treating me the way she did.

One beautiful day, I left school because I decided to do what I wanted. My mom got a call from school and called me on my phone. When I got home, my mom yelled. I was drunk, so I went off on her. We started arguing and I was all up in her face. She thought I was going to hit her, but I wasn't. My brother and sister got between us and I pushed them off. My mother got scared and called the police.

At that point, I walked down the stairs. The police were there already. I tried to fight them off, but at the end they cuffed me and put me in the police car. They took me to the Tenderloin police station and I waited to see what would happen. I was nervous. I waited for two or maybe even three hours until the cop lady came and said they were going to take me to the San Francisco Youth Guidance Center (YGC). I didn't think that was a punishment. I just thought it was going to be an overnight thing and that's it. But that's not what happened. Nobody thought it would get as serious as it did. I guess my family thought I would just be in jail for a while, get out on probation, and be out. Unfortunately, it didn't end up being like that.

I didn't feel safe in jail because the kids in there found out I was gay. I couldn't be myself; all I did was stay in my room and read books. Kids picked on me because of the way I was. This got me so mad because I didn't do anything to them to be treated the way I was. All I had was me, myself, and I.

In jail, I could only make phone calls every Friday, Saturday, Sunday, and Monday for a couple of minutes at a time. About a week later, I got released, but then I got transferred to another jail. They cuffed me and put a chain on my waist, tying me down like an animal. On the way to the new place we passed through my city, my hangouts. It was emotional for me because we passed Castro and Market Street, where you would have found me before—my late night kick-it spot. I had so many memories of myself with my dude and family. I thought this would be the last time I'd see the mall, parks, restaurants, and family. All I could do was cry.

Later they brought me some lunch: three slices of bread with two pieces of bologna, carrots, a cookie, and a packet of mayonnaise and mustard. To drink they just gave me a bottle of water. They told me I was flying to Oregon that same night. I was terrified when they told me I would be taken that far away. I didn't even know where Oregon was. The agent cuffed me and put a big beanbag thing in my left leg. Trust me, it was heavy! We got to the San Francisco Airport and waited for two hours for the plane. We got on and I sat all the way in the back like a criminal. It was my first time on a plane, and I was scared out of my mind. It was about an hour-long flight. We got to Oregon around midnight, then we had to take a taxi ride that was another hour to the Northern Oregon Regional Correctional Juvenile Facility (NORCOR).

When I got to NORCOR, I had to take a shower and get my room. My room was small and concrete, with just a small mattress and pillow for a bed. I had a sink and bathroom but no privacy, because anybody could pass by and see me. All I had in my mind was to call my mom to let her know I was okay, but they didn't let me because they had rules. I couldn't get to sleep until 1:00 a.m. but they woke me up at 5:45 a.m. to eat breakfast and take a shower. Then I was in lockdown for twenty-four hours because I had to take a test. The test was about the rules the facility had because they were very strict. I took the test and then was able to have lunch and do activities with the group. The daily activities were school, physical education, and chill time with people. But all I wanted to do was call my mom and tell her I was okay. Finally I called her and told her how everything was. She was sad to hear that I was really that far away and that I was in jail. Not only was she sad, but practically all my family was sad, because nobody wanted to see a person they love in a position like that. Life in jail isn't easy, especially if you're gay. You can't trust anybody but yourself.

It was so hard not to have more contact with my loved ones, especially my boyfriend. My parents thought he was a bad example for me. From the time I was in jail, I only got to contact him once. He tried to come see me when I was in San Francisco, but he couldn't because he wasn't family. He contacted my cousin Elizabeth to see what was going on. She tried to go see me as well, but they didn't let her because she didn't have permission from my probation officer.

I was terrified of losing my boyfriend because he was my everything. It was so hard not to have someone I loved by my side. I didn't even know if he was still going to be by my side. Even though we had been going out for a year, I felt that he wasn't going to wait for me.

Every day that I was in jail I prayed to God and asked him to let me out of jail soon so I could go back to my regular life. I wanted to be back at my house with my parents, my brother and sisters, to see my friends, and most of all the love of my life, David. I would stay up all night and cry because I didn't know what to do with myself anymore.

The time in jail passed so slowly and I hated that with a passion. I met a couple of people that were in the same position as I was. In the beginning of November, I had my first court date and I was nervous because I've never been to something like that ever in my life. The good thing was that my mom got me a lawyer that helped, so that was a major plus. I didn't even have to talk because the lawyer did all the talking. In the process of getting out of jail you need to fill out a whole packet of information about who you are going to be released to. They made sure I got released to a safe and reliable person. I ended up being released to my auntie, and she had to come pick me up. She came all the way to Oregon with my uncle and my parents; I didn't even know they were going to come get me. It was the best surprise of my life. They picked me up on Thanksgiving Day and took me to eat breakfast. The ride back was so long that I got bored after awhile. It was about twelve hours. I talked to my parents and auntie and told them what jail was like and how sad I got every day.

The reunion with my family was exciting; there was a lot of crying and my parents and aunties were telling me how much they missed me. My family reunion happened in my uncle's house in Daly City. They made a carne asada for me and I felt so special and loved. I got to see my friends when I came back to school after so long. My friends all ran up to me and gave me hugs and kisses and told me they missed me and thanked God I was out. And the best part was that I got to see the love of my life once more, my boyfriend David. That was the best. I missed him so much and I was so happy he was still by my side through all this. I was happy to be out of jail because I missed my freedom.

Looking back, I remember how I also felt like I was at home the moment I arrived in the United States from Mexico. I remember starting school at the age of four and I was a nervous wreck. But learning how to read wasn't as hard as I had thought it would be. I learned very quickly. The first time I started to speak English I said, "How are you?" and my parents were so proud. I still remember my first American food: a cheeseburger. Cheeseburgers were so good. That's all I would eat at the beginning. You might say I got used to the American life. I love it here. I feel so free. I feel more American than I do Mexican now, but I still have a lot of that Mexican spice in me.

Today, it's hard to believe all this happened to me because I feel like it happened in just a minute. It changed my life drastically. Now I am back at school, making up all the work I missed so I can graduate this year. I want to make my family proud. I want to be successful and have something to live for. I want to make my life here with the person that matters the most.

People have many types of dreams. My dream means a lot to me. Believe me, I know, because I almost fell through the cracks, but I climbed back up. But that's okay, because sometimes you have to leave home to find home.

SUEÑOS

by CECILY MARIE ALFARO

MY GRANDMOTHER LIVES in San Salvador, El Salvador. She lives in a very small home by herself since her mother, my great-grandmother, passed away. The house is a two-story house with no roof, and the floor is very rough, almost like walking on sandpaper and rocks, so it's impossible to walk around barefoot. When you walk into the house the first thing you see are the kitchen/store and a hallway leading to the back rooms. There are only two rooms downstairs without any doors and a stairway with no railing next to the wall. As you walk upstairs there is no roof and one room that is isolated from everything else. There is also a shower there, but it only has cold water.

My grandmother isn't very rich, but she isn't that poor. She is a saleswoman who sells candy right out of her own kitchen. Her kitchen isn't very big, but when you walk into the house the kitchen also becomes the candy store. There are shelves full of different kinds of candy and *pan dulce* that she buys or makes herself. There is a small old cash register on the right-hand side very close to the wall that she uses daily on sales or to see what her profits are. The only problem about having the store in the kitchen is that there can only be at most four people in there at a time, including my grandmother. I would say that the store gets crowded sometimes but not every day. Living off of only this income isn't very stable, and it's difficult for her to pay her bills. For her, living is a struggle day by day.

She didn't always live like this. One day very long ago, around the nineties, my grandmother, Mama Luce, and my great-grandmother, Mama Chuce, left their wattle hut in El Salvador to move to San Francisco in hopes of opening a store and starting a new life. Navigating the city was difficult with their limited English and little money. They didn't think the changes would be so drastic. After staying at hotels every night, they came across a store/apartment in the crowded Mission District. People came to the Mission to shop and find deals on many different things. So, where else is a perfect place to open a store? My grandmothers looked at the place and thought that they could make it work out with the little money that they had left.

My grandmothers walked into a bank to apply for a loan wearing their best traditional dresses. They felt out of place as they noticed a man walking toward them in a dull gray suit. They looked up and down at themselves, feeling ashamed of how they were dressed. They looked around at their surroundings and noticed that everyone in the room was wearing dull clothing. The man in the suit walked up to them and asked in Spanish if they needed help, and my grandmothers thought that it would be easier to speak to him in Spanish since they didn't know that much English. The man explained to them that they couldn't get a loan because of not having the right documents and that they would have to go get their residency in order to get a loan.

My grandmothers thought that having a store and moving to San Francisco would help them out in a huge way, but it wasn't as easy as they thought. They tried to open a store and find an apartment at the same time, without much money or many experiences with the new way of living. Since they didn't open the store right and didn't have enough money to survive here anymore, they decided it was time to go back to El Salvador and try to work out what they wanted there. In the end what happened to my grandmothers was not what they wanted at all, but at least they can say that they tried.

The idea of "making it in life" means a lot to me in many ways, such as getting by socially, mentally, and economically. It's a way of being able to do all the everyday things and also making a living in a job. I think that if you really want the American Dream then you really have to put all your heart and soul into it. Success to me is about what obstacles I have to go through to get what I want, all so that it would be all worth it in the end.

The amount of effort you put into it will show where and how much closer we all get to our dreams, even if they are just little ones.

Most people find the American Dream a way to get out of certain situations they may be in, a way to make a better life for themselves. To me it's just a dream that might not really come true all the time, no matter how hard you may try. I'm not fully negative about it, but I mostly think that it is just something that is not very obtainable for most people. I do find that it is false hope to some people, especially to most people who come from other countries. I do have an American Dream, you could say; it's like any other dream that I can think of that I can try to make come true.

I plan to go to college after I graduate high school, and when I finish a four-year college, I want to go to medical school to be a pediatrician. I've had this dream for as long as I can remember and I've been trying all throughout high school to achieve it. I had a downfall in my plan in my junior year, and there was a moment where I thought that I wasn't going to make it. I had surgery on my appendix and on a cyst in my ovary, so I wasn't able to walk and make it to school, therefore I wasn't able to finish my finals for most of classes. Now it's my senior year and I'm struggling to pass all my regular classes as well as some extra classes at night school. I'm taking seven classes plus three classes on the side to get all my A–G requirements to go to college. My dream was to go to University of California, Berkeley as soon as I finished high school, but since I didn't finish the classes my junior year, I have to settle for City College of San Francisco for two years until I can transfer to a university of my choice. My dream isn't fully achieved yet, but it does seem like a struggle to get there, and at this moment it doesn't seem like I'll be able to make it any time soon. I feel that since I had that setback my junior year it might take me a couple of years longer to get what I want.

A very important thing in being able to achieve my goal is that I need to pay for all the tuition, books, and living expenses. My family is economically challenged, as in we can't pay for me going to college. I would be the first member of my family to actually go to college. Since my parents didn't go to college, or even finish high school, I think that it is a good dream to have. But since my family didn't go to college, they can't make enough money for things like my college tuition. My family's struggles help me see that every dream isn't always easy to get, and that most people can't finish what they want to do. Everyone has his or her own imperfections, but that's what makes us unique.

New CHAPTER

by JOCELYN RODRIGUEZ

AS CHILDREN GROW UP, they believe that the all-time American Dream is to graduate from high school, go to college, and have a good career. This was also my parents' dream for me. My own dream was to graduate and then attend San Diego State. But as months have passed, I've been making dumb decisions that lower my chances of getting into college. Once a child grows up and finally sees reality, her dreams may change, just like mine did.

My eighth-grade year, I went to a private school called St. James in San Francisco. That year, every eighth-grader did high school applications. At the time, I was attending an after-school program in San Francisco called Making Waves. I joined Making Waves because my fifth-grade teacher thought it was a good opportunity for me to succeed in life. He saw potential because Making Waves is a program that helps students get into college and make something of themselves. It gives students a space where they can do their homework and get help if they need it. I've been attending Making Waves since I was in fifth grade. Throughout the years that I've been there, the program has helped me academically, and also when I needed an adult figure who wasn't my parent. There's always someone there for me to talk to. Plus, the staff helped me do my high school applications. Then I had to go to an open house, show up, shadow the school, and if possible, go to the interview on my own.

Making Waves helped me apply to two charters schools—Gateway High School and Leadership High School in San Francisco—but their preference was for me to attend the private school, Immaculate Conception Academy. I'd never heard of that school, but once I found out it was right next to my middle school, it seemed pretty cool. ICA is an all-girl private Catholic school, and it was a type of school I really wasn't used to. I wasn't such a big fan of being stuck in a school full of girls, or in a school that has to deal with Jesus.

As acceptance letters were coming out, I was anxious to see if I had gotten in. But once the news came and I saw that I wasn't accepted, I was bummed out because most of my friends were going to that school and I wasn't going to be with them. Making Waves told me I could probably get in if I went to summer school before the year started. So I went to summer school, and I did well. I had to re-interview for ICA, and then I found out I was accepted.

Freshman year came and it started off rough. I wasn't used to the workload or being at an all-girls school—it was just too much for me. My grades slipped, but I can say at least I tried. But the year came to an end and I realized that "trying my best" wasn't good enough. Report cards came out and I found out I had to go to summer school to make up my Ds. I went to summer school because most colleges aren't fans of Ds. It turned out that summer school was easy. There was no homework and the tests just felt like classwork. But during that summer I had a boyfriend, and once we broke up in August, it added to my existing stress. With my schoolwork and that breakup, I just didn't care anymore.

Sophomore year came, and at first I felt okay since I saw my friends again, but academically I wasn't so happy. My attitude became a problem; I didn't really care about anything. I would come to school out of uniform, I got more detentions then usual, and my grades slipped. I had to go to a meeting with the principal and the dean. The dean, Ms. Diaz, told me I had that "I don't care" attitude, and I agreed with her because I really didn't. But then something hit me in the head; I thought to myself, "What am I doing? I really don't need to be acting out, because where am I going to go?" So I changed toward the end of the year. I was on top of my stuff—or so I thought. Once again I was wrong; it was too late to change. Even though I was turning in my work, it was already too late because it was the end of the quarter. I got my report card and I knew I was going to be on academic probation. Again I went to summer school and made up my Ds. I passed summer school with an A and a C.

That summer, a friend called me one day and asked, "Jocelyn, you know Sister is kicking people out?" I asked how she knew, and she said, "Because I was supposed to have a meeting and I didn't go, so she told my mom I wasn't invited back." My dad told me I was also having a meeting at school. I was confident, since I thought I had changed my ways. I hoped the school saw that. I told Ms. Hernandez, a woman who worked at Making Waves as the junior mentor, about the meeting. She told me that she also didn't believe I was going to get kicked out because she saw that I was changing so there was nothing to worry about.

When the day of the meeting came, my dad, the principal Sister Janice, the dean Ms. Diaz, and a person from Making Waves were all there. Standing outside the room made me really nervous, yet confident. I thought I wasn't going to get kicked out—but you never know.

When we all sat down, it was awkward. Sister Janice started with, "Well, you know you're on academic probation." I was shocked; why would she tell me that? Then Ms. Diaz started to talk about how I was acting, my attitude, my detentions, and my grades. They kept going on and I really didn't want to hear it anymore, but then the bomb came down. Sister Janice ended her lecture with, "Sorry, but I won't be inviting you back." I looked at her with a face that said, "You're playing," but she assured me that I was not coming back. I started to cry, bawling tears, but I didn't know why. On one hand, I didn't want to be at ICA; but on the other hand, I did, because my friends were going there and I didn't want to end up in a public school.

The meeting was over and I just kept crying. I knew I had disappointed my family. But as my dad and I were making our way to the car after the meeting, he was supportive. He told me, "Jocelyn, stop crying. There are other opportunities out there. This isn't the end. It's a new beginning." I looked at him with the saddest face because I was sure I had disappointed him. When we got into the car, he talked about how high school was for him. He told me that he messed around at school too, but then he realized that it was just hurting him, so he started to get his act straight and got As and Bs in school. That showed me that he only wanted the best for me. I was shocked that he was not mad at me. It was all good.

Toward the end of that summer, my mom and I went to San Francisco Unified School District to put me in a public school. I didn't have too many options. Most schools were full, since it was almost time for school to start. My first choice was Lincoln, but it was already full, so I put myself on the waiting list. The only schools left were Burton and O'Connell. Since my best friends applied to O'Connell, I just signed up for that school. At first I was not so sure that was the right decision, but since I wasn't going to be alone, it was cool.

O'Connell is very different from ICA. There I have more freedom than I did at ICA. At O'Connell, the work is easier and I can handle the workload. We get less homework, so I don't have to be stressing myself out if I don't bring my book home or if I don't finish everything. Coming from ICA, I am prepared because that school is college-preparatory and the staff expects a lot from you. At ICA, they gave out detentions for the smallest things—like if you wore a jacket without a sweater underneath, were chewing gum, or came late to school. But at O'Connell, they don't give you detentions, and that's a good thing, because we don't have to waste forty-five minutes of our life just looking at nothing.

Throughout this journey I learned not to take things for granted or push my luck. My dream was to be a successful young lady and to graduate from a high-quality school, to go to college, to pursue my career, and live a wonderful life. But I've learned that in life people are not going to give you many chances. I've learned that the hard way. In addition, people also have high dreams of succeeding in life, but these dreams can get taken away because of choices that a person makes. I learned that change is a good thing, and maybe now that I've messed up I can redeem myself and try to strive for my dreams and not be a failure. The reason I want this is because I have a younger sister and brother looking up to me, and I want to be the strong sister.

The key to success is that there are going to be obstacles, but there is always going to be a way around them. The reason I will succeed is because I want to become someone in life. My motivation is my future. In my future, I see myself living on my own, making my own money, and being able to help my parents out. I also want to prove to my siblings that no matter what kind of dream they have, it will always be possible to get to if only you put your mind into it and try your best. If you don't do it, then who else will?

How the Chinese Kid Keeps Hold of the AMERICAN DREAM

by KENNY LAU

JOSÉ HAD BLACK HAIR, brown eyes, and was about five feet tall. He was a Mexican kid and pretty buff, and he liked to wear a gray sweater with pockets. His face looked like a rotten egg: gray and without color. Being Chinese means being smart and getting good grades in school. That was probably the main reason José asked me for the answers to the math homework. Bullies threatened people like me for homework all the time. I was in seventh grade and was thirteen years old. I was very shy and didn't want people to notice me. I am a Chinese kid, and José decided to target me for no reason that made sense to me. At that time he destroyed the thought of the American Dream for me.

By the time I was in elementary school, I thought the American Dream meant having a lot of money, many cars, and a family with a wife, a son, a daughter, a dog, and a cat. We would all be very happy living together in a big, comfortable house—like in the movies. *Mission Impossible* ends with Tom Cruise romantically kissing his girlfriend on the beach while the sun is setting. As always, they'll live happily ever after. I wished I was the Chinese version of Tom Cruise!

The story isn't the same for me. Immigrants have a tough life. Being illiterate in English limited my parents' opportunities. They relied on me a lot to understand the world. They still do. Every time I brought home permission slips, I had to translate what they were about. I also translated our rental agreement, and helped show them where to sign their names. If I were them, I would have learned English. My life would have been a lot easier.

In the beginning, I thought it wasn't a big deal that José bullied me because it only happened once or twice. I thought that he was only playing around. I didn't take him seriously. But I was wrong. He wouldn't stop. One day, when I was going to lunch, there were a lot of people rushing past me, and most of them were trying to get to the lunch line. José demanded I give him my math homework. I refused and turned away from him, but he pushed me into the counter where the silverware was. The corner of the counter stabbed into my ribs, and a sharp pain shot through my entire body. He turned away without looking back. I believe that he didn't know how much pain I was going through. The spectators did not pay much attention. All they cared about was lunch—chicken nuggets or a burrito. José walked away and I didn't run into him for the rest of the day.

José didn't stop there. During class he would crumple up paper balls and throw them at the back of my head. Even though the teacher witnessed this, she would only give him a verbal warning and he would stop momentarily. Then he would continue when the teacher wasn't paying attention. I was angry with her. Why didn't she stand up for me?

It seemed like a never-ending cycle. When my classmates saw José throwing paper balls at me, some of them would try to help by saying, "That's messed up" or "Stop doing that!" But José was tricky—he knew that he would get in trouble, so he would stop. My friends stayed silent when it was happening, and tried to comfort me afterward. "They're cowards," I thought to myself. I felt isolated in my own world.

In front of other kids José liked to call me a stupid Chinese kid and a "yellow banana." He would laugh with his friends and point at me until I ran away. I would usually hide in the bathroom and cry. Probably if I weren't Chinese, José would have left me alone. We Chinese don't fight back that much. We try to avoid conflict. At times, living in this world seemed meaningless and a waste of time.

I remember my mom telling me, "You need to get good grades, so you will be able to go to college and all that stuff." And I had, until I met José. Then my grades plummeted. My parents wondered why and I just told them that I got lazy. They scolded me, but then they dropped the subject. I thought that if I told them about José, they would probably create more problems for me. Maybe they would contact the school district, and they would make José and I go to parent conferences with school administrators. I would feel embarrassed that I was being bullied. Other kids might laugh at me because I wasn't brave enough to deal with José by myself. I thought that if I kept up my grades and avoided José, my parents would not interfere, and my life would be much easier. But I couldn't concentrate on my schoolwork. I was lost. The idea of my big house, my Mercedes, my wife and kids, exploded into pieces. José had destroyed my dreams. The only thought going through my mind was how to get rid of him. I was just trying to survive. Nothing else mattered.

If I saw José walking anywhere near me, I would take a different route. I would try to sit as far away from him in class as I could. I would walk behind other people so José would not notice me. My strategy was effective, until a month later, when he figured out my plan.

Although I knew that José wouldn't kill me, I couldn't stop replaying the images of his bullying in my mind. I noticed that I had a nervous habit. I was constantly clearing my throat and swallowing my saliva. I really wanted to tell an adult. I hadn't told my parents or my teachers since the bullying started. The longer I thought about it, I realized that none of them would be able to help me. My teachers would probably make José and I apologize and shake hands like in kindergarten. That would just make matters worse. And my parents didn't speak English, so I didn't tell them because it wouldn't have made any difference. It's amazing how one person can be so cold-hearted and have such a negative impact.

José was a brick wall in my path. I wanted to be able to graduate from high school. I wanted to be able to get a job, or go to college. But if I got bad grades, I wouldn't be able to get scholarships, and without them, I wouldn't be able to go to college. If I didn't go to college, then my chances of getting a good job would be slim. And without a job, then I wouldn't have money. Without money, I'd have to say goodbye to my dreams.

After we graduated from middle school, José and I went to different high schools. Thank God. I never saw him again. He didn't come find me. I tried to forget what happened. I looked forward to a new life in high school where I didn't know anyone.

Now that I'm older, I have more confidence in myself. My life in high school is fantastic. My teachers and classmates support me. Surviving José has made me a stronger person, and I realize that a lot of people are helping me succeed. My grades have gone back up, and I am actually not so miserable anymore. I look forward to coming to school and learning.

To all readers: Be strong and fight for your dreams. Anything can be achieved if you believe in yourself. You have a lot of people who care and want you to excel. Life can be brutal at times, but trust yourself, and a new road to your destiny will appear. The Chinese kid *can* reach the American Dream.

STRUGGLE

and

SUCCESS

by SANDRA ALARCON

I REMEMBER WHEN MY GRANDMA came to my room and told me that my parents had decided that my brother and I would go to the United States to be reunited with them. I started to jump up and down with happiness. I was so excited to see my parents again; immediately I was in a dream. I ran to find my brother Alberto to let him know what Dad and Mom had said. I told him, but he was acting like he didn't care. My brother's attitude at that moment was really hard to describe; I think that he was in shock. I went to school and I was so happy that I started to tell to all my friends. They were asking me, "Are you coming back?" I said, "Of course, I'm just going to visit and then come back." That's what I used to think. But my parents' decision was to live in the United States and in the summer go to visit Peru.

My parents decided to move to the United States because they wanted my brother and I to have a better education and life. My mom was the first member of the family who arrived in this country. My dad was next. My parents were living in a small room at my aunt's house for several months. Their situation in this country was really tough because of the language; they spoke Spanish and no English. Because of that, they started to attend a community college to learn the language. Unfortunately, they didn't have enough time to attend their classes because of the work that they were doing. My dad always used to study in his free time, but it was not enough.

Mom used to call us every day in Peru, but eventually she stopped. Every second of the night and day, I missed my parents a lot. Although I was living at grandma's house, it was not the same. Alberto started to hang out with his friends more frequently, to have fun and not feel depressed because he missed our parents. Obviously, my grandma did not let me go out with my friends because of my age. I was too little to be outside.

Finally the big day came. I was going to the United States! Alberto and I were waiting at my house for my uncle's ride, and my grandma started to give us advice: she told me I had to be good in school, responsible, and respectful to my parents. She was sad, but not crying. It made me feel really sad. I hugged her and my brother. I wanted to cry but held my tears to act strong. I said to my grandma, "Mami, we're coming back." My grandma was so protective, which made me feel happy; she was always taking care of me. I will never forget that great experience of living with my grandmother.

Uncle came. He grabbed the luggage and bags. We finally got to the airport. My brother and I sat in blue chairs waiting for our flight. Once we were on the plane, I got bored. Then, in the blink of an eye, I was sleeping in a strange bed and heard my mother's voice. I was at my parents' house in San Francisco. I started to cry a river. My mom's words were, "Don't worry, Sandrita, we're together now." It made me feel really good.

Living in the United States was an exciting experience because it was something new for me: all the differences between Peru and the United States, and how the lifestyles differ from each other. In San Francisco, the first time that I saw the Bay Bridge, I fell in love. It's pretty amazing how people have built the bridge. The houses in Peru were a lot larger than in the United States. Walking down the streets and observing the Chinese restaurant and other restaurants made me curious. I wanted to taste those types of food. The language was really different. We bought some clothes at the mall, and when my mom was paying, the cashier asked her some questions, and I was confused just to hear the words that she was saying. However, my mom started to talk to her. I pretended that I comprehended their conversation. It's intriguing to see many different nationalities of people living in this country, because most people speak another language besides English.

On the first day of school, I was so nervous. I kept saying in my head: It's my first time in middle school! Most students spoke English, which made me feel intimidated because I didn't know how to communicate with them. I had been quiet for the whole first period and for all my classes that first day. However, there were students who helped translate in some classes. My classmates would talk to my teachers and let them know that I was a newcomer, and most teachers were friendly. My brother and I were really studying hard. Alberto was like my teacher. He used to teach me five words per day, and he always wanted me to learn more every day.

Alberto has always been my role model. He's a nice person and also smart. I like the way he sees things and the way he tries to improve his bad attitude. He wanted to go back to Peru, and then he just changed his decision. I started to feel the same about going back there—having my education in my own country and coming back to visit my parents at winter break. When my brother explained his intentions to go back to Peru and why he wanted to study there, it was because he wanted to separate from this country because of the confusing idioms that are in the language. He made me understand that life is not always as we want; most of the time we struggle a lot, and that's the basis for becoming successful. So I realized that I would just have to struggle and survive in this country.

It took about three months for my brother to learn English. He was improving with the language more and more each day. After several weeks, I was getting used to my classes and I was feeling pretty good about them. However, my brother was struggling a lot in high school; he started to get frustrated with himself. He wanted to learn English immediately. My sixteen-year-old brother started to be in a depression. He wanted to go back to Peru. My brother's attitude was really frustrating for our family. Mom started to feel guilty.

After two months at school, my science teacher assigned us a project about the periodic table of elements. The assignment consisted of presenting each of the elements that the teacher assigned to each student. I was so scared, I was sweating like an ice cream cone on a hot day, and I heard some students making noise. They started to act angry. I started to feel extremely afraid; just imagining presenting my element made me so nervous. The project was due on Monday, and presenting was the main grade of the project. During the weekend, I kept thinking about the project and how I would present in front of twenty-one students and the teacher. At least we had a week to work on the project, but it was not enough time for me because of my fears of speaking aloud in English in front of the class.

Presentation day came; I still remember everyone's faces. My friend and I were the last two people to present. My friend Noemi went first. She started by describing her element, cobalt. Noemi was a shy girl, but on that day, she made an excellent presentation. During her presentation, I couldn't stop watching the clock. I prayed in my head. I was so scared. When my turn came, I felt everyone staring at me. It made me feel insecure. I wanted to disappear. I started by describing my element, sodium. I felt nervous every time I spoke. While I was introducing my project, half the room was talking, and they started to laugh. That impacted me more. I just wanted to cry and leave the classroom. I looked around, waiting for the teacher to tell the students to be quiet. I was waiting to hear her voice, but I never did. The teacher was laughing too. It totally killed me. After that I felt sad because I felt like a clown in front of the class and angry because I didn't want to obey my mom and start a new life in this country. I felt really humiliated, which caused me a lot of pain. It also motivated me to learn more about the language.

The next day I did not want to go to school. I explained to my parents what happened during the presentation and they were surprised. They let me stay at home. When I returned to school, I felt nervous, like on my first day there. I saw my friends and they were acting the same. I was silent. I started to feel happy because all the students did not mention or seem to remember the presentation. I felt secure and confident and I started to act like my normal self.

Education at the moment seems to be better. I started to feel confident and friendly with my classmates a few weeks after the presentation. I realized that I can motivate myself by keeping in mind that I can do this. Having that phrase in mind helps me a lot. I feel more confident now; I feel secure and not as scared as I was before I learned English. Now, as a junior at my high school, I see how I'm improving in English each day. Additionally, every time I do presentations, I feel free to speak in English in front of my classmates. I don't have those nervous feelings that I used to feel before.

I used to think that my life in the United States would be like Disneyland: a perfect place of happiness. But the reality was to struggle first. After that, I was able to enjoy my Disneyland. Luckily, I don't miss Peru that much because during summer I go to visit my country.

My parents and brother are always there to support me, even in cases when I feel like giving up. Now I feel strong because I know that I am able to handle any hard moments. My brother is in college and also works a part-time job. Alberto is still acting as my teacher. He is always saying, "Do your homework and do not give up."

For my family and me, our goals came true. Now I feel happier than I used to. I feel like talking to anyone on the street, or if someone asks me some question, I respond quickly and feel like I am speaking my own language too. My mom just got a new job, and she spends more time with us. Also she is taking some classes in a community college. On the other hand, my dad is working two jobs; he is busy all the time, except on the weekends.

The dream for my parents and brother seems not to be that balanced because my parents are still struggling as employees, and most of the time they feel exhausted. This shows me that my parents want the best for us. That's why they are working and getting tired each day. But for my brother and me, our American Dream was to learn a new language, and I know we achieved that.

THE AMERICAN DREAM:
Is It the Same for Everybody?

by RAFAEL GURROLA

IT WAS A NICE, sunny day and I was coming back from Stockton. It was Friday, so it was time to party. We were cruising around, the '64 Chevy box was sitting on some old rims, but that didn't matter. My big homie was driving the car, showing his tattoos, repping his affiliation. The phone rang as I looked out the window, searching for females to accompany us. My friend was on the phone saying he was having a house party, so we decided to go over there.

As we got to the house it was already turning dark. What happened in the house was a crazy and unforgettable night. It ended in me getting booked into juvenile hall. As the night ended, I wished I could change being locked up, and I did a lot of thinking about how my life would turn out.

Now that I have gotten out of there, my mind is free. I still think about my actions and how they led to that event. Our dreams are affected by how we live our lives. I believe that when we are younger, we want different things out of life. As we get older, our actions decide our new dreams. Before this happened to me, my dream was just to be what I am today. But now it's different. I did a lot of thinking when I was locked up. As human beings, we get to choose what we want, and others cannot change our thoughts. Nobody has the same dream because if we did, then what would be the point? In this society we need people who think differently and try to expand their minds with different ideas.

I say that nobody has the same dream because society has already given us life, liberty, and the pursuit of happiness. This is not true for some people, though. When we are still young in our years, we have different goals. As we get older our minds start to change. For example, when we are younger, we want to be a police officer or something that catches our attention. Throughout our years, new things catch our attention and we focus on those subjects.

My mother had a different dream than me. When she was a young teenager, her dream was to come to the United States. Now her dream is for me to get an education and help her out when I grow up. Most people want money or fancy materials that don't really help them be who they are. I am not materialistic, though; I just want to be alive in the long run, and also maintain a positive lifestyle.

Nobody has the right to choose our dreams, because if our dreams were all the same, the world wouldn't be very creative and each person would be dull. A mind is a terrible thing to waste, along with its creative ideas. Life is full of wonders and different experiences. Our experiences shape how we see life through our own eyes. We choose our own paths and how we end up in the end.

My American Dream is different now that I have been locked up. Now, I want to be a functional member of society. But at the same time, I am not so sure I will still want to be this way in the future. We have many stages in life, but nobody is sure how long we're going to stay in one stage or if we will follow it throughout life.

The way my mind has evolved gives me many perspectives. Most of us don't wonder what certain people have gone through that makes them who they are today. Americans make judgments based on their ideas and way of living. When it comes down to dreams and goals, people shut them down for what they already are. What society doesn't want us to know is that they are trying to choose our paths without us thinking about it. Society does this by trying to see who we are, and then labeling us without knowing us. They want us to be a bad influence or negative to our communities so that we can't follow our own dreams and goals. I believe that they can't handle our intelligence because of the way we are starting to think and wonder more about life.

I ask people to wonder about their American Dreams, and how they change as we change, and also to remember to never give up, because if we do, then why dream? We have the right to follow our own paths, and no one else has to have a say in it. What do you want out of life?

Where Is THE AMERICAN DREAM?

by KRISTI VARGAS

HAVE YOU EVER BEEN in your house and not felt safe? Feeling safe inside my house is something I question, not because there's violence in my house, but because people might come inside my house and hurt us. There have been moments in my life that I have been inside of my house and I have not felt safe.

You might ask where I live and why I think that this neighborhood is so bad. I even get embarrassed when people ask me where I live and I tell them "Hunters Point," and they tell me, "How can you live up there with so much violence? You must be hella ghetto." I didn't always live there. I used to live in Richmond, CA.

One day we came to San Francisco to apply for public housing, and three months later we were told that we could come move into our new house. We had no choice but to take this opportunity. So many people told my mom that it was very dangerous in Hunters Point, but she said that we had to try it out. It's really funny, but when we went to get the keys to our house we were introduced to a police officer. He told us that before we moved in we had to get an alarm for the house, and that you can never be too safe. He also told us to get bars for the windows. He explained that when we move in, we should put everything in boxes and not show anything of value because someone might break in. I never thought it was so dangerous, but I was wrong and I would soon experience it.

One day I was in my kitchen washing dishes. It was about 9:00 p.m. and I was very tired after washing two piles of dishes. I needed fresh air, but I didn't want to go outside because it was too cold. So I decided to open the window right in front of the sink. I was holding out my hand to pull the curtain to the side, and as I pulled the curtain, I didn't even open the window because I saw someone outside. I looked really hard because it was very dark. I saw a man standing outside. He was holding a gun, and when he saw me, I entered a state of shock and I didn't move at all. I was so scared, I didn't know what to do; I wanted to move my feet so bad, but I couldn't. I felt like screaming. I crawled to the light switch and I turned off the light. I heard gunshots and I ran upstairs to my mom's room. My boyfriend was sitting in the living room, and he ran to see why I had run upstairs and what was happening with the gunshots. I got upstairs and I was scared and I couldn't even talk, I was shaking. It took me about five minutes to talk and then I told everyone what had happened. I was still shaking.

My experience with the man and his gun can't be erased from my memory. I live that day every day I step outside of my house. I have to deal with seeing him and thinking he will try to kill me because I might tell.

Sometimes I'm scared to leave my house, but life keeps going; it will never stop just because I'm scared. You think that once you come to America you will be safe, but you really aren't. Everywhere you go there is some type of danger, even in the perfect neighborhood. I go to church on Tuesdays at 7:00 p.m., all the way in Richmond. I get back around 11:00 p.m. and sometimes I wonder if I will make it inside my house. And I always hope that when I get back home, my house will be the same way we left it. I have to walk thirty-four steps to get to my porch, and in those steps I could get jumped, robbed, or shot. Every time I go down those steps it looks like I'm running. The scariest part is at night when someone is behind me. I never look back because I'm too scared. The faster I get to my house, the faster I feel safe.

In my neighborhood there is no rich class. Everyone around me is low-income, people who struggle at getting a job. Everyone is scared to leave their houses at night because you might get robbed or shot at if they confuse you with someone else. They won't think twice about breaking in, and they don't care if you are inside your house. I'm not a really negative person, but this is what I see every day.

In my case I don't believe in the American Dream. I think that it does not exist because even rich wealthy people are committing suicide because they are not happy with their lives. If living the life of rich people is the American Dream, it is killing us all because everyone is trying so hard to get that white picket fence and house that they forget about their health and suffer strokes and heart attacks. It is only a fantasy that is making us want more even when we have enough to live on. But it is never enough.

Five years ago, I was in the store in line to pay for food my mom and I were buying. There was a black woman in front of us. She had paid and it was our turn next. The cashier had scanned all of our food and the black lady was still in the line and I told her, "Excuse me." She didn't hear me the first time so I told her again, and she did hear me this time because she looked at me and turned around. She ignored me. She was done packing her food but I don't know why she was still standing there. I told her again, and this time she responded and told me, "I heard you the first two times and you don't have to say it again, and I ain't gonna move for a stupid Mexican."

I felt like I wanted to kill the woman. I responded, "I'm not Mexican and I'm not stupid in the first place just because I want you to move." Everyone was getting mad behind us. My mom told the lady that she didn't have to make a big scandal, that all she had to do was get out of the way. My mom is very religious and doesn't believe in fighting. So she was calm, but I felt like I had the devil in me because my face was as hot as a volcano and my hands were shaking. I was thirteen and I knew I could not fight with a thirty-year-old. My mom told me, "Calm down and don't get out of control, let God handle it." So I tried to listen, and then the lady left. When we were outside, though, she was parked right next to our car, so I told my mom to wait and let them leave. The lady got in her car and she pulled over to the sidewalk and told me, "If I ever see you out in the street, you better watch out." I will never forget this because I'm not the only one it has happened to and I'm not going to be the last person it will happen to.

After I got home I thought to myself, "Where is the respect?" When you come to this country you think people will accept you for who you are and not put you down because you look different. It's like you hit a wall and fall on your back when you really notice that people in this country don't accept you. It's very funny how I was born in this country and I am treated like an alien from another planet. My parents are from El Salvador, they came here because of the civil war there. Everyone had told my mother about America and how it was like heaven, so beautiful and perfect. When my mom came here she was impressed with the money and tall buildings, but when things started to fall apart she saw that this was not heaven. In my personal opinion, I think you have a lot more problems in this country, like gangs, drugs, and alcohol, all things people choose to do just to fit in with the crowd.

I know that I can't do anything about all the things that have happened in my life, but I'm going to graduate pretty soon and I have to get my family out of this neighborhood. I will do my best to not let them suffer anymore, because if my mom could not get that education, I will be the first one in my family to do it. I will get a good job and take them somewhere that doesn't have so much violence.

My life is not all fear and pain. I do have very happy moments outside school and my house. I have dreams to become a nurse and help people in physical pain. I like helping people even though I can't change the racism and the violence by myself. There are so many people that do try to help others with violence issues, but they can only get so far, they can't get everywhere all by themselves. If people wanted to change their environment they could get help, but I guess people are so used to it that they just feel like it's normal.

I live in a country that some people would die to live in, because this country is supposed to be a free country. They supposedly would have a better life in this country, but they are wrong. There is more money here, but if you're an immigrant you have to work really hard to get a good job. There is a lot of opportunity, but if you don't have documents you have less of a chance of getting a good job. I think "the American Dream" is only a phrase, it's not something you can ever touch, smell, or hear. It's so out of this world that you can't even see it. It is supposed to give you freedom and help you feel safe and have money. But freedom is not something you can have by coming to this country. You can't live where you want because you don't have enough money to pay a mortgage or rent. If you question this, then why are there so many families living in shelters and so many homeless people? People don't just decide to become homeless or go and live in a shelter; that is their only option, and if they had a good job that would never happen.

The idea of the American Dream is very different for everyone. It might just be to get to the United States and send money to one's family in another country. But it's very hard to get that perfect house and to also find a perfect neighborhood, when everywhere you go, there is so much violence. The American Dream is not for me because there is so much racism, and where is the freedom and security that guarantee you won't get shot or robbed when you step outside your house?

La Vida
RANCHERA

by JEANNIE MUÑOZ

IN THE MORNING, the knocking at the metal door woke me up. It was only 8:00 a.m., yet everyone in el pueblo de San Nicolas De Barra knew that we had arrived. The first thing that came to my mind was, *It's too early, I can't believe that the whole pueblo is up!*

My family and I had arrived the night before in Jalisco, Guadalajara, Mexico after traveling by car for three days. It was nighttime by the time we got there; therefore it was too dark to see anything. Exhausted from the trip, we all went to sleep inside the house my dad built. A year earlier, after purchasing the land, my dad, who had studied architecture in the United States, had made the blueprints for the house and then contracted construction workers in Mexico to build it. Constructing a house in Mexico was very affordable for my dad because an American dollar is worth ten Mexican dollars. He built the house so we would have a place to stay when we took winter vacations. Also, my parents built the house with the plan to move back to Mexico once my three younger siblings and I could take care of ourselves. My parents want to make enough money to retire and move back to their native home. But that's their dream, not mine.

Standing there half-awake, I could see a lot of people—mostly relatives—at the door. Everyone was friendly and greeted us with hugs and kisses. It was very crowded at the door, so we stepped outside. There were so many people that I couldn't even tell who my cousins were. They hadn't seen me in many years. I was a child in their memories of the last time they saw me; now I was a teenager. They asked me if I was engaged, married, or had any children. These questions shocked me, as these things were not on my mind. The fact that all these people had come over early in the morning to welcome us so warmly made me feel special.

The sun was blazing high up in the sky. I felt like I was in a Wild West movie. The women wore dusty, casual jeans and t-shirts. The men wore their pants all the way up to their waists, with rodeo belt buckles. It was kind of weird to see men with their pants like that, since I grew up in a city where guys wear their pants sagging down.

Outside, other than the people speaking Spanish, I could hear the farm animals—cows, horses, goats, sheep, pigs, chickens, dogs, and cats. I could smell the Mexico countryside and the dusty soil beneath my feet. It seemed as if everything around me was full of life. I was in the middle of a rural country far away from home and anything familiar. I could see small houses facing east; to the west was wilderness. The air was filled with humidity and the sun was evaporating the morning dew.

When some of our relatives came inside our house, they noticed that we didn't have anything except two mattresses. Without warning, they all left and came back with furniture, dishware, and decorations for the house. We were not used to this custom of sharing and caring. They were very generous people. At first, my parents didn't want to accept their help, but they also didn't want to reject their hospitality. My parents remembered that life used to be like this when they lived in small pueblos.

All was going well until I told my parents I was going to go shopping. At that moment, many relatives started to whisper with each other. I asked what the fuss was about. They told me that it's not proper for a girl to go anywhere by herself unless she is accompanied by a family member or chaperone. I was about to crack up about this ridiculous rule, but then my brother said he was going to go out "somewhere," yet no one stopped him. That's when I noticed the inequality that existed based on gender. Despite what I believed was right, I held my tongue and obeyed their rules. I agreed to bring an older cousin with me because I didn't want to ruin the good mood everyone was in.

Later that day, I went to my grandma's house, and there were a lot of chores that had to be done. I noticed that there were only women doing the house chores. I asked my grandma where all the *muchachos* were.

She told me that they were out "somewhere." Personally, I never liked doing my chores back home in the United States, but here in rural Mexico, it was like a third-world country—there were no machines or technology to help us. In the United States, we just toss our laundry in the machine and go watch TV. In Mexico, we had to do all the chores by hand.

I found out that not all the chores were done by women; the farm chores were done by men. I had always loved to work with animals so I was more interested in doing the farm chores. I felt discriminated against when I was expected to stay in the house and do only house chores. I felt I had to speak my mind, so I told them I wanted to do farm chores. The women in the house instantly gasped at my comment. My aunt grabbed me by the arm and took me to my mom to tell her what I just said. My mom didn't say much, though, since she hadn't explained the rules to me yet. The only reason why everyone in the house was shocked by what I had said was because, unlike them, I was born in the United States, where everyone has freedom of speech.

I thought I was going to be eating Mexican grill food like what I was used to. But I was totally wrong; there, people only ate beans, eggs, and tortillas—for breakfast, lunch, and dinner. After a week of this food, I started to rebel. I no longer ate what my family was eating. I would eat what I wanted to eat and not what I was served or told to eat. To do that, I had to do major grocery shopping. The only place nearby that had the food I wanted was Chapala—a city eleven kilometers from the village where I was staying. Because there was no gas station in the village, my dad had to drive into Chapala every five days to get gas. So I would go with him and bring back as many bags of food as I could carry.

You might be surprised, as I was, that in the village that I stayed in, meat is a luxury and not something you eat every day. People only kill their animals on special occasions or when it's necessary. They don't believe in killing unless they are going to use and eat every part of the animal. I liked this about their culture. In the Unites States, we are very wasteful. The best thing about being born an American is that I can take these Mexican customs with me to America and practice them. I have the freedom to make my own choices.

I had never seen an animal being slaughtered before, since I was used to buying my meat in cellophane-wrapped packages in the grocery store. In Mexico, I saw how meat ends up in our grocery store. December in Mexico is a month full of festivals, so I was able to see animals being slaughtered for a special festival. My uncle works as a butcher, so he was in charge of killing the animals. He had to kill a goat to make *birria de chivo*. The goat was large and couldn't be taken down so easily, so my uncle Ramon got the goat drunk. Then he and his helpers tied ropes around its neck to lead it out of its pen and into the yard. They did this because otherwise the other goats would cry when they saw this goat killed. Once in the yard, my uncle and his helpers tied all the goat's legs down. I felt sad for this goat as it tried to struggle to break free of the ropes. All its efforts were useless. They slit its throat. Even if it was drunk, the poor goat had to die a painful, slow death. That night, when *la birria de chivo* was served, I didn't want to eat it because the memory of the poor goat struggling kept playing in my head.

One night, the men and boys were going to hunt *tlacuaches* (opossums) to make *chicharrones* for the festival. I was told to stay at my grandma's house with the other females, but I was not about to sit down and watch Spanish *telenovelas* while I knew that my younger brother was having the adventure of his life. I got a rifle and tagged along. It was very dark once we left the village and started to walk into the deadly wilderness. Fortunately for me, growing up in America gave me a sense of adventure and independence, which helped me. In the darkness there were scorpions, coyotes, snakes, tarantulas, and supposedly a lion that had run away from a circus. We all had flashlights but didn't use them until we would find a *tlacuache*. As we traveled in the dark, I kept stumbling over rocks and bushes. Finally, after we had walked a lot, someone spotted something moving in a tree. We flashed our flashlights at the tree, and there was a *tlacuache*, looking like a deer caught in headlights.

My parents bought me a horse in Mexico, which I thought was really cool. In the United States, many girls fantasize of owning a pony. I was sort of angry when I was told how to ride my horse, though. Women there are not allowed to ride a horse unless they ride cross-legged with a long dress. I started to ride without crossing my legs, and wearing jeans. I also got involved in rodeo, which is considered a predominantly male sport there. Soon the whole village started to speak and gossip about what I was doing. My parents didn't know what to do under the pressure of country society. I was very self-conscious about what people were saying. In the end, I told myself, *Forget what everyone says. My personal happiness is more important than what people think.*

I'm bicultural and bilingual and proud of it. I'm happy that I grew up in America because I have been given a lot of choices and the ability to choose my own path. I'm eighteen years old and have decided to get married, out of love, unlike my cousins who get married because of social pressure and economic restraints. A lot of people say that I'm too young to get married, but I feel that in America I have choices to determine my future, that I can continue my education even after I'm married.

After my trip to Mexico and experiencing a totally different lifestyle, I'm glad that I was born in the United States. Thanks to my parents, who took me on trips to Mexico, I take pride in my language and my roots, but I would still rather visit my ancestral home than live there. As a U.S.-born citizen, I can freely travel the world without any problems. All my cousins in Mexico were discouraged from going to school because their parents believe that in order to work the farm lands you just need physical strength and not brains. The women are discouraged from getting an education when they are still single. Instead, they are told to do household chores and prepare for their matrimonial life. They are not allowed to pursue their education after they marry. I'm grateful for being born in the United States and having the freedom to do as I please with my life.

_My_ AMERICAN _Dream_

_by_ NIAT SEBHATLEAB

ADDIS ABABA, ETHIOPIA. My father built a beautiful house for my mother after they got married; it had three bedrooms, two bathrooms and servants' quarters. We had a backyard where my dad put in a swing set for me when I was old enough to use it.

My mother used to get up early in the morning to go to work in her business uniform, her long hair tied up into a neat ponytail. She worked for Ethiopian Airlines. My dad got up around the same time to head to his office. He dressed more casually than the others who worked in the office because he was the supervisor. As a child, everything came easy to me because both my parents worked really hard to make the best living they could for our family.

When I was little I cried when my dad left for work because I hated to see him leave. Some days, he took me to work with him and I sat in the office until his lunchtime when he would take me out to eat or maybe get some ice cream. Some nights when I could not sleep, my dad would come home from a long day of work and take me for a long drive through the city until I fell asleep. Other nights, before it was time for me to go to sleep, my mother would make me a glass of warm milk and read to me until I fell asleep. In the United States this would be really close to what most of society pictures as the American Dream: two parents working full-time, three children, and a pet dog.

As I got older, I had to start preschool. My mom would take my braids out and wash my hair and re-do a different design of braids. It would take my mom hours to comb it out and braid, but somehow it always got done, even with all my fussing and whining. I remember going back to school with my hair freshly done. Every day, without fail, my father used to take me to school, and when school was dismissed he was there to pick me up and take me home. We would come home together and he would eat lunch and take a little nap, then go back to work. I stayed at home for the rest of the day, trying to keep myself occupied. For the most part I would take my bath and get started on my school work. When I was done, I would watch the housekeeper cook dinner in the kitchen.

I watched as she stirred food in all the different pots. She started by pouring equal amounts of olive oil into each pot and letting it heat up while she cut onions. Once the oil was warm enough, she added onions and let them cook in the oil. The smell of the onions would then travel all through the house. She added different spices into each of the pots. The aromas were so strong I could almost taste the flavor. She would pour water and chop up meat to cook with the flavor, or she would cut potatoes and carrots and add them in a different pot; these were the traditional plates. When I did not want to be in the kitchen I would go out into the backyard with my teddy bear that I had since birth. This was my most prized possession and I took it everywhere with me.

In June of 1997, my mom got promoted to sales manager of Ethiopian Airlines. That sounds excellent, right? No. As happy as this made my mother, this meant that we had to leave everything we had in Ethiopia to start a new life in a country that I barely knew anything about. We had to move to Nairobi, Kenya, where my mom found us a nice cozy house in this complex called Duncan Court. Two months after we got there, I started school. I was really enjoying it and I was really comfortable.

In May of 1998, the tension that was building up between Eritrea and Ethiopia broke out into yet another war. Over time, the war got out of hand. People were getting tortured, arrested, or killed for being at the wrong place at the wrong time. My mother was an Eritrean, and this resulted in her losing her job for Ethiopian Airlines. I assume my mother already knew this, and that is why she took us on a trip halfway around the world. Little did my brothers and I know that this vacation would be permanent. My father flew out from Ethiopia to accompany us in our visit to Germany, where my mother's sister lived. We stayed there for about a week as my aunt and my mom caught up on old times and tried to keep us occupied. On our last day, my aunt took us to an amusement park. I was almost five years old, and I recall not being able to get on any of the rides but still being fascinated by everything I saw. I was having so much fun I never once stopped to think that maybe this would be the last time my family would be together for a very long time.

The next morning my aunt drove my family and me to the airport. I really believed in my heart that my dad would be coming to San Francisco with us. When we got to the airport I saw this sad look on my parents' face, as my dad said bye to the four of us and we went our separate ways. I suddenly started crying, realizing that my dad was not coming with us.

San Francisco, California. My mom was on her own and she had to take care of three little kids who were all depending on her. This was a huge struggle for my mom. We stayed with her cousin as we settled in and started a new life. She went to San Francisco City College and learned something that could help her get a job so she could find a place for us to live and get us enrolled in schools.

I now live with my mother, father, and three brothers in a three-story building in a quiet neighborhood. This is nothing compared to Ethiopia. When I was in Ethiopia, most things seemed easy and simple to get taken care of. Now I notice the struggles that my parents have to go through when trying to provide everything that my brothers and I all want and need. Everything may not be the same, but I can definitely say that we are a happy family. Both my parents work full-time. Although they may not have careers in something that they had hoped to do when they were younger, they have enough to support our family.

My brothers and I are all trying to get an education. I learned the hard way that getting an education is a huge competition, and you will only get a good education if you put forth enough effort. With a scholarship to attend an all-girls' school, Immaculate Conception Academy, I stopped caring because everything came so easy to me. That is also when I lost everything that came so easy, including my scholarship and my spot in the school. After this, reality set in for me. I realized I had to start putting more effort into everything so I could achieve my goals and dreams. I clearly understand that I have been blessed and I am grateful, but I do have high hopes to one day visit the country that I am originally from, Eritrea, and also go back to Ethiopia. This is where my happiness originated, and I can almost bet that my mother and father were happier there than in San Francisco because my family's true relatives and friends are in Eritrea and Ethiopia.

As I get older, my memories slowly begin to fade, and sometimes I am scared that they will all disappear before I get a chance to go back. To bring back many priceless memories, I keep a 24kt gold chain with a 24kt piece on it shaped like Eritrea. It's so cold against my skin, but it's blazing hot near my heart. Well, here I am now, in America. I am not at a point where I can say that I am working to achieve the American Dream because my memories are nearly all my dreams. I want things to be how they used to be. What I had is not necessarily what I would call the American Dream, but I was happy and I felt complete.

A majority of the United States population came here with the hope that achieving the American Dream would not be difficult, that getting an education would be easier, that jobs would be better and with much better pay. They come with high hopes, but they do not have the slightest idea how much difficulty they would have coming to the United States from third-world countries such as Eritrea or Ethiopia. Both are very poor countries that have limited opportunities, especially if one does not have an education. These conditions are similar to those in America.

I don't see why it is called the American Dream. I think anyone can have this hope and anyone can achieve it if she works hard enough. The harder you work, the easier things come to you. I can't say that I have an American Dream besides the desires I have for myself, which include getting a college degree, getting a well-paying career, and supporting a family while enjoying life without stress. Many would call this the American Dream and I don't blame them. Yet is that not what all people want? Is it not happiness, safety, security, education, and complete success?

ABOUT *the* AUTHORS

 Ali Sharhan was born in Yemen and moved here when he was thirteen. He likes to play football and watch sports. He is looking to pursue a degree in accounting because he enjoys math. He considers himself a hard worker, because he is a full-time student and works.

 Angel Santiago is from San Francisco. His nationality is Puerto Rican. He's athletic, smart, and handsome. His favorite football player is Hall-of-Famer Jerry Rice. Angel is a very family-oriented person who also loves to hang out with friends and have a good time.

 Angelica Verdugo was born in San Francisco and raised in the Bay Area. When she's not playing volleyball, she likes to write poetry and draw in her sketchbook. Many of her drawings are inspired by photographs that she takes in her free time. She hopes to one day travel to the East Coast and study at NYU.

 Ares Almendares was born in the Mission District of San Francisco. He had many obstacles while growing up and now is trying to pursue his dream in hip-hop music. He plays a lot of basketball after school, but his first sport was baseball. In the future, he plans to move to Brazil and live the good life.

Brian Hibbeler is a native San Franciscan who was raised on the belief that one could pursue their personal aspirations through perseverance and determination. He is an Oprah devotee, enjoys writing in his spare time, and reading literary greats such as *Gone with the Wind* and *Anna Karenina*. Brian hopes to become a chef, entrepreneur, and fiction writer. His essay critiques society's lack of motivation to strive for its dreams.

Carlos Rivas is from El Salvador. He likes to play video games and hang out with his friends in school. Carlos likes to go watch movies, take care of his little brother, and also work with his dad. He hopes he can become someone important in life and is planning to attend City College of San Francisco.

Catherine Esmeralda Olvera was born and raised in San Francisco. Her hobbies include listening to music, going to the movies with family, and hanging out with her best friend in the whole wide world. Catherine's favorite books to read are *Twilight*, *Shadowland*, and *Night World*. Her dream is to attend the Academy of Arts and have a career in writing and photography.

Ccarlos Gonzalez was born in southern California and now resides in Oakland, California. He likes skateboarding, watching YouTube, eating at cheap restaurants, and keepin' it real. He hopes to go to college and get a nice job, as long as he is happy. Ccarlos is a quiet person who is nice and likes life.

Cecily Marie Alfaro is seventeen years old. She enjoys spending time with her two older brothers. She secretly enjoys reading and writing and loves to listen to music 24/7. She's the type of girl that likes to stay at home and mostly spends time by herself. She has very few close friends because she's shy, but once you get to know her she's very nice. She likes to live every day like it's the last day and is overall a content person.

Cristian Soto was born in Mexico, and he moved to San Francisco when he was young. He appreciates the little things in life. One of his favorite pastimes is observing the people and buildings of the city. In the future, he hopes to travel and explore different places around the world.

David E. Flores was born in San Francisco. He likes to use his computer to go onto the Internet and play video games. When he is not using his computer, he likes to play his Xbox 360, chat, and play with his friends from school. He also likes to have good grades in school so he will get accepted to college. When he grows up, he wants to study computer engineering and a bit of graphic design.

Doris Medrano likes to shop and just hang out in her spare time. Some things she values a lot are her family and friends. Her essay is about driving and the obstacles people face.

Eduardo Caamal was born in Cozumel, Quintana Roo, Mexico, and raised in San Francisco. Eduardo likes playing soccer while listening to music because it makes him feel relaxed and concentrated on what he is doing. Some movies he enjoys are *2012*, *The Twilight Saga: New Moon*, and *From Mexico with Love*. His essay is mostly about his relationship with his brother and what brings them together and keeps them apart.

Elizabeth Alvarado was raised in the Mission District in San Francisco. Her parents are both from Mexico; they moved to the United States for a better future. She likes reading urban fiction books. Elizabeth is planning on attending San Francisco City College after graduation. She wrote about how school can be hard and described her struggles.

Elizabeth Garcia was born in a diverse community in San Francisco, with a lot of family support around her. She feels like music is a way of expression and freedom. When she gets out of high school, she wants to go into criminal justice and help her community. As a young Chicana, she is able to understand people's problems. She likes to help people and prove her point. She speaks her mind and believes that family is everything, no matter what.

Fiki Mehari lives in San Francisco. Fiki is a positive, friendly person who is good at basketball. In his free time, he likes to read books and watch TV with family. His favorite show is *House of Payne*. Fiki dedicates his essay to his family and will always be there for them.

Helda Ponce was born and raised in San Francisco. Helda is a fun person to be around. She is a trustworthy person who makes her friends laugh and is there for them whenever they need her. She likes to read book series like *The Vampire Diaries* and *Twilight*. Helda wrote about being successful in life and how completing her education and becoming a photographer is her American Dream.

 Horacio Campos was born in Encarnación de Díaz, Jalisco, Mexico, and immigrated to the United States at the age of seven. His favorite hobby is playing PlayStation 3. Horacio's favorite food is Mexican food. He hates writing and reading, but he likes doing math.

 Jaizel Robles was born in San Francisco and raised in the Philippines. She likes to take long walks on the beach. She is easily irritated by the world, yet she has big hopes and dreams. She loves bananas! Napping is her #1 hobby.

 Jamon Balberan was born and raised in San Francisco. He likes to explore the city, meet new people, and he leads a life of leisure. Although it is sometimes a struggle, he tries to remember that his glass is half-full. He hopes that his creative mind will lead him to a good place in the future.

 Jasmine Antone was born and raised in San Francisco. Her hopes for the future are to finish high school and to go to college and make something of her life. Her essay is about the different struggles in life that people have to go through to achieve their American Dreams. She put her own experience in the essay about how her family's American Dream changed throughout certain events that took place in their lives.

 Javier Lopez was born in San Francisco, on December 15, 1992. He lives with his mom, older sister, and one-year-old son, Javier Jr. He likes to take his son to the park and push him on the swings. He looks forward to graduating high school and continuing his education in college.

Jeannie Muñoz was born in San Francisco in 1991. Both her parents were born and raised in Mexico, and she makes a yearly trip with her family to her ancestral pueblo, in San Nicolas de Barra, Mexico. Jeannie believes that her personality is dynamic and unique because of her bicultural experiences. She is proud of her Mexican roots and proud to be American.

Jeffry Kondo, sixteen years old, was born near Manila in the Philippines and moved to the United States with his family when he was four years old. Through Jeffry's parents, he has an immigrant's perspective on life in the United States. Jeffry loves being with his friends both in school and in games, such as massive, multi-player online games. He is very shy and was diagnosed with socially limiting issues at age eleven, but Jeffry is busting out of his shell!

Jennifer Neron Singh, sixteen years old, was born and raised in San Francisco. She likes to draw, listen to music, and watch movies. Her family and friends come first because of the strong love she has for them. She chose to write about her uncle because he's very special and one of her greatest role models. She's friendly, respectful, and one day she hopes to travel the world.

Jocelyn Rodriguez is a young lady who was born and raised in the lovely city of San Francisco. If you ever want to make her happy, you should buy her a can of Coca-Cola and a bag of hot chips. She enjoys playing softball, hanging out, and learning new things. She is a very lovable and energetic person; you'd love hanging out with her.

Juan Valdivia was raised in the Tenderloin area of San Francisco. He likes to go out and have a good time. He likes to go shopping, and his dream is to go to college and work in the medical field. He tells us about the obstacle he had to overcome and how it's not going to stop him from getting what he wants.

Karen Martinez was born in San Francisco. When she is not in school, she likes playing soccer and softball. Her hopes for the future are to become a successful scientist and a role model for her brothers and sisters. Karen is a hard-working, positive student who likes vanilla ice cream.

Karla Hernandez, a.k.a. Morena, was born in Guanajuato, Mexico, but now walks the streets of the Mission District in San Francisco. She likes playing basketball even though people think she is too short. Her hobbies are writing poems, listening to music, and having sing-alongs, especially to her favorite song, "Differences" by Ginuwine, which is about love. Her hope for the future is to become the best psychologist in the whole world.

Kathia Ramos is sixteen going on seventeen. Her favorite things to do are draw and hang out with friends, family, and her dogs. After she graduates high school she wants to go to art school. She would like to open her own store and have her own clothing line.

Kenny Lau is a sixteen-year-old Chinese American kid born in San Francisco. He enjoys playing badminton and card games on the weekend. When he graduates from high school, he will enroll at a four-year university within the Bay Area. He believes in helping people in his community, and in the future would like to volunteer at 826 Valencia to help students like him write better.

Kimberly Solares was born and raised in San Francisco. She likes to read books and especially enjoys reading vampire books. She likes to go to the movies, to the pier, and taking long walks. Her family and closest friends call her Micky. She is a calm, quiet, shy, friendly, and down-to-earth girl. She loves being with animals, and this is the reason she wrote about her bunny.

Kristi Vargas moved to San Francisco about a year ago and lives in Hunters Point. She wrote her story based on what has happened in her life. Kristi's favorite hobbies are reading and going out with friends.

Leonardo Aguilar was born in Honduras. For fun, he likes to play soccer. He is an athletic, active, and focused person. In middle school, he worked with 826 Valencia and had his poems published in a book.

Lisett Rodriguez is a native San Franciscan. She enjoys photography, hanging out with friends and family, and wandering the city. Her mother grew up in Mexico City and her father grew up in a small pueblo in Mexico. Lisett is very quiet, indecisive, and doesn't know what to do with her future.

 Marc Cesista was born in the Philippines and lives in the Bay Area. He likes music, dance, and enjoys eating out. His essay is about his life and his dreams to play in the NBA. Marc is a smart and fun person who is playful and loves basketball.

 Nestor Javier Muñoz, of Salvadorian descent, was born in San Francisco, on November 17, 1993. He lives in San Francisco's Mission District with his mom, his brother, his brother's girlfriend, and his dog, Chico. Nestor spends most of his time at wrestling practice or hanging out with friends. When he grows up, he wants to study medicine.

 Niat Sebhatleab, sixteen years old, was born in Addis Ababa, Ethiopia. She has three younger brothers who she enjoys spending time with. Niat is an honest, caring, and lively person. She finds joy in listening to music, writing poetry, and solving mysteries. Niat hopes to graduate high school, go to college, and find a fulfilling career.

 Nicolas X. Naval-Mora's family is special to him. He lives with his mother and three younger sisters in the Third Street area of San Francisco. His sisters inspire him to be a good example, to be respectful toward his family, to take responsibility for his own life, and to be mature even in difficult times. He is seventeen years old and works four days a week at Safeway. He is an aspiring bass player.

 Oscar Pineda was born in San Francisco. He likes to play video games on his Xbox 360 and eat at fast food restaurants with friends. After high school, he plans on applying to a four-year university. Afterward, he wants to become a doctor, make a lot of money, and be successful.

Rafael Gurrola is a Mexican American and lives in San Francisco's Mission District. He hopes that he will have a good life and live positively. In his spare time, he likes to walk around his community and spread his ideas. After high school, Rafael would like to go to San Francisco City College to study psychology.

Reca Averilla was born in the Philippines, where she grew up, before moving back to the United States. She misses spending time with her cousins in the Philippines who grew up with her. She visits the Philippines yearly. She likes to go shopping on weekends and is very religious. Education plays a very important role in her life, and she is looking forward to going to college.

Roberto Hernandez was born in León, Guanajuato, Mexico. He has two sisters and two nephews. He loves to spend time with his friends Angelica, Jessica, Beverly, and Mika. He likes to write in his free time because that's a way for him to express his thoughts.

Roberto "Potato" Hernandez is a kid whose American Dream is traveling and going to different places. He likes to play a game called *Call of Duty: Modern Warfare 2*; he is really good at this game. He is funny and outgoing, and also kind of crazy. His favorite food is pizza cheese sticks with tomato sauce on the side.

Ronaldo Perez was born in San Francisco, into a poor Hispanic family that has progressed over the years. In his spare time he enjoys music, baseball, and reading short stories. His hopes for the future are to attend San Francisco State to study medicine, and he would love to be a fireman in the city he grew up in. Ronaldo has pride for where he comes from, his roots, and his family history.

Samantha Mattos loves to read books in her spare time. Samantha wants to become a scientist and work at NASA. She loves to go on long walks with her friends and listen to music. She would like to write some books here and there as a hobby in the future.

Sandra Alarcon was born in Peru but moved to San Francisco in 2005. She is a fun, responsible girl who enjoys playing soccer and writing in her journal. She hopes to one day become an engineer or a journalist. Sandra wrote about the struggle to learn a new language while living in a new country.

 Takeya Smith was born and raised in San Francisco and is a fun, outgoing, energetic sweetheart. She enjoys writing personal poetry, singing, hanging out with friends, relaxing at the beach, and playing volleyball. She wants to travel the world when she's older. She plans to begin her journey in Louisiana, where her family's Creole roots originated.

 Thalia Andrade was born and raised in San Francisco, in a household of four. She is very involved in school: she is the junior class president, was on the softball team, and was also involved in peer mediation. She has a lot of positive qualities: she is very outgoing, fun to be around, real, a great friend, and an unbeatable personality. Thalia wrote her story to help youth realize what their parents sacrificed for them and appreciate their parents while they can.

 Veronica Siliezar was born in San Francisco, on September 21, 1993. She is an only child and lives with her single mom, who was born and raised in El Salvador. Veronica enjoys art, playing softball, learning about cars, and watching soccer with her family. After high school, she plans to pursue a career in the medical field to become a nurse or an optometrist.

ACKNOWLEDGEMENTS

THIS YEAR'S YOUNG AUTHORS' BOOK PROJECT would not be possible without 149 devoted volunteers, one amazing school, two inspiring teachers, and fifty highly insightful students. This publication is the product of a community that dedicated countless hours to bring to life the students' experiences of the American Dream.

Ms. Leathers and Mr. Rose, the two teachers who spearheaded this project, were exceptional to work with. In past years, 826 Valencia had worked with Mr. Rose's class on personal statements, so we were excited for the opportunity to work more extensively with O'Connell. From the start, it was clear that these teachers believed in their students' capabilities to write the most heartfelt essays they'd ever written, and they treated the students with enormous respect while also pushing them to craft and share their stories with the world. To both excellent teachers: this book could not have been written without your support.

We would like to thank California College of the Arts for their immense support. Last year, we met with Mark Breitenberg, provost of CCA, to discuss possibilities of collaboration, and it was very clear that this project was the best way to match our programming to the brilliant and dedicated student minds at CCA.

826 Valencia owes the consistently high tutor-to-student ratio in large part to our inaugural partnership with CCA, specifically Assistant Professor Amiee Phan, chair of the Writing and Literature Program, who formed a course allowing her students to serve as tutors throughout the

entirety of the project. We are very lucky to have worked with such a hands-on educator as Aimee.

Tutors from 826 Valencia and the CCA class worked with students twice a week for six weeks to develop the heartfelt stories in this collection. The tutors and students bonded with one another, and during each session, pairs were engaged in deep discussion or quiet writing and revising. By the end of the project, tutors had connected with the students on a personal level and wished for the realization of each student's American Dream. 826 Valencia couldn't have asked for a group more dedicated or generous with its time and energy.

Many thanks to the students of the CCA course for their enthusiastic commitment to the project: Alexandra Sasha Gainor, Allison Cole, Angelic Williams, Beth Bloom, Christine Meade, Douglas Waters, Emily Jern-Miller, Emma Bernsohn, James Goss, Julie Littman, Kimberly Kim, Laura Garcia, Laura Ramie, Lisa Gordon, Mev Luna, Nicole Santucci, Quinn Graddy, Rae Thomas, Rheea Mukherjee, Seth Singleton, and Stephanie Suggs.

Thanks to our ever-dedicated and wonderful 826 Valencia tutors: Adam Donovan, Alex Miley, Alicia Mckean, Alicia Soon Hershey, Amber Matthews, Amy Popovich, Ana Soriano, Anna Crawley, Ben Shattuck, Brian Martin, Bucky Rosato, Caitlin Murphy, Caitlin Pulleyblank, Cheryl Tyler, Chris Reade, Conan Putnam, Cortney Rickman-Green, Daniel Brownstein, Deanna Beach, Denise Miller, Elana Aoyama, Greg Rasmussen, Hannah Colbert, Ilana Bain, Janice Greene, Jeff White, Jessica Hansen, Karina Utter, Kate Bueler, Kerri-Suzanne Kyle, Kevin Stark, Lauren Ladoceour, Mark Krahling, Mary A. Rose, Mary Elaine Akers-Bell, Merle Rabine, Michael Howerton, Nancy Kivette, Nancy Ware, Nick Janikian, Noelle Rozakos, Patrick Coffey, Rachel Sadler, Sabina Rocke, Seth Mausner, Shannon David, Sondra Hall, Stacy Barrett, Stephen Rosenshein, Tiffani Carter, Tom Molanphy, and Wendy Trevino.

To offer even more editorial support during the writing portion of the project, we asked teams of volunteers to offer suggestions that we then took back to the students in class. We'd like to thank the weekend editors who paid careful attention to student voice and offered invaluable advice: Anne-Marie Cordingly, Ben Castanon, Ben Shattuck, Brandon Vaden, Caitlyn Nora Murphy, Caroline Kangas, Christy Susman, David Brownell, Edward Opton, Evelyn Krampf, Frank A. Lee, Gina

Abelkop, Hannah Edber, Heather Haggarty, Henry Arguedas, Holly Alderman, Jeff Guarrera, Jess Goldman, Jill Dovale, Lara Fox, Lillie Chilen, Maggie Wooll, Mike Winters, Nancy Park, Natalie Abbott, Rachel Sadler, Renee Ashbaugh, Samantha Riley, Sarah Bruhns, and Tate Garibyan.

Once the students finished writing, a student and adult editorial board worked for four weeks to edit the collected essays into a cohesive book. Twice a week, over pupusas or pizza, they debated punctuation and discussed structure late into the evening. We were very fortunate to have this large and extremely passionate editorial board led by longtime volunteer Lara Fox, whom we'd like to thank immensely for her guidance in editing and organizing the book. Ellen Goodenow spent many hours carefully editing in the final round, in addition to attending every evening meeting: we'd like to thank her for being our super editorial volunteer. And, in between all the serious discussions, everyone had a great time; lots of laughter could be heard from our writing lab. To the editorial board we are especially indebted: Abner Morales, Alex Miley, Ana Soriano, Brian Martin, Carolyn Beaty, Cristina Giner, Eamon Doyle, Elana Aoyama, Evelyn Krampf, Jill Dovale, Jocelyn Rodriguez, Julie Dyer, Karen Schaser, Katie Savchuk, Kelley Leathers, Kerri Suzanne Kyle, Kimberly Connor, Lara Fox, Lauren Markham, Lillie Chilen, Linda Gebroe, Linda Puffer, Mark Krahling, Mary A. Rose, Mike Winters, Nancy Park, Natanya Biskar, Neekta Khorsand, Rachel Sadler, Shannon David, Suzie Hill, Tate Garibyan, Todd Myles Carnam, and Valerie Witte. We'd especially like to recognize the group of students who got out of sports practice, asked their bosses to switch their work schedules, and read essays on the weekends and at school during breaks; they made it a priority to put their signature mark on the book. An awe-inspiring thank you to this core group of students: Angelica Verdugo, Brian Hibbeler, Cristian Soto, Jaizel Robles, Karen Martinez, and Nicolas Naval-Mora.

We had the honor of inviting our friend, author Daniel Alarcón, to write the foreword to this book. During his visit to the classroom, Alarcón shared his own writing advice: that most importantly, writing takes patience, sincere thought, and revision after revision. The students realized that even professionally published authors need to edit, that good writing is truly hard work. We'd like to thank him for his participation in the project and for bringing his experience, talent, and wisdom to the students of O'Connell.

This year's book was designed by the talented Jody Worthington, who pours her heart into her work and always takes care that the students' voices and ideas are heard through her design. Thank you Jody, for bringing another kind of beauty to the words.

Huge thanks also to Oriana Leckert for giving a careful eye to copyediting the entire book, and to Oona Lyons, who lent her photo expertise and took portraits of the students for the book.

Thanks to our invaluable 826 interns who supported this project: Caroline Kangas, Jeff White, Karina Utter, Sarah Bruhns, and Shannon David. We'd especially like to thank Ben Shattuck, who gave focused attention to all parts of the project and worked long hours expertly editing student writing.

Huge thanks to Ryan Lewis, 826 National Operations Manager, who played an essential role in the classroom throughout the writing process. Ryan stepped in when we needed his support, with wholehearted dedication to the project.

Finally, we'd like to thank the National Endowment for the Arts for their generous support as our primary fiscal sponsor for the 2010 Young Authors' Book Project.

We are endlessly proud to have worked with the students at O'Connell as they turned their dreams into words, the wisdom they've gathered into honest essays, and their collective voice into a book. We watched their transformations during the process; each student took leaps in bravery, honesty, and hard work by sharing their experiences of the American Dream with us, and to them we are profoundly thankful.

Sincerely,

Marisa Urrutia Gedney, *Programs Director*
Miranda Tsang, *Programs Assistant*

About

826 VALENCIA

MISSION STATEMENT

826 Valencia is a nonprofit organization dedicated to supporting students, ages six to eighteen, with their creative and expository writing skills and to helping teachers inspire their students to write. Our work is based on the understanding that strong writing skills are fundamental to future success, and great leaps in learning can be made when skilled tutors work one-on-one with students.

HOW WE DO IT

826 Valencia consists of a writing lab in the Mission District of San Francisco (our name is our address), a student-friendly pirate supply store that partially funds our programs, and two satellite classrooms in nearby middle schools. More than fourteen hundred volunteers—including published authors, retired teachers, magazine founders, advertising copywriters, SAT-course instructors, and every other occupation under the sun—donate their time to work with more than six thousand Bay Area students each year. These incredible volunteers allow 826 Valencia to offer all its services for free.

Students thrive when they receive one-on-one attention from trained and caring tutors, and they work hard when they know that the community at large will read their writing. Our project-based approach allows students ownership over the learning process and empowers them to express themselves clearly, confidently, and in their own voices.

PROGRAMS

826 Valencia offers a full schedule of free programs that reach students at every possible opportunity—in school, after school, in the evenings, and on the weekends. Here are a few of our most popular offerings:

In-school Support

We dispatch teams of volunteers into local high-needs schools to support teachers and provide one-on-one assistance to students as they tackle school newspapers, research papers, oral histories, college-entrance essays, and more. Our in-school visits are a great way for us to support students who wouldn't, on their own, reach out for help.

Writing Workshops

826 Valencia offers free workshops designed to foster creativity and strengthen writing skills. They focus on everything from cartooning to starting a 'zine. All our workshops—from the playful to the practical—are project-based and taught by experienced professionals.

Field Trips

Up to four times a week, 826 Valencia welcomes an entire class into its writing lab for a morning of high-energy learning. Students may participate in a roundtable discussion with a local author, enjoy an active workshop focused on journalism, or, in our most popular field trip, write, illustrate, and bind their own class book—all in two hours.

Tutoring

Five days a week, 826 Valencia buzzes with neighborhood students who come in after school and on Sundays for one-on-one tutoring in myriad subject areas. We serve students of all skill levels and interests.

Summer Programs

During the summer, our tutoring program caters to English-language learners. Our project-based curriculum focuses on basic vocabulary, phonics, reading, and writing skills. We also host an intensive writing camp for high school students, in which campers write all day every day and work with celebrated authors and artists such as Michael Chabon, ZZ Packer, and Spike Jonze.

Writers' Rooms

Our Writers' Rooms at Everett Middle School and James Lick Middle School are warm, in-school satellites where our volunteers serve every student in the school over the course of the year. These spaces allow teachers to reduce their class sizes and students to receive the one-on-one attention that leads to success.

STUDENT PUBLICATIONS

From our various programs, 826 Valencia produces a variety of publications, each of which contains student writing. These projects represent some of the most exciting work done at 826 Valencia, as they expose Bay Area students to publishing experiences otherwise largely unavailable to them. Each year we publish scores of chapbooks from workshops, field trips, and special projects with teachers and classrooms. We also collect this work into our student-edited *826 Quarterly* at least twice a year.

The book you are holding is the most recent in our Young Authors' Book Project series, which represents the most involved publishing project we undertake each year. Below is a list of previous Young Authors' Book Project publications, all of which are available for sale online and at bookstores nationwide.

Show of Hands: Young Authors Reflect on the Golden Rule, 2009

These stories and essays by juniors at Mission High School reflect on the Golden Rule, which tells us that we should act toward others as we would want them to act toward ourselves. The young essayists' voices are impassioned, surprising, and most of all, urgent.

Seeing Through the Fog: A Gateway to San Francisco, 2008

This collection of stories and essays written by seniors at Gateway High School will guide locals, tourists, and armchair travelers alike to new places and new ways of seeing through the San Francisco fog. It includes a foreword by San Francisco Mayor Gavin Newsom.

Exactly: 10 Beavers, 9 Fairies, 8 Dreams, 7 Knights, 6 Princesses, 5 Dogs, 4 Otters, 3 Old Men, 2 Robots, 1 Traveling Shoe & Everything Else It Takes to Make a Great Children's Storybook (More or Less), 2007

This showcase of fifty-six children's tales written by students at Raoul Wallenberg Traditional High School includes vivid illustrations by professional artists, resulting in a delightful storybook for readers of all ages.

Home Wasn't Built in a Day: Constructing the Stories of Our Families, 2006

Essays by students at Galileo Academy of Science and Technology offer insightful stories that explore the myths and realities of what makes a family a family. The book includes a foreword by actor Robin Williams.

I Might Get Somewhere: Oral Histories of Immigration and Migration, 2005

This compelling collection of personal stories by Balboa High School's class of 2007 reflects on the problems and pleasures of life in new surroundings. It includes a foreword by author Amy Tan.

Waiting to Be Heard: Youth Speak Out About Inheriting a Violent World, 2004

This anthology by students at Thurgood Marshall Academic High School offers passionate, lucid statements about personal, local, and global issues—the way high school students would have you hear them. It includes a foreword by author Isabel Allende.

Talking Back: What Students Know About Teaching, 2004

Students from Leadership High School discuss the relationships they want to have with their teachers and the ways they view classroom life.

STAFF

Executive Director: Leigh Lehman
Development Director: Anne Farrah
Design Director: María Inés Montes
Programs Directors: Marisa Urrutia Gedney and Vickie Vértiz
Programs Coordinator: Emilie Coulson
Volunteer and Events Coordinator: Margaret McCarthy
Programs Assistants: Cherylle Taylor and Miranda Tsang
Pirate Store Manager and Publishing Director: Justin Carder

THE BOARD OF DIRECTORS OF 826 VALENCIA

Barb Bersche, Brian Gray, Thomas Mike, Abner Morales, Bita Nazarian, Alexandra Quinn, Mary Schaefer, Vendela Vida, Richard Wolfgram

FOUNDERS

Dave Eggers
Nínive Calegari

What's hiding under your

MATTRESS?

Whether it's loose change or heaps of cash, a donation of any size will help 826 Valencia continue to offer a wide variety of FREE literacy and publishing programs to Bay Area youth. We would greatly appreciate your support. Please make a donation at:

www.826valencia.org/helpout/donate

or mail a check to:
826 Valencia St., San Francisco, CA 94110

...

Thank you!

Your donation is tax deductible. What a plus!

826 Valencia Street
San Francisco, CA 94110
415.642.5905
www.826valencia.org